WARSAW GHETTO POLICE

WARSAW GHETTO POLICE

The Jewish Order Service during the Nazi Occupation

KATARZYNA PERSON

Translated by Zygmunt Nowak-Soliński

Published in Association with the
United States Holocaust Memorial Museum

CORNELL UNIVERSITY PRESS
Ithaca and London

First published 2021 by Cornell University Press

Library of Congress Cataloging-in-Publication Data

Names: Person, Katarzyna, author. | Nowak-Soliński,
    Zygmunt, translator.
Title: Warsaw Ghetto police : the Jewish Order Service
    during the Nazi occupation / Katarzyna Person,
    translated by Zygmunt Nowak-Soliński.
Description: Ithaca [New York] : Cornell University Press,
    2021. | Includes bibliographical references and index.
Identifiers: LCCN 2020022419 (print) | LCCN 2020022420
    (ebook) | ISBN 9781501754074 (hardcover) |
    ISBN 9781501754081 (epub) | ISBN 9781501754098 (pdf)
Subjects: LCSH: Jüdischer Ordnungsdienst—History. |
    Holocaust, Jewish (1939–1945) —Poland—Warsaw. |
    Jews—Poland—Warsaw—History—20th century. |
    Getto warszawskie (Warsaw, Poland)
Classification: LCC DS134.64 .P48 2021 (print) |
    LCC DS134.64 (ebook) | DDC 940.53/180943841—dc23
LC record available at https://lccn.loc.gov/2020022419
LC ebook record available at https://lccn.loc.gov/2020022420

CONTENTS

List of Illustrations   vii

Acknowledgments   ix

Abbreviations   xi

Map of the Warsaw Ghetto in November 1940   xiii

Introduction   1

1. Establishment of the Jewish
   Order Service   4

2. Organization and Objectives
   of the Service   33

3. Violence and Corruption in the
   Exercise of Daily Duties   49

4. Police in the Eyes of the
   Ghetto Population   76

5. Policemen's Voices   89

6. Response to Violence   102

7. Spring 1942   111

8. Umschlagplatz   121

9. After Resettlement   139

10. The Courts   147

Conclusion   155

Appendix 1. Sanitation Instructions for Precinct Patrolmen *159*

Appendix 2. Official Instruction for the Order Service *161*

Notes *179*

Bibliography *215*

Name Index *223*

Subject Index *227*

Illustrations

Map of the Warsaw Ghetto in November 1940   xiii

1. Jewish Order Service functionaries, Fourth Precinct   2
2. Adam Czerniaków and functionaries of the Jewish Order
   Service by the ghetto gate on the corner of Żelazna
   and Grzybowska Streets   2
3. Adam Czerniaków with functionaries of the Jewish Order
   Service and the Polish Blue Police   7
4. Józef Szeryński with his adjutant, Stanisław Czapliński   11
5. Bernard Zundelewicz   13
6. Marian Händel   15
7. Members of the "Reserve"   18
8. Doctors of the Jewish Order Service   25
9. Members of the Jewish Emergency Service   32
10. Maksymilian Schönbach   34
11. Functionaries of the Gmina Precinct   37
12. Functionaries of the Anti-aircraft Defense Department   38
13. Member of the Jewish Order Service   40
14. Members of the Anti-epidemic Company   51
15. Jewish Cemetery gate   55
16. Central Lockup   67
17. Children imprisoned in the Central Lockup   69
18. Female guards in the Central Lockup   71
19. Policemen of the Jewish Order Service with detainees in
    the Central Lockup   77
20. Adam Czerniaków with functionaries of the Jewish Order
    Service and the Polish Blue Police in the courtyard of the
    Jewish Council   85
21. Jewish Order Service functionaries, First Precinct   93
22. Jewish Order Service functionaries, Second Precinct   99
23. Members of the Disciplinary Section   104
24. Staff members of SEPOR   108

25. Jewish Order Service functionaries, Third Precinct   115
26. Jewish Order Service functionaries, Fifth Precinct   117
27. Jewish Order Service functionaries, Fifth Precinct   118
28. Anti-epidemic Company   126
29. Jewish Order Service functionaries, First Precinct   136
30. Jewish Order Service functionaries, First Precinct   150
31. Ghetto gate at Grzybowski Square   157

ACKNOWLEDGMENTS

My research on the Jewish police in the Warsaw Ghetto and the writing of this book were made possible thanks to the postdoctoral fellowship at Yad Vashem and the European Holocaust Research Infrastructure fellowships at Memorial de la Shoah in Paris and at King's College, University of London. Colleagues from these institutions generously provided me with guidance and invaluable help and have been a great source of support in the early stages of my work. I also benefited greatly from numerous, often very lively discussions of its contents and from advice received at conferences and workshops where I presented my work. I would especially like to express my thanks to Natalia Aleksiun, Giles Bennet, Jakub Chmielewski, Boaz Cohen, Barbara Engelking, Maria Ferenc, Gabriel Finder, Jan H. Issinger, Marta Janczewska, Kamil Kijek, Ewa Koźmińska-Frejlak, Justyna Majewska, Dan Michman, Antony Polonsky, Agnieszka Reszka, Noah Shenker, Paweł Śpiewak, and Andrzej Żbikowski for their generous help and encouragement.

I am greatly indebted to my home institution, the Jewish Historical Institute in Warsaw, which houses most of the material quoted in this book and which showed confidence in my work by publishing the Polish edition of this book. At every step of the writing, I benefited immensely from the expertise of my colleagues in the institute as well as from their personal support and friendship. I especially owe a deep debt of gratitude to all wonderful scholars involved in the full edition of the Underground Archive of the Warsaw Ghetto, without whom this book would have never come into being.

I am extremely grateful to Emily Andrew at Cornell University Press and Claire Rosenson at the United States Holocaust Memorial Museum (USHMM) for their invaluable contributions to this manuscript, as well as to production editor Karen Hwa, copy editor Don McKeon, translators Zygmunt Nowak-Soliński and Krzysztof Heymer, and the staff at Cornell University Press for their wonderful work. I would also like to thank the peer reviewers for their insightful comments.

I dedicate this book to the memory of my teacher and doctoral supervisor, David Cesarani, a wonderful and courageous historian, who believed in this book much more than I ever dared to.

Beyond all the professional support, this book would never come into being without the support of my family. Thank you.

My most heartfelt thanks go out to the children and grandchildren of the Warsaw Ghetto policemen who agreed to speak to me of their fathers' and grandfathers' experiences and their postwar lives. It was only thanks to them that I could attempt even to begin to grasp this topic.

Abbreviations

AAN	Archiwum Akt Nowych w Warszawie (Polish Central Archives of Modern Records), Warsaw
APW	Archiwum Państwowe w Warszawie (State Archive in Warsaw)
ARG	Ringelblum Archive
DP	displaced person or persons
GFH	Ghetto Fighters House
IPN	Instytut Pamięci Narodowej (Institute of National Remembrance), Warsaw
JHI	Żydowski Instytut Historyczny (Jewish Historical Institute), Warsaw
JHIA	Archiwum Żydowskiego Instytutu Historycznego (Archive of the Jewish Historical Institute), Warsaw
KdS	Kommandeure der Sicherheitspolizei und des SD (Headquarters of the Sipo and the SD)
Kripo	Kriminalpolizei (Criminal Police)—criminal police in Nazi Germany
MŻIH	Muzeum Żydowskiego Instytutu Historycznego (Museum of the Jewish Historical Institute), Warsaw
Orpo	Ordnungspolizei (Order Police)—uniformed police force in Nazi Germany
Polish Blue Police	Polnische Polizei im Generalgouvernement (Polish Police of the General Government)—police force in occupied Poland, consisting of prewar state police members, under German leadership
Polish State Police	Polska Policja Państwowa—prewar Polish state police force
RG	record group
RSHA	Reichssicherheitshauptamt (Reich Main Security Office)—organization overseeing security and police forces in Nazi Germany

SD   Sicherheitsdienst (Security Service)—intelligence and security agency of the SS and Nazi Party in Nazi Germany

SEPOR   Sekcja Pomocy Rzeczowej dla Funkcjonariuszy (Section of Material Assistance for Order Service Functionaries)

Sipo   Sicherheitspolizei (Security Police)—state security police in Nazi Germany

USHMM   United States Holocaust Memorial Museum

YIVO   YIVO Institute for Jewish Research, Archives & Library Collections, New York City

YVA   Yad Vashem Archive

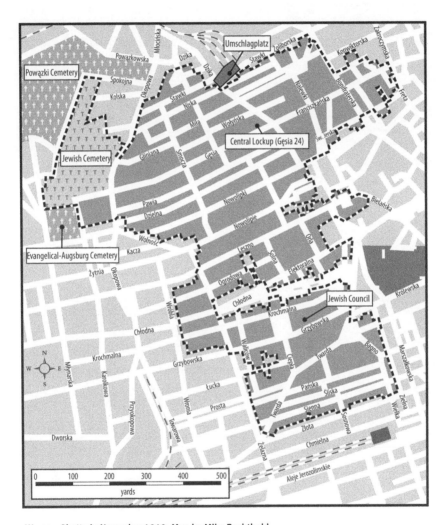

Warsaw Ghetto in November 1940. Map by Mike Bechthold.

WARSAW GHETTO POLICE

Introduction

They were lawyers, engineers, young yeshiva graduates, and sons of businessmen with connections. They came from Warsaw and its suburbs, and many came from Łódź. In the autumn of 1940, they reported by the hundreds to a collection point in the Jewish Council building. They received hats and batons, and the poorer ones were given shoes. They were quickly trained and sent into the streets. "At the time, we treated it very naturally, they gave us a wage after all (and you could not even dream of getting a job) there wasn't much work to do and we got food rations. It was even considered a success—to get into the police," one of the inhabitants of the Warsaw Ghetto recalled after the war.[1]

In a German propaganda film from the spring of 1942, the ghetto policemen differ very little from German soldiers.[2] They stand in two rows, facing one way. When they march, the cameraman concentrates on their shiny boots. Then we see them at work—the kind of work usually associated with German soldiers—they check the identification papers of passersby, stand at the gates of the ghetto, and brutally beat detained children.

In the official album of the Jewish Order Service created at the time, ghetto policemen pose for a photographer at their workplaces.[3] Here, they are focused on officials filling out forms behind massive desks, typists, officers conducting briefings, guards supervising prisoners at work. Some are smiling. At first glance, it looks like any other wartime police precinct.

If you look closely at these photographs, however, you can see worn-out coats, suits that are too large, the damaged shoes of some contrasting with the shining boots of others, the resignation on many faces.

FIGURE 1.   Jewish Order Service functionaries, Fourth Precinct, 1941. Source: JHI, MŻIH E-1/20/4.

FIGURE 2.   Adam Czerniaków and functionaries of the Jewish Order Service by the ghetto gate on the corner of Żelazna and Grzybowska Streets, late 1941. Source: JHIA, ARG I 683-62.

There are other photos, with titles that speak for themselves: "The [Jewish] Order Service 'taking care' of children"; "The Jewish Order Service conducts a search of children 'smuggling' food into the ghetto": "The [Jewish] Order Service organizing a crowd."[4] These photos from the Underground Archive of the Warsaw Ghetto (known as the Ringelblum Archive, or ARG) were taken in the ghetto as an indictment.[5]

As we look deeper into the history of the Jewish Order Service, images clash with images. Jewish policemen are portrayed as dutiful German soldiers, German officials, and, finally, traitors to their own people. Each account, each testimony reveals its own version of the activities of the Jewish police during the occupation. All these narrative threads are reunited on the Umschlagplatz, the collection point by a railway station, where the policemen are burdened with what for many became their final task: that of assisting in the deportation of Jews to the death camp of Treblinka. The question of how they got there constitutes the heart of this book.

CHAPTER 1

Establishment of the Jewish Order Service

Background

On September 20, 1940, the city governor of occupied Warsaw, Ludwig Leist, unexpectedly summoned Adam Czerniaków, chairman of the Judenrat (Jewish Council) in Warsaw.[1] Czerniaków, then fifty-nine years old, was an engineer by training and a prewar social activist who proved to be a very capable administrator, skillfully maneuvering between German demands and the needs of the community entrusted to him. On that day, as Czerniaków wrote in his journal, "a senior official from the district" ordered him to establish a "Jewish Order Service"—a Jewish police force that would be the Jewish equivalent of the Policja Polska Generalnego Gubernatorstwa (Polish Police of the General Government), known as the Blue Police.

As in several other ghettos, in Warsaw the Jewish Order Service was not created as a new entity but was based on an already existing paramilitary organization, in this case the Security Guard of the Judenrat's Labor Battalion.[2] The Labor Department of the Jewish Council, later the Labor Battalion, was established at the Judenrat at the end of 1939 to facilitate the delivery of German-imposed quota of workers for forced labor. The department was at first subordinate to Section IVB of the German Security Police (Sipo) and the Security Service (SD), from mid-April to July 1940 to the Plenipotentiary of the Chief of the Warsaw District, and from July 1940 to the Labor Office in

4

Warsaw (Arbeitsamt). As Czerniaków wrote in March 1940, this institution was set up by the Judenrat "on the one hand to satisfy the demands of the German authorities, and on the other to provide the impoverished population with the opportunity to earn a living."[3] From the beginning of March to the end of May 1940, a Security Guard of 111 people functioned as an extension of the Labor Battalion, dealing primarily with finding men who evaded compulsory labor. After the reorganization of the battalion at the end of May 1940, a separate unit was created from the Guard, and this became the nucleus of the later Jewish Order Service. At that time, the responsibilities of the Guard became much broader. Its members were among others overseeing the construction of a wall around the area of the future ghetto. Beginning in the summer of that year, the Guard patrolled the Jewish Cemetery, where gravestones had been defaced and broken.[4] It also provided security in the Labor Office building and other Jewish Council offices.[5] In late July and early August 1940, official instructions and internal regulations were drawn up for the Guard.[6]

The transformation of the Security Guard into the Jewish Order Service was defined by the Germans as part of the Selbständige Autonomie (Self-Regulating Autonomy) of the Jewish community in Warsaw. This was also the general feeling on the ghetto's street.[7] On March 29, 1940, historian Emanuel Ringelblum, the founder of the Underground Archive of the Warsaw Ghetto and an extremely astute observer of wartime reality, wrote, "Today, there were rumors that the fences around the ghetto area will be replaced with walls. In connection with this, [the prospect of a] ghetto in Warsaw is again seriously discussed, as are the several hundred Jewish policemen the Gmina [Jewish Community, meaning the Judenrat (Jewish Council) and all subsidiary organizations], it was said, is to recruit. Everyone is pulling strings to get these sought-after positions."[8]

While similar Jewish guard organizations responsible for ensuring security had been created in almost all the larger ghettos in occupied Poland, the establishment of a Jewish law-enforcement body is not mentioned in any of the documents regarding the creation of ghettos in the General Government—neither in the express letter of September 21, 1939, from the head of the Reich Main Security Office (RSHA), Reinhard Heydrich, to the commanders of operational groups of the Security Police, nor in the September 13, 1940, decree by the governor-general of the occupied Polish territories, Hans Frank, or Frank's executive regulations issued on September 21.[9] Heydrich's Schnellbrief mentions only concentrations of Jews from the provinces in larger cities and the creation of a council of elders in each Jewish community, which was to be "fully responsible, in the literal sense of the word, for the exact and prompt implementation of directives already issued or to be issued in the future."[10] Heydrich does not specify what measures of enforcement the Jewish councils would have at their disposal. Frank's decree of November 28, 1939, specified the composition and manner of appointing Jewish councils, but it did not mention auxiliary organs. The regulations for this decree, dated April 25, 1940, reported that all orders for Jewish councils would be transferred through district authorities, which explains the manner in which information on the establishment of the Jewish Order Service was passed to Czerniaków.[11] The governor of the Warsaw District, Ludwig Fischer, included no orders pertaining to the service in the order on the creation of the Warsaw Ghetto issued on October 2, 1940.[12]

Importantly, the Jewish Order Service was not directly incorporated into the German Order Police (Ordnungspolizei, or Orpo). Instead, it was explicitly set up as subordinate to the Polish police force under the occupation authorities, popularly referred to (in order to distinguish it from the prewar Polish State Police and to underline its character as part of the German system of oppression) as the "Blue Police." The Blue Police was established on October 30, 1939, by the Higher SS and Police Leader in the General Government, Friedrich-Wilhelm Krüger, and was strictly subordinated to the Orpo.[13] In terms of composition, it was a direct continuation of the prewar Polish State Police. Its members included functionaries of the prewar state police, excluding those of non-Polish ethnicity; its personnel and organizational structure in Warsaw maintained its fundamental continuity. The police wore the prewar navy-blue uniforms of the state police, except that the Polish eagle on their caps was replaced with the coat of arms of the capital of the district in which they served.

The Jewish Order Service had, in reality, to submit to all the decisions of the Blue Police, and the head of the service had to submit his orders for their approval. The Blue Police also controlled the composition of the service: it approved candidates for employment, promotions, and demotions. In organizational terms, the Jewish Order Service in the General Government was subordinate to the local Blue Police headquarters. In Warsaw, the Jewish Order Service was directly supervised by the Blue Police commander there, Col. Aleksander Reszczyński, although his deputy, Maj. Franciszek Przymusiński (commander after the assassination of Reszczyński in 1943), was much more often in the ghetto and became a link between the two organizations.[14] In everyday matters, the Jewish Order Service reported to the Warsaw-North Command, headed by Mieczysław Tarwid. Members of the Jewish Order Service were also supervised in part by the leadership in Blue Police precincts remaining within the territory of the ghetto. Lack of clear legal guidelines often led to lack of clarity regarding the exact relationship between the Jewish Order Service and various levels of the Blue Police, with Jewish policemen often at a loss as to whom they should be addressing.[15] German authorities in some cases defined the relationship between these institutions—for example, issuing orders for the Blue Police to assist the Jewish Council when requisitioning apartments in "Aryan" houses in the ghetto, after the change of ghetto borders.[16]

Thus, the Jewish Order Service in Warsaw was not, by definition, an independent organization but only an auxiliary service that performed tasks imposed on it by the German administration, the Blue Police, and the Judenrat. The first two of these organs played a crucial role in this system of control; one former Jewish policeman, in his wartime report, described the German authorities as supervisory and decision-making and the Blue Police as monitoring and administrative.[17] At the same time, however, the scope of authority of these bodies constantly overlapped, forcing the service's leadership to dedicate a significant portion of its activity to maneuvering between the expectations of various individuals, often of conflicting opinions, who played significant roles in the Jewish Order Service and who exploited it to achieve their private goals. The formation of the service, as defined by one of its members, lawyer Stanisław Adler, was based on the

FIGURE 3. Adam Czerniaków (in a bowler hat) with functionaries of the Jewish Order Service and the Polish Blue Police, late 1941. Source: JHIA, ARG I 683-58.

shifting sands of German legislation that denied Jewish authorities any real powers.[18] Despite the support of the Blue Police, the real power of the Jewish Order Service in Warsaw until the deportation period in summer 1942 was relatively limited in comparison with similar organs in other ghettos in the General Government. Its power did not increase, and unlike in other ghettos, the Jewish Order Service did not become fully independent from the Judenrat. This seems to be the case not so much due to the strength of the Warsaw Judenrat but to the limited contacts between the leadership of the Jewish Order Service and the German authorities. These contacts were taken over by a network of Gestapo informers—independent of the service and in competition with it—some of whom acted openly under the Office for the Prevention of Usury and Speculation (part of what was widely known as the "Thirteen" [Trzynastka], as they were located at 13 Leszno Street in the Warsaw Ghetto). The Thirteen combined the goals of economic exploitation with quasi-charitable activity and informing the Gestapo about events in the ghetto.

The lack of top-down regulations regarding the appointment and operation of Jewish law-enforcement bodies led to significant differences in the functioning of these formations in various localities.[19] Although the functioning of the security services largely depended on local conditions, in most cases the establishment of the Jewish Order Service had a similar purpose that was related to the registration of Jews and their exploitation as a workforce and later included the seizure and spoliation of property and the assembling of the Jewish population and its supervision.[20]

No evidence has come to light that would establish whether there were any working relations between the Jewish Order Service in Warsaw and similar formations emerging in other ghettos of the General Government. Of course, this does not mean that no contacts were made, especially with regard to Jewish law-enforcement organizations in other large ghettos or ghettos near Warsaw, such as the Otwock Ghetto. According to *Gazeta Żydowska* (The Jewish Gazette), a Polish-language propaganda newspaper overseen by the German authorities and distributed in the ghettos of the General Government, security formations in other localities were modeled on the organization in the Warsaw Ghetto, from which they often asked "for technical guidance and information."[21]

Policemen

Adam Czerniaków received the official order to organize the Jewish Order Service on October 12, 1940, along with information about the creation of the Warsaw Ghetto. The next day, at a meeting of the Judenrat, an inspection committee was chosen to oversee the selection of future members of the service.[22]

In Warsaw, as in other ghettos, the selection of the appropriate person to head the local Jewish Order Service was left to the chairman of the ghetto's Judenrat. According to T. (Tadeusz?) Witelson, an officer of the service and at the same time a contributor to the Underground Archive of the Warsaw Ghetto, the commander was elected at an informal meeting held at 69 Pańska Street, in the apartment of Leopold Kupczykier, the owner of a confectionary factory and a member of the Judenrat in Warsaw.[23] Also said to have been present were Judenrat member and prewar judge Edward Kobryner, Adam Czerniaków, and Józef Szeryński. The latter was a candidate for the position of commander of the Jewish Order Service in Warsaw, a convert to Catholicism, and a prewar officer of the Polish State Police, currently an office worker.[24]

Józef Szeryński

Józef Szeryński, a man gifted with great ambition and talent, was in many respects an ideal candidate. Born in 1893 as Józef (?) Szenkman, he completed his secondary education, served in the Russian army, and in 1920 joined the Polish State Police. In March 1920, he was promoted to commissioner, a year later chief commissioner, and in January 1930 to deputy inspector. In April 1929, he became the head of the newly created Press Department of the National Police Main Headquarters and thus the first press spokesperson of the Polish State Police.[25] From May 1935 to September 1939, he served as an inspection officer of the provincial headquarters in Lublin.[26] Despite his limited education and what was undoubtedly a greater obstacle—the fact that he had not distinguished himself during the First World War or the Polish-Bolshevik War—Szeryński quickly climbed the police ranks. Although many claimed that he was alienated and unhappy as one of the few Jews at such a high level in the state police, it is difficult to agree with this opinion.[27] From the progression of his career, it is clear that Szeryński achieved within the police formation all that was possible given his background.

The great advantage Szeryński enjoyed as the head of the Jewish Order Service was his knowledge of the organization of police forces. In 1922, he joined the delegation that created the state police in Silesia, a region that had just been ceded to independent Poland. The delegation aimed, among other things, at organizing accelerated four-week police courses for recruits.[28] At the beginning of his career, Szeryński thus acquired skills that would prove invaluable for his functions in the ghetto. He was interested in the police as an organization throughout the interwar period, publishing extensively on the topic in the specialist press. Among his articles were studies of the history of the Polish State Police, specialist studies in the field of legal regulations, and detailed descriptions of techniques of police operations amply illustrated by stories drawn from the author's own experience.[29] The most interesting are probably those in which Szeryński touches on the realities of everyday police life, directly and in a lively, dynamic language, pointing out to functionaries the most basic issues, from external appearance to good manners.[30] These texts fully support the view, widely held among the ghetto policemen, of Szeryński as a police officer by vocation, a man who fully identified himself with the institution and treated it seriously, and who at the same time skillfully found a common language with rank-and-file policemen.

As his prewar career demonstrated, Szeryński was equally well placed among the higher echelons. In November 1930, the popular newspaper *Dobry Wieczór* (Good Evening) reported on an elite social group that met every week at the Ziemiańska, the most fashionable café of interwar Warsaw: "15 people belong to it so far. Each member of the club received a nickname. At the club table there is a marble plaque engraved with the hours when it is reserved for them." In addition to well-known industrialists, artists, and lawyers, there was also Deputy Inspector Józef Szeryński.[31]

A similar image of Szeryński as a man who appreciated the good life, while remaining precise and practical, emerges from articles he wrote for the official press organ of the Polish army, *Polska Zbrojna* (Armed Poland) and published under the initials "J. S."—a series of short reports from a trip to the Balkans.[32] Picturesque descriptions of landscapes and exotic urban scenery alternate with practical information on prices of meals and how to keep safe. Even when traveling as a tourist, Szeryński remained primarily a policeman.

From many sources we learn that despite Szeryński's qualifications, Czerniaków offered him the post only after two illustrious Jewish lawyers had rejected it. The first was Leon Berenson, one of the biggest stars of the Polish bar, a defense lawyer famous for his role in the political trials of 1905 and the 1936 Przytyk pogrom trials, who, as the policeman Stanisław Gombiński wrote, "personified for many of us, probably for all, the highest virtues of a Pole, a Jew, a citizen, and a lawyer."[33] Equally important, Berenson had previously been involved in setting up the Labor Battalion. However, in the autumn of 1940 Berenson was already in poor health.[34] The authorities of the ghetto also considered the candidacy of Maksymilian Schönbach, a former officer of the Austrian army and a long-time social activist.[35] Schönbach refused to accept the position, however, agreeing only later to take up the lower post of head of the secretariat of the Directorate of the Jewish Order Service. Many other candidates must have appeared, and the position of superintendent of the service was the subject of various types of political games throughout the existence of the ghetto. In January 1941, *Gazeta Żydowska* published a rather enigmatic note about possible changes in the leadership of the Jewish Order Service aimed at rationalization of its operation.[36] It probably referred to the reported attempt to transfer the leadership to Berenson, who, however, refused to accept it. In spite of this and other attempts to make changes at the highest levels of the service, Szeryński remained in his position until the beginning of May 1942.

According to some sources, Berenson was the one who recommended Szeryński to Czerniaków.[37] According to others, it was the journalist and well-known assimilationist, Stefan Lubliner.[38] In any case, the matter of selecting the head of the Jewish Order Service played out within a small, hermetic circle of polonized Warsaw Jews. Even among those most unfavorably disposed toward Szeryński, there were no suggestions that he received this position by order of the Gestapo or the Blue Police, although his prewar acquaintances with Polish police officers were certainly a great advantage. The choice of a person associated with the Blue

FIGURE 4.   Józef Szeryński (seated) with his adjutant, Stanisław Czapliński, mid-1941. Source: JHI, MŻIH E-1/3/3.

Police, the supervisory body of the newly formed Jewish Order Service, was understandable, and this criterion was applied in other ghettos of the General Government as well.[39] According to Polish Underground reports, Szeryński enjoyed "close, friendly relations" with the first superintendent of the Blue Police in Warsaw, Marian Kozielewski, and the chief of staff, Bolesław Buyko, whom he knew from his work at the state police headquarters.[40] The reports go on to say that both Kozielewski and Buyko had demonstrated their friendship to Deputy Inspector Szeryński under the occupation,[41] and so we may suppose that they helped Szeryński after he arrived in Warsaw or even brought him from Lublin to Warsaw. When Szeryński became superintendent of the Jewish Order Service, Kozielewski was already a prisoner in Auschwitz and therefore could not have been involved directly in his selection. However, his successor in the position of commander of the Blue Police, Chief Inspector Aleksander Reszczyński, also had a prewar association with Szeryński. For one year, from September 1938 to September 1939, along with the future superintendent of the service, Reszczyński served as a superintendent in the district command of the Polish State Police in Lublin.[42]

We do not know how Szeryński reacted to the proposal to take such a high position in an unfamiliar milieu. Supporters said that he hesitated, knowing that as a convert he would not be accepted by the Jews of Warsaw.[43] His opponents claimed that he embraced it with elation resulting both from the bad financial situation he found himself in and his ambition, which much exceeded both his talent and previous professional achievements.[44] In making this decision, he surely could not have known, however, what role the Jewish Order Service would play in the life of the yet-to-be-sealed ghetto. When Szeryński took up his post on October 26, 1940,[45] everything indicated that Czerniaków had chosen the right man to organize the service, which at that time was supposed to be, in the strict sense of the word, an Ordnungsdienst (order service).

Although the Jewish Order Service was initially to be dependent on the Judenrat as one of its departments, thanks to Szeryński's strong personality its subordination was never fully carried out in practice.[46] To a great extent, this was the result of Szeryński's confrontation with Judenrat members heading the Seventeenth Department, which was to oversee the service. It was first led by Leopold Kupczykier, who did not have the training or experience that would allow him to carry out such duties. A growing conflict between him and Szeryński led to his replacement by a social activist, attorney Bernard Zundelewicz, who, again, played only a marginal role in the service (referred to by Adler as "decorative secondary role").[47] Adam Czerniaków's diary and the postwar reports of his colleagues clearly show

FIGURE 5.   Bernard Zundelewicz, mid-1941. Source: JHI, MŻIH E-1/5.

that even the chairman of the Judenrat had limited influence over the Jewish Order Service, though he remained on good terms with Szeryński.[48] They met often, at least once a week, going together to the district headquarters of the Sipo and the SD. On Saturdays they took trips together to the town of Otwock, where Czerniaków throughout his time as the chairman of the Judenrat rested from the demands of his daily work.[49]

Officers

One of Szeryński's first steps was to select his coworkers. Taking over the role, he found in the highest positions many former officers of the Labor Battalion's Security Guard, who had automatically transferred to the newly created Jewish Order Service. From various accounts, it is unequivocally clear that that the Guard was deeply infiltrated by the Gestapo, which placed its protégés in its ranks.[50] One of these was Marian Händel, whom Szeryński appointed as the intermediary between the service and the German administration.[51] As Gombiński wrote, Händel "was used for all slippery services, when a smooth person who presents himself well on the outside, slick and with impudence, is needed. And he knew how to deal with these matters, and he had 'his' Germans, so he grew in importance, means, and corpulence. He had no scruples, he did not 'save the community,' he did not sacrifice himself. In the atmosphere of behind-the-scenes intrigue and scheming dinners, he was the right man in the right place."[52]

There is no doubt that the portrait painted by Gombiński was only slightly exaggerated and that Händel was really a man of great potential. As Marcin Urynowicz writes in his study of Adam Czerniaków, Händel also remained close to the chairman of the Judenrat and served him as one of his most important links with the SS and Gestapo informants. He had particularly good contacts with Ludwig Leist and the head of the Resettlement Department, Waldemar Schön.[53] It was thanks to these contacts that he learned about plans to close the ghetto to the outside world in November 1940 and was the first to inform Czerniaków.[54] Szeryński's attitude toward Händel was decidedly negative, and in the end he managed to a great extent to remove him from power.[55] When Heinz Auerswald became the commissioner for the Jewish Residential District (the ghetto) in May 1941, Händel lost influence among the German authorities to another Gestapo collaborator, Israel First.

Szeryński entrusted the remaining high-level positions in the Jewish Order Service to friends and colleagues from before the war, mainly lawyers coming from highly polonized or assimilated social circles. Despite his prewar position, Szeryński remained alienated—a "man from nowhere" within the Jewish community. Unsurprisingly, he surrounded himself with people he knew and trusted. In this way, he introduced into the service the previously

FIGURE 6. Marian Händel, mid-1941. Source: JHI, MŻIH E-1/6/2.

mentioned attorney and diarist Stanisław Gombiński, who was entrusted with managing the office of the Directorate of the Jewish Order Service. Not everyone the new commander brought into the service, however, had the necessary qualifications. The recollections of those opposed to Szeryński paint a picture of "the Colonel's coterie," where Szeryński "repaid self-effacement and obedience with promotion, various privileges, and . . . shares in profit, but he oppressed insubordinate, recalcitrant, or critical ones with unparalleled ferocity."[56] A symbol of these practices was the rise of brothers Stanisław and Marceli Czapliński. They were small-business entrepreneurs who, after the outbreak of the war, gave material assistance to the future superintendent of the service and helped him find a job when he came to Warsaw from Lublin.[57] Szeryński trusted the brothers so much that despite their lack of experience in this field, he appointed Stanisław as his adjutant and Marceli as the head of the Economic Department of the Jewish Order Service.

This team of officers was then joined by lawyers who were brought in by others involved in the creation of the service. One of them was an associate with the Ringelblum Archive, lawyer Zygmunt Millet, who described his recruitment in this way: "In the second half of October 1940, a friend informed me that plans were being made to create a Jewish police force. There was no announcement. My friend told me to hand in my application to him directly, and he would give it to Zundelewicz for assessment. He added that I should try for an officer position because it would be better paid. Indeed, I submitted my application to my friend, enclosing a reference from lawyer [Leon] Berenson. Next, I turned to lawyer Rozensztat, who endorsed my application in writing."[58]

This process was described similarly by Stanisław Adler, who joined the service at the same time:

> On October 19, 1940, I went to the Legal Department of the Jewish Council to begin my campaign for a job that would provide physical and economic survival in that terrible period. Once more I was told that there were no vacancies. However, while I was in the building, I met my colleagues F[ryderyk] Teszner and J. Ajzenberg, who attempted to persuade me to join the "militia" that was being formed. . . . My colleagues were of the opinion that it would be a very socially significant thing to have the ranks of the new organization filled with honest people, especially lawyers. . . . I allowed myself to be persuaded by my colleagues and drafted an application consisting of a single sentence only.[59]

Rank and File

As decided by the verification commission for future Jewish Order Service functionaries, the conditions for admission were from twenty-one to forty years old, completion of six grades of secondary school, adequate health, height at least 170 centimeters (5 feet 7 inches), weight at least 60 kilograms (132.4 pounds), military service completed, impeccable past (no criminal record), and references from two people well known in the district.[60] The recruitment attracted enormous interest. *Gazeta Żydowska* reported that "many thousands of applications were submitted" and on November 8 informed the readers that further applications would not be accepted.[61]

Recruitment was divided into stages. According to the Judenrat chairman's reports, "the composition of the Jewish Order Service was completed very carefully and its members were evaluated in terms of their mental, spiritual, and ethical qualifications."[62] After submitting the application, the candidate stood before the committee, which verified his application and directed him to the examinations carried out by the medical committee. If the outcome was positive, he still had to present himself before the so-called superexamination—a commission led by Szeryński (with time, as Gombiński writes, the commission became a one-man body), which made the final decision. Szeryński thus enjoyed great independence when it came to the composition of the service. However, it is difficult to say whether this was a conscious decision on Czerniaków's part and a sign of his trust in Szeryński or, rather, an omission resulting from the enormity of the tasks that fell at that time on the Judenrat and its chairman. Either way, the Jewish Order Service enjoyed a certain autonomy from the beginning; the influence of the Judenrat and even the German administration on its formation was relatively limited.

Szeryński's decision was approved by the secretary of the Committee of Judenrat Councilors, who had conducted a background review of the candidate.[63] *Gazeta Żydowska* described the activities of the commission: "In response to the application, a request for completing a detailed questionnaire with a description of all qualifications was received. After some time: Medical Committee—weight, height, breathing in and out, ten push-ups, any illnesses. And, finally, the menacing, dignified, piercing look of ten pairs of eyes at the candidate-designate, 'the superexamination.' Fear in anticipation of the decision. Judgment."[64] According to the Judenrat reports, the medical committee examined 1,312 candidates, and 1,000 of them were finally considered fit to join the Jewish Order Service.[65]

Not all of the detailed rules of admission to the Jewish Order Service were strictly observed. In addition to the unclear criterion of "spiritual qualifications,"

FIGURE 7. Members of the "Reserve," mid-1941. Source: JHI, MŻIH E-1/22/3.

the recruitment committee did not have the ability to establish that a candidate had no criminal record. Adler, deputy district commander in the service's Organizational and Administrative Department, who participated in the work of the recruitment commission, describes in his memoirs several colorful figures, known prewar criminals, who used all the means available to them to try to enter the service. According to Adler, at least ten candidates were removed from the list of those accepted after negative outcomes of the verification of their records on the so-called Aryan side of Warsaw—that is, outside the ghetto.[66]

There was also a problem with finding candidates for higher positions who were familiar with Yiddish. In December 1940, *Gazeta Żydowska* reported that "due to the fact that some of the members of the Jewish Order Service do not speak Yiddish difficulties often arise in the performance of their functions. The Jewish Order Service Directorate launches Yiddish courses for those who do not know this language. In the future, care will be taken to see that candidates for the Jewish Order Service, along with other qualifications, have knowledge of Yiddish."[67] Despite these assurances, the Polish language remained the only one used in the internal administration of the service through the entire existence of the ghetto.

Candidates for the Jewish Order Service also had to submit references from well-known figures in the ghetto. The apartments of the members of the Judenrat and other influential people were stormed by close and distant acquaintances hoping to benefit from their influence.[68] On November 28, 1940, Mojsze Bursztyn, living at 53/6 Twarda Street, even wrote to the Inspectorate of the Jewish Order Service at the Judenrat in Warsaw, citing the authority of Mejer Bałaban, a professor at Warsaw University and one of the most illustrious Polish Jewish historians of his day:[69]

> In connection with the ongoing recruitment to the Jewish Order Service, I kindly ask you to count me among its members. I am twenty years old. I am a graduate of the "Tachkemoni" training program in Warsaw. I am healthy, strong, well built, and disciplined. I also have basic training in military preparation, which I had at the Jewish scout organization "Betar." I have been working voluntarily for six months as deputy clerk of Social Benefits in District II of the Jewish Society for Social Welfare. The references for me can be given by Prof. M[ejer] Bałaban and Dr. M. Alter. I hope that my qualifications, Dear Sirs, will meet the requirements and this application will be considered favorably.[70]

Although the support of the Judenrat was of the highest value, *protekcja* (patronage) was sought from the widest possible variety of sources. Zygmunt Millet, an employee of the office engaged in the recruitment of candidates for the service, wrote that over a hundred applications supported by the references of the Gestapo agent Józef Ehrlich had passed through his hands, although we may assume that many of those who sought references from him regarded him as simply a well-connected man, not realizing the source of his connections.[71] Another person from these circles, whose protekcja was considered to be particularly valuable, was Marian Händel, then the deputy commander of the Jewish Order Service. Another future member of the service recalled:

> They could catch you for work . . . young people especially. I was afraid to sleep at night. . . . I had a friend, he was a policeman. . . . His name was Chaim. I said, "Chaim, what should I do?" He said, "Become a policeman." I had someone—it was my cousin's friend who worked in the Judenrat. . . . I went to him, and he gave me instructions—how to pass the doctors and everything. And after that, I became a policeman. It all took me three, four weeks. As a policeman, they couldn't catch me for work, you know.[72]

Thanks to similar intercessions with the service, young men under the age of twenty-one, almost all from wealthy or well-connected families, were accepted as messengers in the service.

The first recruitment to the Jewish Order Service came to an end in the autumn of 1940. In mid-November 1940, the number of service functionaries amounted to 1,635 people.[73] Additional recruits were still accepted in January 1941, increasing the number of policemen to 2,000, although it is not known what that recruitment looked like. *Gazeta Żydowska* informed readers only that Chairman Czerniaków gave an order to present him with candidates for the service.[74] New members were also incorporated in groups, as the scope of the service's activities increased. In the summer of 1941, two hundred policemen were added to the service with the establishment of the Anti-epidemic Company,[75] and subsequently others were added with the liquidation of the Thirteen in the summer of 1941.[76]

There were also other changes in the police personnel. Figures for persons removed from the Jewish Order Service from the moment it was created until the end of 1941 can be found in the supplementary notes to a study on the subject of the service deposited in the Ringelblum Archive.[77] According to the information provided there, 184 functionaries were removed from the list during this period, including fifty-six at their own request, seventy-one by permanent absence, seven who were deemed unfit for service, and nine who died. Another sixteen were removed while verifications were being carried out, including seven because of criminal records. Twelve others were removed on the orders of other organs of authority (nine by the Blue Police, three by German authorities). Finally, the remaining twenty-two were removed for disciplinary reasons: eight as a result of "loss of trust," two after the decision of the Disciplinary Section, and three for abuses committed; the latter were sent to a forced-labor camp. According to the reports of the chairman of the Judenrat, in the first half of 1942, ninety policemen were removed from the service, and replacements were immediately found.[78]

The main reason for the fluctuation was the resignation of those who were unable to stay in unpaid positions any longer. The only ones who were receiving a regular salary were former members of the Security Guard of the Labor Battalion who in November 1940 moved to the reorganized Jewish Order Service as well as several other individuals, including Szeryński and Lubliner. It was only in November 1941 that all high-ranking officers, numbering about one hundred people, began to be paid on a regular basis.

Employment in the service became particularly attractive during the round-ups for the labor camps in the spring of 1941; as the secretary of the Ringelblum Archive, Hersz Wasser, wrote that at that time, any vacant place in the Jewish Order Service was valued at its weight in gold.[79] One of the officers commented:

Any vacant post in the [Jewish] Order Service was considered invaluable, and exorbitant sums were paid. In this branch of the business, however, the [Jewish] Order Service had to share profits with the Blue Police, whose recommendation or approval was necessary for each applicant. Basically, negotiations with "clients" were done by the [Jewish] Order Service only, but there were instances where the Polish Blue Police did their own business on the side and gave the [Jewish] Order Service a command to be carried out. If a client was pressed for time because of the round-up for the camp, the admission to the [Jewish] Order Service, usually quite a complicated and lengthy affair, was dealt with within several hours: this gave way to the saying famous in the Service: "in the morning—a box [with money], in the evening—a number [in the Jewish Order Service]."[80]

Another wrote that prices for a place in the service were widely known and listed on the "ghetto stock exchange."[81] This demand could be exploited by selling candidates' certificates to interested parties—that is, certificates authorizing the acquisition of vacant posts in the service, which were also considered protection against forced labor.[82] Because the Polish Blue Police, who were receiving bribes for approving candidates as new policemen, was also to profit from this trade, only particularly well-connected candidates could get into the service without any fees. The structure of the service was artificially enlarged to give work to as many people as possible. One of the young messengers, the son of a businessman from Włocławek, recounting his work after the war, described it as "delivering various communications from one place to another . . . instructions or various forms, dusting, cleaning. . . . It was really a phony appointment. . . . I think I primarily got this appointment through my father's connections with some other people."[83] Similar opinions appear in the memoirs of officers dealing with the administrative service. Jerzy Lewiński, administrative director of the Third Precinct, recalled after the war that lawyers working in the precinct stayed in the offices for two or three hours a day and were constantly looking for other ways to earn a living.[84] Similarly, Gombiński worked in the Directorate of the Jewish Order Service only before noon,[85] and Adler wrote that he was in the office from nine thirty in the morning to three in the afternoon. He recalls in his memoir, "Compared with my pre-war functions, my present work is childishly easy and absorbs a minimum of time. I am not pressed by deadlines. I am not responsible for anything; it is enough if I work with my usual precision to produce satisfactory results."[86]

A separate case is that of the group of "no assignment" policemen—that is, those who were formally members of the Jewish Order Service and were entitled to the resulting privileges but did not have to participate in daily service. One of these was Abram Wolfowicz. Born in 1917 in Łódź,

Wolfowicz came to Warsaw with his parents in 1939. Because his father was a producer of cold cuts and the owner of a grocery in the ghetto, Wolfowicz started to oversee a meat factory (in the courtyard at 2 Leszno Street) and the sale of meat and bread (at 4 Nowolipki Street, under the company name "Łodzianka"). After the war, Wolfowicz described the mechanism of obtaining the patronage that enabled him to join the service:

> My father went to Dr. Dobrin Berthold, at 36 Leszno Street. [Dobrin] worked and had influence in the Judenrat. Dr. Dobrin put [Marian] Händel in touch with my shop, and Händel began to buy there tea, coffee, cocoa—[products] hard to obtain at the time. After getting to know Händel, I told him that I could get a constant supply of food and other items from the Aryan side, but I needed to be able to move freely. . . . Finally, after numerous attempts with the help of articles of food and, most importantly, interventions by Dr. Dobrin and Councilor [Abraham] Gepner, Händel appointed me as permanent liaison of the [Jewish] Order Service without any specific assignment.[87]

According to the account of T. Witelson, a member of the Jewish Order Service and one of the contributors to the Ringelblum Archive, the largest professional group in the first recruitment were office workers (28.7 percent of the original service), then merchants and industrialists (23.2 percent), representatives of free professions (16.7 percent), technicians (15.2 percent), craftsmen (10.3 percent), and students, pupils, and dependents (5.7 percent).[88] The service was therefore first of all made up of representatives of groups who had either strong social connections or funds for bribes.[89]

As a group, members of the Jewish Order Service were thus relatively well educated, but they were by no means homogeneous. Yet policemen came for the most part from one generation (born between 1900 and 1919) and so had their personality shaped in interwar Poland. They were usually strongly acculturated and at the same time experienced firsthand the growing antisemitism of the 1930s, which often significantly affected their professional prospects. The core subgroup among its high-level members, and one that the service was most associated with, was lawyers. At the end of the 1930s, unemployment in this professional group, especially among the youngest of its representatives, was high.

According to data provided by Gabriela Zalewska, in the academic year 1929–30, Jews constituted over a third of the students in the Department of Law and Political Science at the University of Warsaw. After the introduction of *numerus clausus* (Jewish quota), their number decreased, but in 1934–35 it was still relatively high—23.5 percent.[90] Few of them had any chance of finding a job. In a painful blow, the registry for attorneys was closed in 1938; in addition, the largest professional organizations continued to limit the number of Jewish lawyers. In practice, young Jewish lawyers were thus barred from completing professional apprenticeships, and their path to a professional career was closed.[91]

One of those affected by the closure of the attorney lists, Stanisław Gombiński, was admitted to the Administrative-Organizational Department of the Jewish Order Service and later became head of the secretariat. Gombiński, despite the fact that he was a lawyer, was not entered on the list of attorneys before the war; he worked as a legal clerk in the Workers' Housing Association (Towarzystwo Osiedli Robotniczych).[92] One can therefore understand that young, unemployed lawyers were eager to work in the newly forming Jewish Order Service, where they would have at least some opportunity to use their learning for the first time. They finally got a chance to prove themselves professionally under the supervision of such famous personalities as Maksymilian Schönbach and Leon Berenson—an opportunity that had been taken away from them as antisemitism rose in the 1930s.[93]

During and immediately after the war, many claimed that admitting so many lawyers to the police was a part of a deliberate German policy aimed at demoralizing the Jewish intelligentsia or, conversely, that it was a deliberate action of the Judenrat, which wanted to save the Polish Jewish elite from labor camps and to entrust the authority and power of the police to people with a high social standing.[94] These opinions, however, are not confirmed in the sources. Rachela Auerbach, a writer and colleague of Emanuel Ringelblum, is correct in saying, that lawyers seeking a job in the Jewish Order Service simply had better protekcja.[95] Therefore, the "overrepresentation" of lawyers in the Jewish Order Service resulted from the recruitment mechanisms and not from any particular features of this group.

Many young graduates of well-known high schools in Warsaw claimed after the war that some of their prewar friends had found work in the service. One of the candidates for the service, a graduate of the prestigious Stefan Żeromski Private High School, said in a postwar interview that among the policemen were many of his schoolmates. He himself did not join the service only because he had waited too long to submit an application for admission.[96] But among its members we also find people who grew up exclusively in the Jewish environment, had a traditional Jewish education, and even came from Orthodox families, such as Rabbi Srul Berensztajn. Many other biographies do not fall into the category of "assimilated Jews," to which all policemen were eagerly cast after the war in order to underline their distance from the ghetto community.

Szaja Nusbaum, a native of Żyrardów, had moved with his family to War-saw before the outbreak of the war. In Warsaw, he and four of his siblings began their studies at a Polish state school catering to Jewish pupils, a so-called *szabasówka*, and continued later in the secondary school run by the Gmina (the formal Jewish communal organization). All five also received reli-gious education. Yiddish was spoken in the family home and, as Nusbaum's brother recalled after the war, their entire family, social, and educational lives unfolded within a closed Jewish circle. In September 1939, Nusbaum and his younger brother fled to the East. After a year, they returned to Warsaw and started to trade in groceries. After the ghetto was sealed, Nusbaum joined the police to help his brother in smuggling goods.[97]

Another policeman, Jakub Epsztajn, came from a Hasidic family. In Kozienice, where he was born, he received a religious education and began studying at a public school. Before the war, apart from dealing with Polish clients in the mirror factory in which he worked, he had no contact with non-Jews. Epsztajn was in the ghetto from the moment it was closed to the outside world.[98]

Among the policemen were also sympathizers and members of the Pol-ish Socialist Party (Polska Partia Socjalistyczna), Jewish party activists, such as Zionists Arie Grzybowski,[99] Yehuda Engelman,[100] and Israel Kanał,[101] as well as Bund member Mieczysław Dąb.[102] The name "Luxembourg" also appears in the reports, probably identifying Abram Luksenberg (service number 896).[103] Some former policemen testified after the war that their parties directed them to the service, but this is not confirmed in other sources. They did, however, carry out political tasks, such as distribution of the underground press.[104]

Reports from the ghetto also do not confirm the postwar stereotype of a predominance of Christian converts in the Jewish Order Service. It is true that some of the closest collaborators of Szeryński were baptized, but there were also known cases of candidates for lower positions in the service who were rejected after they were suspected of having been converts to Christianity.[105]

Other Employees of the Jewish Order Service

In addition to the policemen, fourteen or fifteen people were employed in each precinct: a secretary, two instructors working in shifts, two or three clerks of the Officers' Assistance Department for the Jewish Order Service and the Order Service Fund (responsible for enforcement of tax collection for the service), kitchen staff, and tax collectors. The secretary's task was to supervise the correspondence and official records of the station: registration of detainees, crime reports, and others, as well as to prepare reports for the Blue Police, the Jewish Council administration, and the Directorate of the Jewish Order Service. Furthermore, in each precinct, about forty people worked as auxiliary staff: typists, cleaners, and employees and concessionaires of the cafeteria and kitchen. These extremely desirable jobs were reserved almost exclusively for the families of high-ranking officers and those with well-placed acquaintances. One of the employees of the secretariat was the well-known translator of German, Melania Wasserman.[106]

It seems, however, that unlike in the Judenrat offices, work in both the precincts and the Directorate of the Jewish Order Service was well organized. Szeryński, as an experienced organizer, transformed a group of recruits into capable officials who efficiently navigated between the absurdity and the nightmare of ghetto reality.[107]

Among those associated with the Jewish Order Service was also a group of medical professionals. Physicians associated with the service in time were granted the right to wear police caps marked with the Rod of Asclepius; as members of the service they also enjoyed other benefits, such as the right to move around the precinct day and night. They were treated de facto as non-uniformed policemen.[108] The chief doctor of the service was venereologist Dr. Zygmunt Fajcyn, the chief doctor of the Judenrat, who received patients at the clinic at 6 Twarda Street. Among the other nine doctors who were

FIGURE 8. Doctors of the Jewish Order Service. In the middle of the front row is Dr. Zygmunt Fajcyn, mid-1941. Source: JHI, MŻIH E-1/13/1.

involved in treating the members of the Jewish Order Service were Julian
Lewinson, Ignacy Rejder, Włodzimierz Zadziewicz, and Henryk Makower
from Łódź, who was also the head of the infectious ward of the Bersohn and
Bauman Hospital.[109] Reports from the ghetto confirm that here as well contacts were also the key to getting jobs in the service. Makower, for example,
had links to two prominent Judenrat councilors, Edward Kobryner and Józef
Jaszuński, with whom he initially shared a flat.[110] While doctors were treating members of the Jewish Order Service, their families in theory did not get
any medical assistance, but it is not clear if this is how it worked in everyday
practice.

Gestapo Collaborators in the Structures of the Jewish Order Service

The Jewish Order Service was subordinate both to the German civil
administration—initially created at the Resettlement Department (Umsiedlung) under the direction of Waldemar Schön (later the Commissioner of
the Jewish Residential District, Heinz Auerswald), and to the Kommandeur der
Sipo und des SD (KdS, Commandant of the Sipo and the SD), the Department IVb of the Gestapo (dealing with "Jewish" matters) led by Karl Brandt
and Gerhard Mende. The service's contacts with the occupation authorities
should therefore be considered on several levels.

There is no doubt, however, that up to the spring of 1942, Auerswald's
influence was the most visible in the ghetto and in the daily activities of the
service. It was he who made decisions that influenced the everyday life and
work of the policemen: he decided on the rationing of food and which buildings were to be allocated as command posts. It was the commissioner of the
ghetto to whom Szeryński provided highly detailed daily and weekly reports.
Archival documents show that this was not just a formality: the reports were
read carefully in the commissioner's office, and in case of doubt, the superintendent of the Jewish Order Service was asked for clarification.[111]

Although Szeryński knew German well, he kept his contacts with the
German authorities to a minimum, and there is no evidence confirming
that he enjoyed any special treatment. On the contrary, Czerniaków had
to intervene with the SS on behalf of Szeryński after the superintendent
of the Jewish Order Service came into conflict with one of the military
commanders.[112]

While it is difficult to say to what extent the soldiers of the Wehrmacht
who were stationed at the ghetto came into contact with members of the
Jewish Order Service,[113] an important role in the everyday functioning of

the service was also played by the Orpo, which directly supervised the Blue Police, which in turn oversaw the Jewish Order Service.[114] Functionaries of the service also maintained everyday contacts with the Germans through the Transferstelle employees and German businessmen managing workshops in the ghetto, where members of the service were often employed as guards and as escorts for groups of workers.[115]

The Gestapo at that time played a smaller role in the life of the Warsaw Jews. Its contacts with the Jewish Order Service were limited to supplying Brandt with translations of the daily orders and formal approval by the Gestapo of new police candidates. It seems, as police reports confirm, that the Gestapo was not interested in the composition of the Jewish Order Service and only in a few cases openly introduced "their" people into it.[116]

Although it was said in the ghetto that the Directorate of the Jewish Order Service had already "won the war" because "they are vaccinated against typhus, they are protected from starvation and befriended by the Gestapo,"[117] unlike in Łódź, Cracow, or Radom, there were relatively few people in the Warsaw Jewish Order Service who, in a more or less direct way, provided information to the German authorities and would therefore have been identified in the ghetto as informers. Nor were any allegations of this kind made against Szeryński. The exact number of informers or their status is impossible to determine, although it seems that there were not as many as was rumored in the ghetto. As one policeman wrote, "There is no question that [among] 2,000 people are many who are in the confidential services of the Germans. However, it would be difficult to determine their number, tasks, or names."[118] It is also difficult to determine what type of information interested the German authorities. The only surviving report from an anonymous informant from the Warsaw Ghetto contains, almost exclusively, widely known information about life in the ghetto, mainly rumors and reactions to events in the ghetto and beyond its borders.[119] The second report known to us, "Jewish Residential District in Warsaw from November 16, 1940 to November 1, 1941," has been lost, its content known only from an article written by Adam Rutkowski in the early 1950s.[120]

What the real opportunities were for collaborators in the ranks of the Jewish Order Service is not clear today. Certainly the rumors that spread in the ghetto greatly exaggerated them. It was said, for example, that when the Germans changed the borders of the ghetto, Marian Händel was able to negotiate with the Germans, for the price of two kilograms of gold, the incorporation of one side of Sienna Street into the ghetto.[121] Similar rumors circulated about Józef Ehrlich; according to one of the underground newspapers, two Blue Policemen who beat him up were in revenge tortured to death by the Germans.[122] However, it seems that Ehrlich's contacts, like those of the majority of Gestapo informers, were limited to individual policemen and were based on common economic interests.

Ehrlich and others like him were probably much more interested in using their contacts with the Gestapo for their own interests than the Gestapo was in strengthening its position within the Jewish Order Service structure. The rather limited scale of these interests is demonstrated by the applications submitted by Ehrlich to the German authorities. The first, from May 27, 1941, addressed to the SiPo, begins with the words "Józef humbly asks!" Next, Ehrlich writes, "Because I am your loyal coworker and up to the present day I fulfill my tasks to your satisfaction, I kindly ask you to kindly intercede with the Transfer Office regarding the granting of permission for me to import lemons to the Jewish Residential District in Warsaw. I am privileged to plead bowing humbly over this matter, which is of great importance to me, because I have no means to ensure the maintenance of my large family consisting of twelve people."[123]

On the same day, and in similar words, Ehrlich turns to the Security Police with a request for permission to open a cinema in the ghetto.[124] The third letter, from August 1941, contains a request for permission to sell tobacco products in the ghetto. Ehrlich describes himself as "employed by the Security Police, and to the full satisfaction of this service."[125]

Information confirming the influence of the Gestapo protégés on the day-to-day functioning of the Judenrat in the first months after its establishment is found in Adam Czerniaków's diary. However, again the information concerned relatively minor matters, such as pressure for better apartments or work. The only more significant demonstration of Gestapo protégés' influence recorded by Czerniaków took place in early November 1940, when the chairman of the Judenrat was detained in Pawiak Prison for one night as a result of an intervention by a Gestapo informer who held a grudge against him for failing to allocate him an apartment.[126] Later, Czerniaków's daily journal is filled with entries about people "threatening him with a phone call [to the Gestapo]," but he and the Judenrat employees usually ignore them.[127] It seems that those who had the most influence in the ghetto and made a real profit for the German authorities, such as businessmen Moryc Kohn and Zelig Heller, leaders of the ghetto underworld and the most highly placed Gestapo collaborators, did not need favors from the Judenrat.[128]

The ghetto organization most strongly identified with the Gestapo was undoubtedly the Thirteen. The Thirteen was not a single institution but an entire network of institutions, offices, and organizations. The best known

of these was the Office for the Prevention of Usury and Speculation (Preis-
überwachungsstelle). Control over prices and trade in foodstuffs and other
necessities in the ghetto was one of the most important tasks that the Jewish
Order Service was to take over from the Blue Police. According to the reports
of the chairman of the Judenrat, in January 1941, this was still the priority
of the work of the Jewish Order Service. Already in the next month's report,
however, we read that "all actions in the fight against usury and speculation
were abandoned as a result of a command of the [Blue] Police." These tasks
were officially entrusted to the newly created Thirteen. Members of the
Thirteen received hats with a green band (hence they were sometimes called
"gamekeepers") and a band with the name of the office. They were exempt
from the obligation to work and, according to some, also from paying taxes
to the Judenrat; they also had passes allowing them to leave the ghetto legally
for short periods.[129]

The members of the Thirteen were not subordinate to the Blue Police or
the Judenrat; Czerniaków wrote in his journal that he had not received any
official orders about this and did not initiate official contacts with them.[130]
According to the only surviving fragment of the Thirteen's statute of January 25, 1941, it was an office directly subordinate to the governor of the
Warsaw District.[131] It is not clear to what extent and how it was controlled
by the German authorities. According to the statute, the Thirteen's tasks
were "to protect the consumer against various manifestations of usury and
smuggling through the offer of objects of everyday use. Everyday items are
things that serve to meet the everyday needs of people and domestic animals." This protection consisted of, among other things, controlling prices
and the extent of profits. As part of the report on statutory and propaganda
issues, a special cell was created to "explain generally the consequences of
profiteering for the community and, further, of the behavior of the public
in the event of usury or in the event of an attempt to spread panic of usuri-
ous prices."

It seems that the leaders of the Thirteen were conducting independent
activity focused primarily on their own profit; one can also suppose that in
order to increase their profit, in the long run, they planned to seize power in
the ghetto. The details of this activity, as evident from postwar testimonies,
were not widely known. The profits of the Thirteen's officers (similar to
those of the officers of the Jewish Order Service, who were, however, acting
on a much smaller scale) came from shares in enterprises, shops, entertainment venues, and smuggling rings. The office also took over the management of apartment houses on Orla, Leszno, Karmelicka, and Nowolipie
Streets.

In the ghetto, the Thirteen was referred to as the "Jewish Gestapo," and it was widely recognized as an institution comprising individuals who collaborated with the Nazis. There were various rumors, especially about its leader, the journalist and refugee from Łódź Abraham Gancwajch.[132] It was said that before the war, Gancwajch had been a pimp; that he had his own office at Gestapo headquarters at Aleja Szucha; and that well-known actors and writers took part in drinking parties organized by the Thirteen.[133] How exactly Gancwajch came to power is not clear, but it is certain that he acquired this position thanks to his German contacts. According to Adler, Gancwajch was first supported by Wilhelm Ohlenbusch, head of the propaganda department at the office of the Warsaw District.[134] This theory seems probable, taking into account the propaganda in favor of the Thirteen, which can be traced in *Gazeta Żydowska*. Later on, the Thirteen was dependent on the Gestapo.[135] Gancwajch's protector in the Gestapo, as is evident from postwar testimony in particular, was SS-Unterstürmführer Gerhard Stabenow from Department IIID (economic) of the SD (Sicherheitsdienst, the security force responsible for investigation of internal or external opposition to Nazi authorities) in Warsaw.[136]

Competition between the Thirteen and the Jewish Order Service was primarily a result of overlapping areas of responsibility. Price control and trade in foodstuffs and other necessities in the ghetto was one of the most important (and profitable) tasks that the service was to take over from the Blue Police.[137] According to the reports of the chairman of the Judenrat, this was still the priority work of the service in January 1941. In the following month's report, however, we read that all actions in the fight against usury and speculation had already been abandoned on order of the Blue Police.[138] These tasks were officially entrusted to the newly created Thirteen. The Thirteen's annual report, titled "The Jewish Residential District in Warsaw from November 16, 1940 to November 1, 1941," shows that this office was also carrying out its own investigations and acted as a judicial authority.[139] Undoubtedly, those who remained at the edges of the law were afraid of the Thirteen much more than they were of Jewish Order Service. This was because, among other things, the Thirteen successfully confiscated luxury goods, which the Jewish Order Service did not manage to do. As one of the policemen wrote, "Members of the Thirteen dealt with the owners of the shops more uncompromisingly—the German way. They simply confiscated the goods, loaded them in carts, and either the owner later bought them back at the 'office' or the food went to be divided among the officials fighting poverty."[140] The secretary of the Ringelblum Archive, Hersz Wasser, wrote in his diary that there was a belief in the ghetto that the Jewish Order Service was "shaking with fear of the Satan from Leszno 13."[141] The Thirteen's agents had a very clear picture of the activity of the service and reported on it to the authorities.[142]

In the summer of 1941, the Thirteen fell victim to the competition between the German civilian administration, the SiPo, and the SD. Gancwajch, a protégé of the SiPo in Warsaw, lost his privileged position after the civilian administration gained power in the ghetto. On August 5, 1941, quite unexpectedly, the activity of the Office for the Prevention of Usury and Speculation was suspended, and all documents, aside from personnel and disciplinary files secured by the Second Security Police Department, were destroyed.[143] Thanks to Gancwajch's efforts with the Gestapo, two hundred members of the Thirteen were incorporated into the Jewish Order Service; thus the number of its members increased to two thousand. However, they were not granted the special powers that Gancwajch sought.[144] On the basis of files entrusted to it by the Gestapo, containing applications, résumés, and personal questionnaires, the Jewish Order Service qualification commission chose former members of the Thirteen with better reputations. Present at the meeting were representatives of the Directorate of the Jewish Order Service and the Blue Police. Those who were chosen received lower ranks than those they held at the Office for the Prevention of Usury and Speculation. Although no senior officials of the Thirteen were admitted to the service, the transfer of its members to the service certainly did not contribute to improving its image. As Ringelblum wrote, "There is a justified fear that if there are still some decent people in the Jewish police, they will be completely morally corrupt now."[145] Similar developments took place in other ghettos of occupied Poland. For example, in the ghetto in Radom in April 1942, twenty Gestapo informers were admitted into the Jewish police following reports that the policemen were not fulfilling their duties effectively.[146]

After the dissolution of the Thirteen, Gancwajch withdrew from public life and took up trading, although from time to time he tried to play a role in the ghetto. In April 1942, when the mass executions in the ghetto began and when it was announced that the former Thirteen leaders faced the death penalty, he went into hiding from the Gestapo on the Aryan side. Thereafter he appeared in the ghetto only occasionally.[147] Nevertheless, rumors of Gancwajch's return to power, and of his taking over the leadership in the Judenrat, circulated in the ghetto even after the deportations.[148]

Despite the dissolution of the Thirteen, some of its agencies were still operating in the ghetto, including the Jewish Emergency Service established in May 1941. Said to "provide quick and emergency assistance in street accidents,"[149] it was first and foremost a refuge from forced labor for former

FIGURE 9.   Members of the Jewish Emergency Service, mid-1941. Source: JHIA, ARG I 683-26.

members of the Thirteen and their families.[150] Its members received identification cards similar to those held by functionaries of the Jewish Order Service, as well as the same food rations, and were able to access the services of the Section of Material Assistance for Order Service functionaries.

The Jewish Order Service, in contrast to the hated Thirteen, was, after all, widely regarded as an institution of the Jewish administration. Hersz Wasser, who usually assessed it very harshly, wrote in a postwar expert opinion that while the members of the Jewish police were tolerated, the Thirteen was surrounded by distrust and contempt.[151] With time, however, many service members began to use methods more and more reminiscent of those used by Gestapo informers.

Chapter 2

Organization and Objectives of the Service

Organization of the Service

After finishing his description of the intake to the Jewish Order Service, Stanisław Gombiński turned directly to the reader of his memoirs:

> The reader, if he [or she] had lived at that time in the Warsaw Ghetto, would probably stop reading at this point, reach back to [his or her] own memories, and . . . indignantly ask, "So, why was this the state of affairs? If indeed human selection was so careful, so cautious, why were these people so bad, why did they harm the population so badly, why did the people hate them so much?" Let the reader withhold judgment . . . and first become familiar with the actual state of affairs in its entirety. Then try again, for the hundredth time, for the thousandth time, to grasp our reality.[1]

The Statute of the Jewish Order Service was presented to the German authorities on November 12, 1940,[2] and approved by the governor of the Warsaw District on November 29. Stanisław Adler, one of the creators of the Jewish Order Service regulations and author of its statute, based it on the regulations of the prewar State Police and the official instructions of the Blue Police.[3] These regulations were supplemented with instructions contained in the daily orders of the commander. In May 1942, Service Instructions for

FIGURE 10. Maksymilian Schönbach, head of the secretariat of the Directorate of the Jewish Order Service, mid-1941. Source: JHI, MŻIH E-1/7/1.

the [Jewish] Order Service were attached to the regulations, which contained detailed provisions regulating its functioning.[4]

The Jewish Order Service consisted of higher ranks (the commander, his deputy, precinct commanders, and their deputies) and lower ranks (group commanders, section commanders, and policemen). As in other ghettos of the General Government, members of the service were not uniformed; the attribute that immediately distinguished them from other ghetto inhabitants was their cap.[5] Lower ranks received dark blue caps with a light blue band (those who had higher education also had a white and blue cord around the crown) and the emblem of the Jewish Order Service. Policemen also wore yellow armbands with an inscription in Polish and German "Jewish Council in Warsaw—Order Service" and a service number, worn on the right arm between the elbow and the wrist. The lower ranks were marked on the silver braid around the edge of the caps' brims and on the band with yellow pins attached to a black rectangle and others with silver stars (from one to four) embedded in a plush or velvet backing. The officers did not have to display their service numbers on their outer garments, although they always had to have them with them. The rank between the higher and lower ranks was that of the "group commander on plush," who was given the right to wear three pins on a plush or velvet backing.[6] Fees for these distinctions were paid in part by the policemen themselves and in part from the funds of aid organizations. The City Welfare Committee financed, for example, the purchase of twenty-five pairs of shoes and ten pairs of replacements for worn-out soles.[7] The policemen were equipped with batons, and as in other ghettos they did not receive firearms.[8] Those directing traffic had white sleeves so as to be visible at night.[9]

During the first two months of its operations, the Jewish Order Service occupied two rooms in the Judenrat Building at 26/28 Grzybowska Street. As Stanisław Gombiński wrote, "The first served as a law office, in which several officers from the former Guard of the Labor Battalion were busy arranging business and segregating the piles of applications that filled the corner of the room. . . . The second room was the office of the headquarters, where Kupczykier or Händel would 'pop in' for a few moments, where Szeryński met with some of his closest associates. There were also representatives of the Committee of Judenrat Councilors who, before Szeryński took office, processed applications."[10]

At the end of November 1940, the Directorate of the Jewish Order Service first received its own premises, seven rooms in the former school building at 12 Prosta Street. The building, still equipped with school desks,[11] was, however, completely unsuitable for office needs and too small to accommodate the rapidly growing management staff. For this reason, in January 1941, the Directorate moved to 32 Krochmalna Street and then to 17 Ogrodowa Street. The Directorate of the Jewish Order Service consisted of the secretariat and three departments. Department I (administrative and organizational), was responsible for the organization of the entire formation and individual units, the editing of orders, and the training program (after basic training policemen took further courses as part of their service) and consisted of organizational and administrative units as well as service and training.[12] Department II (personnel) dealt with recruitment, maintained personnel files and an index of policemen, and handled misconduct inquiries. The tasks of Department III (economic) were to supervise business premises and purchase of equipment, office supplies, and cash registers; it included SEPOR—the section for assistance to members of the Order Service (see chapter 6). Aside from the three departments, there was the Adjutant's Department for the commander of the Jewish Order Service.[13] The internal structure changed over time. Order and disciplinary units as well as services and training became separate departments. With time, other units were included in the service, subordinated to its superintendent: the Central Lockup and Hospital Sentry Section, the Anti-aircraft Defense Department (established in May 1941 at the Directorate),[14] and a press office for the services of *Gazeta Żydowska*, a particularly important unit because it was through that newspaper that the service shaped its image and circulated information and announcements. This included all information related to the day-to-day functioning of the service that needed to reach ghetto inhabitants, such as announcements on recruitment, changes to the borders of precincts and their headquarters, and changes in the duties of police members. *Gazeta Żydowska* was an extremely important propaganda tool; it was to shape the image of the Jewish Order Service as an element of the "new everyday life" of the Jews of Warsaw shut within the walls of the ghetto. At the same time, as Marta Janczewska wrote, "*Gazeta Żydowska* had to balance between the rules of the game under the occupation and a sense of realism for readers who had to find in it a reflection of their experiences and problems."[15] In order to retain this realism, *Gazeta Żydowska* also occasionally mentioned the abuses of the Jewish Order Service.

The Jewish Order Service was divided into six line companies corresponding to the precincts that were created later; each of these consisted of four platoons, numbering about fifty policemen each. Apart from the companies, there were three reserve platoons, a communications platoon (on bicycles), and an administrative platoon. There was also instructor staff trained to work in the precinct offices.[16] A separate unit, the Gmina (Judenrat) company, was under the personal supervision of Marian Händel and managed by Józef Rode.[17] With a strength of two platoons, it was intended exclusively for the maintenance of order in the institutions and departments of the Jewish Council. This unit was incorporated directly into the Jewish Order Service from the Labor Battalion.

The ghetto was divided into six precincts, the sizes of which changed with alterations in the ghetto's borders.[18] At the head of the precinct was a precinct commander, who had two deputies; one was responsible for the beat patrol duty and the other for the administrative offices and precinct offices. Three platoons served in each precinct, commanded by a deputy precinct commander. The platoons consisted of communications sections and three groups of twelve, commanded by group commanders; each group was divided into three sections consisting of three policemen and a section commander. Line service initially lasted eight hours without breaks; later an eight-hour shift with substitutions was introduced, during which six policemen occupied four posts, turning over every two hours so that two policemen remained in reserve. During the three command shifts, a duty policeman was on duty around the clock.

In April 1941, the organization of an Anti-aircraft Defense Department of the Jewish Order Service began in the ghetto under the strict supervision of the Blue Police.[19] In the Directorate of the service, the Anti-aircraft

FIGURE 11.   Functionaries of the Gmina Precinct, mid-1941. Source: JHI, MŻIH E-1/23/2.

Defense Department was created by Henryk Weisblat.[20] Anti-aircraft Defense reports were also collected from the commanders of individual precincts of the Jewish Order Service.[21] The Anti-aircraft Defense leader in a specific area was the deputy administrative head of the precinct, and the tasks related to anti-aircraft defense were included in the everyday duties of Jewish policemen. Also, in the summer of 1941, the so-called Hospital Sentinel Unit was set up with a strength of thirty to forty policemen. Its aim was to guard Jewish prisoners treated in a hospital in the ghetto.[22]

In the last months before the deportations from the ghetto began, the German administration planned to set up a fire brigade that would operate as part of the Jewish Order Service. Before then, if a fire broke out in the ghetto, the Polish fire brigade intervened, assisted by service members.[23] In February 1942, *Gazeta Żydowska* informed its readers that by decision of the German authorities, "the Polish fire brigade will take part only in extinguishing major fires in the Jewish Residential District. We are to deal with the smaller ones on our own, with the municipal fire brigade providing the necessary firefighting equipment."[24] As one diarist wrote, neither the Judenrat nor the Jewish Order Service sought to establish a Jewish fire brigade, chiefly because of the associated costs and a lack of instructors.[25] But in June 1942, the matter was settled. Jakub Brendel, an officer of the Jewish Order Service and a prewar member of the volunteer fire brigade in Kalisz, was to head the Emergency Fire Service.[26] Two days after the beginning of the deportations, on July 24, 1942, *Gazeta Żydowska* reported that on the order of the commissioner for the Jewish Residential District, an Emergency Fire Service was set up within the Jewish Order Service, with the task of extinguishing small and medium fires. The emergency service had thirty members (they were to receive hats with a red cord around the crown, a service number with a picture of a firefighter's helmet, and an armband with the inscription "Feuerwehrbereitschaft" (Fire Service Guard).[27] However, with the deportations starting, the fire brigade never came into being.

During recruitment, those admitted to the Jewish Order Service were directed to a short training session. Six hundred policemen were trained before the walling in of the ghetto. The training took place in the building and courtyard of the then closed Nożyk Synagogue at 6 Twarda Street under the supervision of the "Reserve" branch headed by Albin Fleischman, formerly a captain in the Polish army. The Reserve was a formation dealing with the organization of the Jewish Order Service that functioned until January 1941.[28]

Rafał Lederman, a lawyer and head of the Service and Training Department, oversaw training of the recruits. By all accounts, practical training amounted mainly to drill exercises. "Policemen were not taught their

FIGURE 12. Functionaries of the Anti-aircraft Defense Department, mid-1941. Source: JHI, MŻIH E-1/12/4.

obligations to the population; instead, they were trained to march and do military exercise without weapons, and later (when the word spread about crowds raiding the Jewish Council in Łódź), they were also taught the wedge march, aimed at breaking up crowds."[29] Theoretical training was modeled, to a large extent, on the training that Blue Policemen went through; according to one of the trainees, a significant part of it concerned criminal law issues, which was not within the purview of the Jewish Order Service.[30] Training of successive groups of recruits to the service continued throughout the ghetto's existence.

Daily Duties

On November 16, 1940, the ghetto was sealed, and the first members of the new Jewish Order Service went out onto the streets. Their duties included the regulation of pedestrian and vehicular traffic on the streets of the ghetto, which was implemented by Blue Police members. Jewish Order Service policemen were also included in the Blue Police patrols. The district police command of the Blue Police in the ghetto was initially located at 56 Kroch-malna Street but was later moved to the building at the corner of Żelazna and Chłodna streets. Before the ghetto was sealed, the following Blue Police precincts were located in what would become its territory: Third Precinct (headquartered at 53 Nowolipki Street), Fourth Precinct (10 Niska Street), Fifth Precinct (4 Lubeckiego Street), Sixth Precinct (10 Waliców Street), Seventh Precinct (56 Krochmalna Street), and Eighth Precinct (52 Śliska Street). Four of them—stations for the Third, Fourth, Fifth, and Eighth—functioned after the separation of the ghetto from the rest of the city. Each had a staff of twenty to thirty functionaries, and therefore about ninety Blue Policemen were stationed in the Warsaw Ghetto.

Polish and Jewish formations together conducted daily patrols in the precinct and carried out anti-aircraft defense supervision. Auxiliary units (including permanent bicycle liaison with the Jewish Order Service) were assigned to each Blue Police precinct. Precinct commanders Capt. Władysław Rodkiewicz, Capt. Wacław Kleczkowski, and Capt. Leon Dymiński also participated in formal roll calls and other gatherings organized by Szeryński.

By calling the newly formed formation in the ghetto Jüdischer Ordnungs-dienst (Jewish Order Service), the German administration aimed to emphasize its subordinate position in relation to the Blue Police (i.e. the "real" police). Of the three areas that were within the scope of duties of the prewar state police—general order keeping, fighting criminality, and protecting the state system—the Jewish Order Service was designated for order tasks only. These were specified in Józef Szeryński's order of December 23, 1940:

1. Preventing Jews from gathering on street corners and in front of houses.
2. Regulating pedestrian traffic on streets, especially at intersections.
3. Removal of obstacles to pedestrian and vehicular traffic, such as wagons and prams, as well as people trading on the streets or carrying any bundles on the pavements etc.
4. Overseeing the cleanliness of pavements and roadways.
5. Supervising the cleanliness of courtyards, staircases, and places of general use in houses.[31]

Other order tasks were set by the commander of the Jewish Order Service and precinct commanders in the daily orders,[32] which also provided information about personnel changes, reprimands, and commendations. In practice, therefore, the scope of duties and the role of the service in the ghetto were much broader than that of the formation from which it originated—the Security Guard of the Labor Battalion.

FIGURE 13. Member of the Jewish Order Service by the fence on the corner of Walicόw and Krochmalna Streets, late 1941. Source: JHIA, ARG I 683-53.

The daily activities of the Jewish Order Service can be recreated today from reports created for the German administration. The archive of the Institute of National Remembrance in Warsaw houses a collection of "Daily Reports of the Directorate of the Order Service for the German Commissioner" concerning planned official activities and confirmed service failures in the ghetto, compiled by the commander of the service and covering the period from January 8 to July 20, 1942. In accordance with their title, they contain information about the daily tasks of the service as well as identified and secured places of smuggling.[33] These reports are complemented by the "Weekly Reports of the Order Service in the Jewish Residential District in Warsaw," sent by the chairman of the Judenrat to the commissioner for the Jewish Residential District in Warsaw from June 1941 to July 1942.[34] They contain, primarily, information on crimes committed in the ghetto but also about the daily tasks of the service.

The reports contain summaries of information on order-keeping in the ghetto and were probably based on the daily reports of heads of precincts submitted every day to the Directorate of the Jewish Order Service. Although the reports of heads of precincts have not survived, we know that they consisted of reports on manpower and situational reports on the events of the day in the precinct, including fires, holdups, murders, suicides, other sudden deaths, discovery of a corpse, construction catastrophes, tram-related accidents, broken tram electrical lines, broken sewer pipes, and broken water mains.[35] Information on the functioning of the service during this period and its daily tasks can also be found in the reports of the Judenrat kept in the Underground Archive of the Warsaw Ghetto and in the state archives in Warsaw covering the ghetto's entire existence. The image of the ghetto coming from the daily police reports, in which the biggest problem is the bursting of pipes, is of course completely different from that created during the work of the Ringelblum Archive.

Roll calls for Jewish Order Service were held every day at six o'clock in the morning in the courtyard of the Jewish Council Building. On January 12, 1941, the service officially began its duties in six precincts. In the order of that day, Józef Szeryński called on all policemen to be "conscientious and zealous in the performance of their duties, to comply with orders, regulations and ordinances, to maintain the dignity of service members both on duty and off duty, keeping in mind that in relation both to the populace and to each other, the Jewish Order Service is a public service, performed in accordance with the social and civic interest."[36]

The central element of service was patrol of the precinct. During the daily patrols, the policemen had, according to their official instructions, "to

walk along the sidewalks beside the roadway (the cobblestones), to provide polite and accurate answers to people's queries, [and] to help anyone
in need."[37] Their duties included ensuring the continuity of traffic on the
roadway and sidewalks, preventing theft, drawing property owners' attention "if any items are placed so that they can be tempting to a thief," and
recording accident damage to buildings, pavements, or streets. Although the
patrols were carried out on foot, in exceptional cases, when it was necessary
to "help (people who had fainted, children, the sick) or carry things that
cannot be delivered on foot to their destination because of the weight," the
Jewish Order Service members were entitled to use horse-drawn cabs, and
the cab drivers were obliged to carry out their commands.[38]

The duty instructions also required members of the service to pay special attention to cases of the abuse of animals, such as horses unable to
work or the overloading of carts. During night patrols, policemen were
obliged to check whether gates, doors, and shop shutters were closed and
pay attention to any suspicious state of affairs, "for example, a light that
was usually on is off or the other way around, or it is brighter than usual,
suspicious murmurs or noises are heard," and to initiate investigation.[39]
Some policemen were sent each day to the permanent posts, where their
tasks included surveillance of the street. They also monitored cars, carts,
and cycle rickshaws for adherence to safety regulations, including proper
lighting, driver's documents, and transported goods. Policemen at checkpoints were also to look out for suspects among the passersby. The official
instruction required that "if a pickpocket or other suspicious person gets
on a tram or an omnibus, the functionary should immediately and confidentially inform the conductor, warn other passengers, and watch the
suspect."[40]

Permanent posts were also created near the walls and at the gates of the
ghetto. After the ghetto was separated from the rest of the city, twenty-two
gates were made in the surrounding walls (later fifteen, as the ghetto was
more hermetically sealed), which were supervised by at least two Orpo members who manned two-hour shifts and two Blue Policemen. The number of
Jewish Order Service policemen at the gate was dependent on the intensity
of traffic. Their shifts lasted from 7:00 a.m. to 1:00 p.m. and from 1:00 p.m.
to 9:00 p.m.[41] In addition to manning the gates, their service included standing guard next to the walls and border barriers, which were guarded from
the Aryan side by the Blue Police. To the tasks of the Jewish Order Service policemen was added the monitoring of people and trucks, preventing
anyone from sneaking through gaps in the walls and fences, and combating
smuggling. They checked the walls every day, taking note of the holes made

by smugglers. They also had to remove the bodies of those murdered at the walls: people caught smuggling or trying to cross over them illegally.[42]

An important part of the so-called normal duties of the Jewish Order Service was monitoring sanitary conditions. With the extreme poverty prevalent in the ghetto, terrible overcrowding, and the recurring outbreaks of typhus, tuberculosis, and dysentery, one of the most important tasks of the service was to monitor the sanitary condition of the ghetto's buildings, courtyards, and streets. The reports reveal that despite constant inspections and interventions with custodians and house committees (self-help organizations consisting of representatives of an apartment block responsible for organizing social aid among inhabitants of that building), the effects of the activities of the service in this field were doubtful. Streets and buildings in the ghetto remained in a catastrophic condition, and the constant battle against the causes of epidemics was thwarted by inadequate garbage collection and inefficient sewer maintenance. The Blue Police, the city council, and the city cleanup council did not cooperate with each other, which of course made the situation worse. As one policeman wrote:

> The City Council of Warsaw does not perform its duties towards the "Jewish district." It does not clean the streets, garbage was not removed, sewer manholes were not repaired, etc. and the commissioners and deputy commissioners of Jewish houses did not contribute money to keep their homes in good sanitary conditions. All together and separately—they complained about the catastrophic state of the ghetto, not knowing or not wanting to know which side was to blame. The [Jewish] Order Service in this case—as in all others—suffered the consequences of their impotence and the lack of funds. So it can be summarised that the orders of the [Jewish] Order Service Directorate (very "energetic" and in a threatening tone) could not be and were not carried out.[43]

Initially, members of the Jewish Order Service were sent out to perform sanitary operations unprepared, as part of their regular daily duties. Later, sanitary platoons were created in each precinct, and these were to cooperate with the Judenrat's Anti-epidemic Department. In June 1941, an anti-epidemic unit was established at the Directorate of the service, led by Deputy District Commander Manfred Talmus. Finally, in November 1941, an anti-epidemic company composed of two hundred policemen was formed under the leadership of Mieczysław Szmerling. The company's task was to support the house commissioners in the fight against typhoid epidemics. Policemen assisted the disinfection columns and, if necessary, performed guard duty at quarantined apartments or entire apartment blocks. At the peak of the epidemic, around two hundred policemen were assigned to anti-epidemic duty each day.

The Jewish Order Service was not authorized to conduct criminal cases. If its members observed a crime, they were obligated to inform the local Blue Police station. Historian Aharon Weiss in his work on the service in the General Government points to three basic areas of activity of the Blue Police in the Warsaw Ghetto: monitoring the work of the Jewish Order Service, directly supervising the Central Lockup at Gęsia Street, and, finally, fighting crime.[44] There are few reports of their monitoring the everyday work of the Jewish Order Service, so it can be assumed that this was not a frequent occurrence. Similarly, supervision of the Central Lockup, which was staffed exclusively by members of the Jewish Order Service, was probably limited to occasional visits. The task of the Blue Police that should therefore be considered the most important was the conduct of criminal cases in the ghetto.

Jews arrested by the Blue Police were transferred to the German prosecutor's office at the German Special Court (Staatsanwaltschaft bei dem Sondergericht Warschau),[45] which then referred the case to a Polish court (subordinate to the occupying authorities), or, when there was a "threat to the security of the German nation," to a German court. The German courts dealt with all offenses against war legislation, including illegal crossing of the ghetto border, not wearing armbands, and illegal economic activity. The Polish courts dealt with common crimes within the scope of the prewar penal and civil code.

Although the task of the Jewish Order Service was to secure the crime scene, detain the suspect(s), and then to transfer further proceedings to the Blue Police, in practice most cases were settled by the service in the ghetto. The weekly reports of Józef Szeryński show that only about sixty people monthly were handed over to the Blue Police.[46] This was primarily due to the fear that the matter would subsequently be referred to the German court, but also due to issues of practicality. The transfer of a case to the Blue Police entailed, among other things, the necessity of bringing the suspect and witnesses to interrogation outside the ghetto, which was a logistical problem for both the Blue Police and Jewish Order Service.[47] No doubt, this is why most of those detained by the Blue Police were immediately released in exchange for a bribe.[48] Although the chairman of the Judenrat stressed in a weekly report in January 1941 that no unit for investigative services was to be set up within the Jewish Order Service,[49] proposals to create a Jewish criminal police (as one might suppose similar to the one functioning in the

Łódź Ghetto or the equivalent of the Blue Police's Kriminalpolizei) appeared from time to time.[50] In June 1942, *Gazeta Żydowska* informed its readers that a criminal investigation bureau had been established within the Directorate of the Jewish Order Service. However, no further information about its actions has come to light.[51]

For more serious matters, or ones concerning ghetto inhabitants with some property at their disposal, the Jewish Order Service organized settlement hearings. In precincts, the person responsible for criminal and civil administration of justice was an instructor at the rank of a group commander "on plush" who issued judgments, usually in agreement with the head of the precinct, after hearing witnesses and crime scene investigators; such matters never went beyond the walls of the ghetto. In the spring of 1942, *Gazeta Żydowska* reported that the mediation activity of the Jewish Order Service enjoyed "the great recognition and trust of the Jewish population," but the reality was much more complex.[52] One officer wrote that he usually managed to bring both sides to a settlement when he used persuasion but also a threat of arrest or detention for one or two days. "In practice, there are still more measures in the form of 'harassment,' such as extracting people from apartments at night and taking them to the precinct station 'to explain,' keeping suspects in the precinct station and forcing them to do dirty and unpleasant work, such as cleaning the lavatories at refugee shelters."[53] The same author estimates the number of cases dealt with as being in the area of around 150 per day.[54]

Initially, most offenses reported to the German authorities were related to noncompliance with sanitary requirements and public order (although it is difficult to say what was meant under the second term). With time, reports of offenses related to noncompliance with anti-aircraft defense, such as failing to observe the compulsory blackout, began to prevail. The weekly reports clearly show that from mid-1941, the number of detected offenses, or at least those reported to the German authorities, was growing very steadily. It is difficult to establish whether this was due to the continuous brutalization of everyday life in the ghetto, the increasing sense of threat and resulting chaos, or an increase in crime; more efficient operation of the Jewish Order Service; or, finally, the greater interest of the German authorities in the internal affairs of the ghetto in preparation for Operation Reinhard, the plan to murder approximately two million Jews living in the General Government.

The Jewish Order Service operated within this organizational framework (with some modifications) throughout the ghetto's existence. However, it was not the ordinances and instructions but rather the practicalities of living in the ghetto that determined the service's daily activities. Life in the ghetto was governed by a peculiar dynamic that forced changes in the functioning of the service. One of the key changes involved the assistance service at the Judenrat.

Although assistance to the Judenrat was not listed among the tasks of the Jewish Order Service, the service from its beginning took over the duties in this regard from the Security Guard of the Labor Battalion. Ultimately, Adam Czerniaków sanctioned it at the end of December 1940, adding to the list of duties of the service the seventh point: maintaining order in public buildings and offices, especially the Judenrat and its institutions.[55]

The permanent duties of the Jewish Order Service in this area included manning checkpoints in front of the Judenrat's buildings; maintaining order within its offices; carrying out various types of debt collection from business owners and shops, individuals, and home committees; monitoring the condition of residences (sometimes evicting and quartering tenants); and registering men for forced labor.

New tasks also resulted from subsequent demands the Germans made of the Judenrat. These included rounding people up for forced labor, escorting groups to labor sites, securing the ghetto walls, assisting requisitions, and collecting payments as well as monitoring blackouts and anti-aircraft defense at night. The policemen also took impromptu action at the request of other institutions. In the period covered by surviving daily orders (November 1940 to January 1941), this included conducting a census of "application offices, typing, and translation offices" and creating "a list of owners of all kinds of horse-drawn vehicles, carts, trolleys existing in the Jewish District. etc.," made on the order of the Industrial and Trade Department.[56]

Benjamin Murmelstein, a senior member of the Judenrat in Theresienstadt, called that ghetto an "as if" town: "as if coffee, as if meals, as if a job."[57] Jews locked in the ghettos of occupied Poland also wrote about the experience of "life as if."[58] In the "as if" world of the Warsaw Ghetto, there appeared in the autumn of 1940 "as if policemen." The policemen were not real, just as Jewish self-government was not real—a parody of the Jewish state closed in behind walls. Their "as if" status was emphasized by the German authorities, who did not call them policemen but rather only order officers of the Jewish Order Service.

Jewish policemen often become symbols of the superficiality of ghetto institutions, of ghetto "life as if." It must be emphasized, however, that regardless of their later corruption and the role they played in German policy, the daily routine of Jewish Order Service was not at all a facade.

After they received nominal training, the functionaries were thrown into the middle of the nightmare of the ghetto, taking over all the tasks carried out to that point by the Blue Police.

Everyday dramas with which the policemen were confronted are well illustrated by the problem of abandoned and orphaned children. Janusz Korczak, in his spring 1942 study "The Child and the Police," described the children with whom the members of the Jewish Order Service had to deal and for whom they had to take responsibility:

1. Infants and those children over a year old who cannot walk yet.
2. Children who, due to disability or lack of strength, unhappy incident, illness, or deep mental retardation, cannot walk on their own and must be taken to a hospital or care facility.
3. Detained children who do not want to be brought to the designated place and who attract a crowd with their cries or their behavior.
4. Children abandoned or lost or brought by temporary caregivers with a request to take care of them—in the late evening hours, in order to ensure that they are given the first night without bathing and disinfection of clothing.
5. Older children and adolescents detained at a place where an offense or crime was committed.
6. Children and adolescents who are handed over to the [Jewish] Order Service by the Blue Police, the gendarmerie [i.e., the Orpo], or persons injured and assaulted.
7. Children who can be identified as or are suspected of being the object of exploitation, forced to beg and to commit punishable acts.
8. Underage prostitutes.
9. Mentally disabled minors.
10. Corpses of children on the street and in communal spaces.[59]

Children were brought by members of the Jewish Order Service to hospitals or care facilities, which either refused to accept them because of overcrowding or were not able to provide them with adequate care. To remedy this, the policemen took the initiative to create so-called detention centers, where children would be detained after the curfew. Initially, they were supposed to remain there only temporarily, but with time the detention centers became de facto children's homes, where about thirty to forty children stayed permanently.[60] Funds for financing the assistance activities of the Jewish Order Service, including detention centers, were collected during concerts of the police orchestra conducted by the pioneer of Polish jazz, Szymon Kataszek, among other events, and during presentations of the short satirical revues titled "In Our Precincts" (U nas w Rejonach), which were performed in various entertainment venues in the ghetto starting in January 1942.[61] The author of the revues was an officer of the Jewish Order Service, Jerzy "Jerry" Ryba, a well-known prewar writer of revue songs.[62]

CHAPTER 3

Violence and Corruption in the Exercise of Daily Duties

Corruption

"In the dirt battalion—extortion of money," Adam Czerniaków wrote on May 19, 1940, describing corruption, which since the first weeks of the Labor Battalion's existence had paralyzed both the battalion itself and the Guard that functioned as part of it.[1] The horror of forced labor and thus the power that the Labor Battalion held over the individual fate of Warsaw Jews undoubtedly provided ample opportunity for abuse. Corruption, often the brutal forcing of "contributions" for the battalion,[2] took place at all its levels—from its leader, Maurycy Halber, to its rank-and-file members. As early as April 1940, Emmanuel Ringelblum described the "new type of catchers" assisting Germans in organizing roundups for labor camps "without armbands and their pockets full of eggs. They took them as payment from Jews. . . . In a word, a new fashion: Jewish catchers."[3] A few pages later he described "Jewish catchers from the Judenrat."[4]

At the beginning of June 1940, the widespread corruption in the Labor Battalion became so bad that SS-Untersturmführer Gerhard Mende, a deputy of Karl Brandt, a reporter for Jewish matters in the Gestapo, intervened in it.[5] There were rumors that the battalion was to be replaced by the Blue Police in the task of escorting Jews to forced labor.[6]

The newly established Jewish Order Service initially offered hope for the end of these practices. The organizational statute of the service clearly prohibited corruption; members "acting for the purpose of obtaining property or personal benefits for himself or for other persons" and those who "assume or benefit from financial gain or its promise for himself or another person" would be penalized.[7] The later internal regulations of the Jewish Order Service were even more detailed—they forbade the "offering of gifts" and "funding of superiors by the collective or individual functionaries of the Jewish Order Service." Gifts were defined as "all items having an exchangeable monetary value."[8] In reality, however, collecting larger or smaller amounts during daily duty became the main source of income for policemen and was reluctantly tolerated by both the Jewish administration and the German authorities.

The corruption of the Jewish policemen affected everyone—from businessmen from whom the money was taken in a Mafia-type manner to ordinary people forced to pay bribes for admission through a back door to an office, alleged violation of the curfew, or noncompliance with the blackout order.[9] Over time, the rumors about the greed of policemen who were ready to do anything for an easy profit became more and more shocking. In September 1941, the ghetto was shaken by rumors about the Jewish policemen guarding the cemetery: they "dig up the graves at night, pull out gold teeth and remove the dead body's shroud."[10] There was also recurring talk of extortionists from the Jewish Order Service cooperating with the Blue Police.[11]

Although *Gazeta Żydowska* tried hard to describe the corruption of policemen as both an element of the ghetto "folklore" and something that was commonly accepted, such actions were almost uniformly considered to be contrary to social solidarity and thus not justifiable.[12] The exception is personal testimonies in which corruption and banditry were perceived as a characteristic of the ghetto's system of government and not the independent actions of policemen. Stanisław Różycki, one of the most attentive observers of everyday life in the ghetto, commented in the spring of 1942 on the corruption of members of the Jewish Order Service:

> This is a very worrying symptom. It is no longer that individuals are guilty of blackmail or rape. It is not even that people at large are guilty of lawlessness, which the authorities tolerate or helplessly ignore. It is rather the overt, official lawlessness, sanctioned by the law and cynically practiced. These pirate methods prove the bankruptcy and absurdity of the political system.
>
> Indeed, you could say that the example is set from above, that it imitates the methods of the occupier. But this argument is invalid because

the occupier, who unceremoniously and boldly exploits the occupied population, can do things that our own Judenrat should not, if it wants to maintain some authority in society.[13]

Corruption in the Fight against Epidemics

Another field of routine corruption, and one that was increasingly linked to physical aggression, was what was euphemistically labeled "the disinfection of apartments"—the basic method of combating the persistent typhus epidemic. In reality, the term "disinfection" amounted to extortions, destruction of apartments, and theft, as well as violence, especially in the bathhouses to which residents were brought to be disinfected.

The disinfection of an apartment block within the ghetto began with the arrival of policemen and the closing of the courtyard gates. Then a succession of people appeared: a doctor, a manager, five so-called triple sections (with sections officers), which were assigned to the apartments designated for disinfection, and a policeman, in case there was a need for intervention (for example, in the event of resistance or a closed apartment). If it was found that there were cases of typhus in the building, the Jewish Order Service blocked the entire building in addition to the specific apartments in which the sick persons lived; they then escorted them and other residents of the apartment to a quarantine site and the remaining building residents to the

Figure 14.   Members of the Anti-epidemic Company, mid-1941. Source: JHI, MŻIH E-1/14/3.

bathhouse. In the meantime, the special team assigned to this duty disinfected the apartments. If the residents of the building were sent to the bathhouse at 15 Spokojna or 93 Leszno Streets, they were escorted out of the ghetto.

The disinfection of apartment buildings between Ciepła and Rynkowa Streets and on Krochmalna Street on August 28 and 29, 1941, and the forced disinfection of their residents became infamous in the history of the ghetto. This *Aktion* (action) was organized by the Department of Health on the orders of the German authorities; according to one witness, more than one hundred functionaries of the Jewish Order Service took part alongside Orpo men and Polish Blue Policemen.[14] The buildings selected for disinfection were inhabited mainly by the poorest members of the ghetto population. A former officer of the Jewish Order Service, Samuel Puterman, described a typical disinfection in his memoir:[15]

> Rifle butts, screams, and shots pushed them into the Market Square, the former area of the Wielopole stalls. The healthy carried sick people, covered by a tarpaulin, a tablecloth, a dress. Wretched hovels spat out other frightened people, in rags, people in rags, thousands of rags. Paralytic, elderly, the sick and children with their young, muffled, swollen eyes and faces of the elderly crawling on the muddy pavement. The eyes of the sick, burning with typhus fever, hundreds of mouths whispered words of prayer, thousands of groans made the humming sound of a whirlwind, and over all this the gendarmes of the [Jewish] Order Service raged.[16]

Residents of houses were kept in the street all night long, in the rain, without food. The Jewish Order Service officers noted in a report for the Judenrat: "A dead five-year-old boy was taken from his mother's arms; a twenty-year-old young woman was found dead in front of the market hall. Women with children in their arms walked all night because it was impossible to lie on the asphalt."[17]

After returning home, the inhabitants of Krochmalna Street found their apartments looted and their remaining belongings destroyed during the disinfection. The Jewish Order Service functionaries were uniformly accused of failing of intervene and to warn residents about the planned disinfection (which would have entailed no risk or cost to the policemen), even though it seems today that only the top leadership of the Jewish Order Service knew about it.[18] Regardless of what happened, this tragic action affected the image of the service. The Jews in the ghetto now saw the Jewish Order Service as partners in the violence of the Blue Police and the Germans, oppressing particularly those who could not afford bribes. Those who could afford to do so were ready to pay to avoid disinfection, and policemen willingly participated in these payoffs.

With the help of the Jewish Order Service, the Department of Health also carried out so-called collection blockades, the purpose of which was to obtain from the residents of a building overdue payments for carrying out disinfections. This blockade, according to the directions of the Health Department, could last no longer than forty-eight hours and usually also included shops and companies located in the building. Sometimes the building's House Committee paid the Jewish Order Service in advance so that they would let out the tenants who paid a fee to the Health Department but could not leave the building because the principle of collective responsibility was in force.[19]

Corruption was apparent in the disinfection operations from the very beginning. Describing the disinfection *Aktion* in his apartment building carried out by the Blue Police before the ghetto was sealed, ghetto postman Peretz Opoczynski wrote:

> Soon screams are heard in the yard: the Polish [Blue] police are hitting people with rubber truncheons; they block every exit from the building so that there is no place to go except into the line for the baths. Some of the police stand in the exits, while others run through the apartments, driving people to the bathhouse. From everywhere screams and cries are heard. The stall keeper's wife, who is pregnant, tries to explain to a policeman that she can't go into the bathhouse in her condition; but he brings his stick down on her head, and her agonizing cry echoes through all the floors.
>
> In truth, the brutality of the police is a first-rate ploy: the butcher calls in several policeman and, locking the door behind them, takes a flask of whiskey from a cabinet, sets a plate of sliced wurst on the table, and even . . . opens up his wallet. Afterwards the police emerge with red mugs, and everything is hush-hush.[20]

As early as the beginning of November 1940, *Gazeta Żydowska* informed readers about a "certain resentment" among residents of the soon-to-be-sealed ghetto with reference to the disinfection units, while at the same time it emphasized their role in the "fight against death."[21] Yet extortion soon became the primary task of the disinfection units and the police functionaries who participated in them. The easiest way to earn money for policemen was to charge for warning residents of a building that was targeted for a sanitary inspection. This is how one of the officers described it: "The [Jewish]

Order Service went into the area of the designated building, alerting the residents and whistling and shouting, 'Everyone downstairs!' The residents, awakened from sleep, were coming down crowding, storming the two men at the doors, one for collecting bribes the other for letting the people out onto the street."[22]

In the first months of the fight against epidemics, when the operations were carried out rigorously and a blockade could last for a week or two, the profit could have been significant even when the inhabitants of overcrowded apartments paid only small sums. Jewish Order Service members were also paid by the house committees to destroy a sanitary doctor's reports about infectious disease found in the building, which the doctors were supposed to send to the Department of Health. At other times, bribes were paid to policemen so the individual could be released from the forced steam bath. One of the doctors employed in a sanitary operation reported for the Ringelblum Archive:

> Shortly after 5 in the morning, [Jewish] Order Service members came to such and such apartment buildings and locked the entrance gates. Next, they contacted the House Committee and, for a pre-arranged fee, allowing the House Committee to take all infected people out of the premises before the sanitary column arrived (the fee was based upon the wealth of the apartment building). . . .
>
> Gruesome scenes ensued: patients with typhus were led through a crowd gathered in the courtyard. They were often seriously ill, with brain and lung complications. When the steam baths were held in the cold season, patients often paid for such trips with severe illnesses and even death.
>
> When most patients had been driven out of the apartment block, the [Jewish] Order Service members proceeded to the second part of their task, namely bathing. Since only the dirty and lice-infested were to be bathed (read: those who could not pay), it was done in a very simple way. The police in the yard caught a handful of weak, ragged beggars swollen with hunger, and triumphantly led them through the streets to the bathhouse, while others were freed from this obligation thanks to a certain amount paid to the police by the House Committee.[23]

Corruption at the Ghetto Walls

The most visible part of the ghetto topography associated to this day with the corruption of the Jewish Order Service were the gates to the ghetto (so-called outlets). Policemen serving at the ghetto entries were referred to as

FIGURE 15.   Jewish Cemetery gate, view from Gęsia, 1941. Source: JHIA, ARG I 683-35.

"players" (*grajkowie*), originating from the popular ghetto saying *szafa gra* (the jukebox is playing), a euphemism for bribery. They were paid by smugglers to negotiate with the Germans the illegal passing of the goods. One policeman described it as follows:

> Characteristically, German gendarmes almost never wanted to do business with the Polish [Blue] police, only with Jews. This would usually begin with a gendarme telling a Jewish policeman that he wanted a bottle of vodka, a chocolate bar, or a bar of soap. The policeman, provided he was smart enough, would reply that he had no money, but that some could be made if only the gendarme would let a wagon with potatoes, flour, or other products into the ghetto. . . . If a smuggler wants to bring a food wagon to the ghetto, he approaches a Jewish policeman and makes arrangements with him. The Jewish policeman tells him the time and agrees on a signal; then the smuggler telephones his supplier on the Aryan side and tells him to send the wagon. At the signal, the wagon arrives, is checked by the Polish policeman, and a gendarme lets it in.
>
> There are policemen who have "their" gendarmes and maintain contact with them. Such a Jewish policeman, known as a player, arranges the smuggling with those gendarmes and pays them their due. The fee

for a wagon with about 2 thousand kg of smuggled goods is usually 400 zlotys. 100 zlotys goes to the Polish policemen (typically there are two of them), the gendarme also gets 100 zlotys; the "player" pays 85 zlotys to the policemen who are on duty at the outlet (usually 8 people), and takes the remaining 115 zlotys for himself.[24]

Szapsel Rotholc, a typesetter by profession—in the 1930s, a famous and immensely popular flyweight boxer and in the ghetto the "king" of players—reported after the war what these "negotiations" and the risks involved looked like:

> Even when it had already been worked out with the gendarme, when he was properly prepared and had promised that a certain truck or car would be let in and when he already had given 100 percent assurance it would happen, until the last second the heart was beating [about whether he] had deceived. . . . There were gendarmes who became immediately agitated if at that moment by chance there appeared some, even the smallest witness; they stopped the truck. It was then said that the truck was burned. There were also gendarmes who, with real German sadism, pledged everything, took the ransom for the truck first, saying that they did not trust Jews, and when the truck came, these gendarmes stopped the truck and the person who had paid the gendarme.[25]

The German authorities estimated that several hundred Jews left the ghetto illegally every day, most of them in search of food.[26] The goods were smuggled not only by entering the ghetto through the gates but also through a wooden fence separating sidewalks belonging to the ghetto from the roadway, which fell on the Aryan side, and through tunnels, sewers, over the wall to which ladders could be attached, and through concealed holes in the wall that the Technical Department of the Judenrat tried unsuccessfully to block. In these cases, Jewish police stood at the intersections of neighboring streets, on guard, on the lookout, and watched the surroundings to warn smugglers of the approach of the German Ordnungspolizei (Order Police). Group commander Marek Passenstein described it as follows:[27] "The alarm signal during the day was usually to say out loud the name of one of the smugglers, passed from mouth to mouth, until the password reached the exit hole. . . . After the pedestrian traffic stopped moving, after the curfew, the warning was a signal light."[28] The German patrol was a threat both for smugglers and the policemen protecting them: "Smugglers quickly disappeared at the gates, hid in tunnels and dens, while policemen had to stand on duty at their posts in this section and expose themselves to the dubious pleasure of answering the gendarmes' questions and looking into the barrels of German machine guns."[29]

Competing smugglers sometimes denounced each other to German authorities; denunciations also came from the Aryan side.[30] Policemen became victims of internal settlements in the criminal world, in which some of them participated, having established cooperation with smugglers. Soon after the ghetto was sealed, a rumor spread about two players who were to be stabbed with a knife while doing business with smugglers.[31] In an entry in Adam Czerniaków's diary from October 1941, we find information about policeman Jakub Katz, who had his head fractured by smugglers.[32] Others recorded rumors that Heinz Auerswald himself, in civilian clothes and with an armband with a Star of David, would check the work of the watch guards.[33] Probably some of the eighty-six policemen arrested between June 1941 and July 1942 by the SD were detained for offenses related to smuggling.[34] In August 1941, the Jewish Order Service conducted disciplinary proceedings against Head of Section Moszek Blumstein and functionaries Mendel Lewin and Jerzy Szejnberg, who, according to a German patrol member who observed the event, allowed a smuggler to escape before their eyes as he was in the act of catching a sack thrown over the wall from the Aryan side. The outcome of the proceedings is not known, so we do not know how effective was the defense put forward by members of the service who blamed the Blue Policemen serving at the wall on the Aryan side for the entire incident.[35] Everyone involved in smuggling took significant risks. Beginning in January 1942, members of the Blue Police also faced the death penalty for smuggling goods into the ghetto or people out of it.[36] Arrests in matters related to smuggling were made even among the Germans guarding the gates to the ghetto.[37]

Smuggling was the basis for supplying the ghetto with food, and the players who took an active part in it were risking a lot—which is why this form of police corruption was treated with greater indulgence than bribery in other situations. The actions of policemen in allowing smugglers to pass were even viewed with some sympathy, as an expression of the vitality of the ghetto and a small victory in the war against the German administration.

Physical Violence

Violence at the gates, and the events described above on Krochmalna Street, are examples of police activities in which corruption was directly connected with physical sanctions authorized by the ghetto administration. According to the "Instructions for the [Jewish] Order Service," the members' tasks included "supporting the authorities it is called to assist in carrying out official actions, removing obstacles and overcoming the resistance encountered."[38] Yet the same instructions prohibited policemen from using force when it was not necessary.[39] In "Lecture on the Duties and Correct Behavior of Members of the [Jewish] Order Service,"[40] distributed in the ghettos throughout the General Government in the summer of 1941, instructor Józef Prussak admitted that the policemen, exhausted from their service and "sometimes by the simply hostile manners" of the ghetto residents, treat them severely, but although they have this right, they should avoid such conduct. He wrote, "Let the courteous policemen become the norm. In characterizing this politeness, they will say with appreciation: 'polite as a member of the [Jewish] Order Service.'"[41] Along with the general content of the lecture came similarly vague legal regulations. In April 1941, during the surge in roundups for forced-labor camps, the Directorate of the Jewish Order Service issued an order stating that the use of force was left to the individual judgment of the policemen guided by "a sense of tact and ethics, and even more so by a feeling for the citizens."[42] *Gazeta Żydowska* elaborated:

> The [Jewish] Order Service is a social-civic organization, its members serving in the most difficult conditions of the particular administrative area, the Jewish district. A [Jewish] Order Service policeman has a more difficult task than any policeman in any country, as the latter has tradition, training, experience, and preparation. A [Jewish] Order Service member had to transform himself into a policeman almost overnight and was immediately assigned to a police station, where he had to perform several difficult duties. In order to do so, he had to be tactful and ethical and have a lot of understanding for the citizens of his area. With these qualifications, the [Jewish] Order Service policeman will solve any problem by himself, at any moment, and in all circumstances and will decide whether and when he is allowed to use force.[43]

More detailed entries can be found in the May 1942 service manual: "It is forbidden to beat citizens, especially detainees. The use of a baton is allowed only as a last resort, after exhausting the means of persuasion [and] after two warnings. In these cases, the beatings were to be on the hands and back. Beating on the head is in any case prohibited, unless it is defense against an armed assailant. The Jewish Order Service policeman, regardless of the fact that the incident has been noted in the official notebook, has to submit a report to his direct supervisor, giving the background of the incident and justifying his behavior."[44]

It soon became clear that this principle had no basis in reality. In the Jewish Order Service day orders, we find that on January 8, 1941, policeman Eliezer

Landau (identification number 267) received a formal reprimand "for brutal behavior toward Alfred Jof on December 30 last year, while serving by the post office building at Zamenhofa Street."[45]

In February 1941, Ringelblum wrote in his diary about a rumor circulating in the ghetto that a young boy who had kicked a policeman was, in revenge, beaten to death in the Judenrat building.[46] Similar information can be found in the underground Jewish press. One widely circulated story was that of a certain Dr. Zusman, an elderly man who died of a heart attack after being beaten on the street by a functionary of the Jewish Order Service. Commenting on this tragedy in light of the recently issued "Duty Instructions," a contributor to an underground Zionist youth newspaper wrote, "It is a pity that Dr. Zusman, who died last week from the beating he received on the head with a rubber truncheon by a person with 'special moral qualifications,' did not read the 'Instructions.' It is also interesting to know with what kind of weapons Dr. Zusman attacked the person who 'is to serve the public as an example.'"[47]

While it is difficult to ascertain whether these specific events actually took place, there is no doubt that Jewish Order Service members did use excessive force, including beatings with police batons. These incidents were mentioned repeatedly, if casually, in Gazeta Żydowska, which at the same time tried to justify the behavior of the Jewish Order Service members by saying they had been provoked.[48] Personal documents and testimonies clearly show that throughout the period of the functioning of the service, the people in the ghetto were convinced of its brutality and often felt helpless when faced with it.

Physical violence often occurred during interventions related to the duties of the Jewish Order Service as an auxiliary service of the Judenrat, including conducting debtors to the Jewish Council offices, participating in evictions and compulsory quartering of tenants, and blockades of apartment buildings whose residents had not paid the police tax. The Jewish Order Service also resorted to violence when collecting fees for the Jewish Council from the house committees. One of the house committee reports contains a description of one such action:

Today, in the morning, the [Jewish] Order Service squad arrived at the closed doors of the apartment block at 23 Nalewki Street and demanded payment from the house committee. The committee members replied that the committee had no money. The commanding officer of the [Jewish] Order Service . . . proposed that the members of the house committee go to the Judenrat offices to negotiate with the head of the Fees and Donations Department, Mrs. Dacha Syrkisowa, which the committee agreed to do. In fact, the [Jewish] Order Service intended to take members of the house committee to the Jewish Council under escort. The members of the house committee agreed the next day to pay on the 24th of this month two thousand zlotys, which had to be paid by one o'clock in the afternoon.[49]

This and other house committee documentation show that such actions resulted in the intended outcome. Not surprisingly, requisitions from private individuals and businesses were carried out in an even more determined manner. As Stanisław Adler wrote, reluctant payers were, for example, rehoused in refugee shelters that were known for horrific sanitary conditions and were ridden with typhus. After one detainee committed suicide by hanging in the jail located in one of the Jewish Order Service precincts, the service had no trouble reaping benefits. As Adler commented, "His case convinced other objectors of the importance of paying the levies, and money started to flow in abundantly."[50]

Reports from the ghetto show that the violence used by the Jewish Order Service was often considered part of the wartime morality of the street. And on the street there was a struggle for survival: those who were unable to buy themselves out or who had no one to denounce were lost. To this category of the weakest and most defenseless belonged child-smugglers, who were beaten with clubs by the same policemen who accepted bribes from wealthy smugglers, and refugees and deportees from Jewish communities outside Warsaw who got lost in the chaos of the Warsaw Ghetto. In a document deposited in the Underground Archive of the Warsaw Ghetto, Salomea Ostrowska, manager of the quarantine for deportees at 109 Leszno Street, describes actions of the Jewish Order Service that had the characteristics of mob-like crime: "The activity of the Jewish Order Service is another saddening chapter. According to deportees and reports (I know that two have been filed), some [deportees] were robbed by [Jewish] policemen. A policeman approaches a woman and takes her bundle, promising to bring it to the designated place. He then leaves with her bundle, and thus the poor woman loses everything she had managed to salvage from her home. A wagon from Łowicz was robbed by policemen because the refugees failed to pay a ransom."[51]

In rare situations, often more readily associated with Gestapo collaborators, Jewish policemen appealed to the Germans to intervene. One such incident was described in April 1942 by an anonymous social activist who submitted his report to the Ringelblum Archive. Policemen who did not receive a bribe during a disinfection operation called for help from the Germans, who beat up the chairman of the house committee:

> It is uncertain whether this was the result of a collective decision of the [Jewish] Order Service officers, or (as they claim) the idea of one of them, a Mr. Michelson. In any case, the German officers ordered the chairman of the House Committee to be summoned. He came after a while. Then the Germans led him to a third courtyard, where he was pushed into a corner and beaten in the usual way for at least 10 minutes. In the usual way—meaning that an individual pushed against the wall was beaten in the face . . . while being kicked at the same time. The Department of Health was notified about what happened, in particular that the [Jewish] Order Service set the Germans against the chairman of the House Committee.[52]

Even by the standards of the brutal reality of ghetto life, this case shook public opinion. It also met with an immediate reaction from the authorities of the Jewish Order Service, who transferred the guilty policemen to another precinct.[53]

Sanctioned Violence: Roundups to Labor Camps

Describing the atmosphere prevailing during the recruitment to the Jewish Order Service in autumn 1940, chronicler Ludwik Landau wrote on September 19, "Roundups of men who were to be sent to labor camps but didn't show up are held every night; because of the news arriving from the camps, almost no one goes voluntarily—despite the repeatedly enthusiastic reports printed in *Gazeta Żydowska* about life in the camps."[54]

Compulsory labor for men from fourteen to sixty years old was introduced in December 1939, although Jews had been sent to forced labor since the beginning of the occupation of Warsaw in September 1939. Initially, Warsaw Jews worked at *placówki* (work sites) in the city and from mid-August 1940 in isolated forced-labor camps. They were also transported to carry out specific tasks at industrial plants, doing drainage work or road construction.[55] The men were taken by private companies or the SS. Those who managed to return to the ghetto, physically and mentally battered, talked about the murderous working conditions, torture, and high mortality.

In the summer of 1940, men from eighteen to twenty-five years old (and later to thirty-five) received orders from the labor offices; volunteers were also encouraged to sign up. This method of recruiting workers, however, did not prove effective—it did not provide the required contingents. For this reason, in the spring and summer of 1941, roundups began. People who failed to appear were tracked down in their apartments, and pedestrians were detained on the street. Jews apprehended by the Jewish Order Service for minor offenses were also sent to camps. Tatiana Berenstein estimates the number of Jews sent from Warsaw to forced-labor camps in 1940 and 1941 at more than fifteen thousand.[56]

The peak of labor-camp roundups came in the spring of 1941 when the Warsaw Judenrat was forced to carry out the German orders under threat of an interruption in food supplies to the ghetto and of criminal sanctions. Fifty-three thousand Jews were needed for the forced-labor camps in the Warsaw and Lublin Districts. The Judenrat's Labor Camps Committee recruitment campaign failed totally—only two thousand men volunteered for work, mainly deportees who hoped that they would be sent to camps closer to their homes.[57] In order to fill the contingents, the Jewish Order Service began roundups in the streets of the ghetto.

Roundups were usually carried out according to an established plan: an apartment building was blockaded, men were brought down into the court-yard, and those who did not have documentation exempting them from forced labor were taken away. An anonymous man reported to the Ringel-blum Archive on what took place in the building where he lived:

> We were about to sit down to dinner when one of the neighbors burst into the room, shouting that the men should hide as quickly as pos-sible. We went over immediately, my brother-in-law and I, to the win-dow and saw the courtyard filled with Jewish police, numbering about 80, under the command of the precinct commander and assisted by 2 civilians from the Department of Labor and 6 Polish policemen, who blocked the apartment building and were guarding all the doorways to the stairwells. We understood what was coming, but it was too late to escape. Suddenly there was banging on the door and a Jewish police officer with two lower-rank policemen came into the apartment.[58]

The men who were rounded up were most often led to the collection point in the Collegium Secondary School Society building at 84 Leszno Street, which in effect became a prison guarded by Jewish and Blue Policemen and officials of the Labor Department. Here they were subjected to a medical inspection, a wash, and a head shave and then sent to the camps. Men were also caught on the streets, and before being sent to the camps, they were kept in other places, including in lockups in police stations.[59] The raids were conducted in restaurants, cafés, and shelters for refugees and deportees.

As members of the disgraced Labor Battalion moved to the newly established Jewish Order Service, so did their practices. It quickly became apparent, for example, that a certificate issued by the Labor Department did not always guarantee release from the work requirement, but release could be ensured by a sufficiently high bribe. The author of the above-quoted testimony wrote that of the 150 men in his apartment block who were subject to the work requirement, only 21 were brought to the Collegium; the others either fled or paid a bribe of fifty to one hundred zlotys.[60] Once at the Collegium, this amount had to be significantly increased, as the bribe was to be divided among larger numbers of policemen. At this stage, bribes were also taken for providing information to families and for delivering packages of food and clothing (very often men had been taken from their homes with no belongings). To replace those who managed to bribe their way out of the Collegium, people were caught on the street—stopped, for example, for violation of the curfew, regardless of their age or state of health.[61] Victims of the roundups were therefore the poorest, those who could not find a safe place to work or who could not afford a high enough bribe. There were rumors in the ghetto that bribery was so lucrative that the Jewish Council stopped accepting candidates volunteering for the camps.[62]

From the beginning of the Jewish Order Service's operations, police functionaries were also sent to serve as guards in labor camps. In late November and early December 1940, along with a transport of 362 workers to the camp in Końskowola, thirty Jewish Order Service functionaries (commanded by an officer) were sent to guard the camp, carry out roll calls, and escort the workers to work.[63] The Labor Department of the Judenrat officially authorized the work of members of the Jewish Order Service as guards in the camps in April 1941, seeing this as an opportunity to calm the ghetto community's fear of German overseers and to limit the evasion of work.[64] The Judenrat also assumed that their presence would prevent the use of torture and bring the situation in the camps under its control to at least some extent. *Gazeta Żydowska*, hoping to encourage readers to go to work, even emphasized that the guards in a given camp were members of the Jewish Order Service.[65]

The policemen in the camps undoubtedly had much better living conditions than the forced laborers; nevertheless, they dreaded this service. Gombiński wrote, "It was not without dramatic scenes, because everyone assumed that guard duty would be connected with a direct danger to life. It was to be feared that the fury and sadism of the overseers would be discharged upon the Jewish guards, that ordinances, with special malice, would be aimed at harassing the guards, that the guards would be held responsible for failings, shortcomings, bad work."[66]

Police doctors and paramedics whom the Warsaw Judenrat Medical Chamber designated for work in the camps had similar concerns.[67] In September 1940, Ludwik Landau wrote, "The Judenrat in Warsaw called for doctors to report for work in the camps; however, there were no volunteers despite the promised three-hundred-zloty salary. This was because of the bad living conditions in the camps and the fear of having to take part in the bullying of workers. The Gmina had to announce that in the absence of volunteers it would have to appoint doctors to camps as workers."[68] Dr. Henryk Makower noted in his memoir that "the trip to the camp was a frightening experience for every doctor."[69] Even if they managed to get out of the camp unscathed, policemen and doctors were subject to an obligatory two-week quarantine.

It is not clear what criteria were used to select policemen for service in the labor camps. There are many indications that recruitment took place under duress. It even happened that Ukrainians escorting forced laborers picked up Jewish policemen they encountered on the streets. One victim of this practice was a group leader, economist Marek Passenstein, a social activist involved in helping children in the ghetto and one of Ringelblum's close associates. Passenstein was taken from the sentry post at the corner of Żelazna and Chłodna Streets. In a letter addressed to the Judenrat, he reported:

On April 25th, 1941, at 21:30 after leaving the headquarters of the Second Precinct of the [Jewish] Order Service, where the night service briefing was held, I was standing on Żelazna Street near the corner of Żelazna and Chłodna Streets with orderlies Rotsztajn and Wizenfeld when we were surrounded by several armed members of the *Lagerschutz* [camp guards], battered with rubber truncheons, deprived of hats, armbands, and service numbers, and, threatened with rifles, pushed brutally into the ranks of the passing columns of camp workers.

My attempts to explain that I was currently on duty, that I had a card signed by the German authorities, and that the [Jewish] Order Service was exempted from work in the camps had the opposite effect and caused a whole new series of blows, with rubber batons, to my face and back.

I tried, as we passed through the gate on Chłodna Street, to appeal to the German sentry there to intervene, but I was forced away by several *Lagerschutz* officers, who threatened that if I even turned my head, they would immediately use their weapons.[70]

The policemen were shepherded to the Eastern Railway Station, and from there they traveled to Garwolin and farther, to the camp in Wilga. After three days, Passenstein was released from the camp as a result of Czerniaków's personal intervention.[71] Passenstein's experience was not exceptional. Jewish policemen were led by force to other camps, including the camp in Pustków near Krosno.[72]

Opinions differed on the Jewish Order Service's guard duties in the camps. In the Underground Archive of the Warsaw Ghetto, for example, there is a report detailing the behavior of a group of twenty members of the Jewish Order Service sent as sentries to the Pustków camp in the spring of 1941. According to the author of the report, their service was easy, and during off-duty hours they circulated around the camp without any duties. Instead of maintaining order in the camp, they wandered around the grounds, played cards, sometimes argued with each other, and were unable to establish their authority over the workers.[73] According to another document from the archive, the functionaries took bribes, beat prisoners, and harassed women from nearby villages until the camp commandant sent them to forced labor and moved them from their separate quarters to the general quarters for the workers. It was said that those for whom the trip to the camp was disciplinary punishment demonstrated particular cruelty toward the workers.[74] Members of the Jewish Order Service were not the only Jewish guards to behave in a reprehensible manner. In May 1941, in the camp in Drewnica, all the members of the camp guard and the Jewish camp doctors were arrested, accused of taking bribes for issuing work exemptions.[75] These cases were widely commented on in the ghetto.

It seems, however, that, after all, in some camps the situation of the workers did in fact improve after the replacement of the camp guards with Jewish Order Service members.[76] In a report from the camp in Końskowola, a former prisoner writes that relations between workers and policemen, who "by skillful approach to workers, were able to win their trust and obedience—without recourse, in the vast majority of cases, to any harsher repression," were good there; however, he emphasizes that this was not a typical situation.[77] The author of another report, from Pustków, tried to explain the behavior of service members: "The functionaries—these young people aged twenty-one to twenty-six—were brought up in a privileged environment, some with higher education. They are far from understanding the fate of the workers in the camp and from willingly and spontaneously easing the plight of workers. Probably none of them had done any social service work before the war, and this is the reason for the discrepancy between the demands placed on them and their possibilities and role in the camp. The possible blame for the selection of such an element, unaccustomed and unable to be deployed to hard camp service, is borne by those delegating teams of the [Jewish] Order Service to the camps."[78]

Irrespective of their behavior in the camps, the guards were uniformly unprepared when they arrived there, and, as the sources available to us indicate, they were almost all recruited under duress. In addition, the experience of "hard camp service," for many traumatic, undermined their power of empathy and had a progressively desensitizing effect.[79] This was often the first step—in effect, an initiation rite—in the escalating use of violence, and one that made later acts significantly easier.

Undoubtedly, the manner of conducting roundups for the camps and in particular the accompanying corruption negatively affected the image of the Jewish Order Service. From the moment of its members' involvement in the roundups, one can observe a clear change in the language used to the described them. The term "catchers" from that moment clung permanently to the Jewish police.

They were thus firmly placed in the history of anti-Jewish persecutions, with diarists comparing them to *khapers*, Jewish community officers in tsarist Russia who delivered Jews to the Russian military authorities as forced conscripts. As the community often chose to protect young men who had their families to support, it often decided to provide minors instead. Olga Litvak commented, "On the one hand, young men of draft age often had families of their own to support. The alternative presented the gruesome spectacle of having to tear children away from their parents. The situation provoked abuse to which the young, the poor, and the marginal fell victim. Contemporaries placed the blame almost exclusively at the feet of Jewish communal leaders rather than the Russian government; the problem, intoned a chorus of Jewish voices, was that "God was high above and the tsar far away."[80] Similarities to the situation in the ghetto could not go unnoticed. As an anonymous writer commented at the time, "In my courtyard the noble work of Jewish catchers began—who knows if they were not a reincarnation of their Jewish great-grandparents, catchers from the time of Nicholas—Jewish policemen."[81] The people led by the policemen to the camps became in the eyes of some in the ghetto "cattle led to slaughter."[82]

Sanctioned Violence: Central Lockup

From June 1941, the Central Lockup at 24 Gęsia Street became the next area of activity of the Jewish Order Service.[83] In the diary of Adam Czerniaków, the first information about the lockup on Gęsia Street appears on June 6, 1941. At that time, the chairman of the Judenrat noted that policemen from the Seventh Police Precinct had fallen ill with typhus, and so there was a problem escorting prisoners to the Aryan side.[84] The chairman then noted

FIGURE 16.   Central Lockup, mid-1942. Source: JHI, MŻIH E-1/25/2.

that there was to be a detention center for 100 to 150 prisoners within the ghetto. The official justification for the lockup was as follows: Jews imprisoned on the Aryan side, deprived of the right to receive parcels, became the first victims of hunger and diseases prevailing in prisons there, including typhus and tuberculosis. There was also a problem with Jewish prisoners escaping from hospitals in the ghetto, where they had been taken for treatment.[85] In mid-July, news of the creation of the lockup was officially reported in *Gazeta Żydowska*, which guardedly informed readers that "the current scope of the local Jewish self-government apparatus has created the need to establish its own lockup, the existence of which will put an end to the troublesome previous procedure."[86]

The Central Lockup was initially located in a building at 22 Gęsia Street, which soon turned out to be insufficient and functioned later as a "small lockup." The main lockup was established in ten cells of the former military prison building at 24 Gęsia Street—"a large, vast gray-white edifice recently repainted with feeble pale white paint with a typical barracks look."[87] For some time, discussions continued between the Jewish and German administration about whether Gęsia Street should function officially as a lockup or a prison (the latter term was originally used).[88] Finally, they was decided on the term: Central Lockup for the Jewish Residential District (Zentralarrest für den jüdischen Wohnbezirk). Jewish prisoners from Warsaw prisons were transported to the Central Lockup, although it still happened that Jews arrested on the Aryan side were held in prisons outside the ghetto.[89]

On July 3, 1941, Czerniaków noted that the lockup on Gęsia was better organized than Pawiak, the largest Gestapo prison in occupied Warsaw, but a month later, after a Gestapo inspection, he noticed that although the ghetto lockup was clean, prisoners received only 130 grams of bread, not 400 as in other Warsaw prisons.[90] The lockup quickly became overcrowded, and there were some unsuccessful attempts to solve the problem by joining more buildings together.[91] Throughout the existence of the lockup, Adam Czerniaków sought to gradually release groups of prisoners, especially children. He succeeded several times, and as a result of his interventions, larger parties of prisoners were released, among others in March (151 prisoners) and April (260 prisoners) in 1942. In July 1942, he strongly approved the plan to set up a correctional institution in the ghetto—a shelter with about two thousand places, to which children and young people in detention were to be transferred and to which the Blue Police could send Jewish children and young people caught on the Aryan side. A building at 31 Nalewki Street was designated as the headquarters. The educational care of children was to be under the Prisoners' Care Section under the general supervision of the Jewish Order Service. The Judenrat managed to obtain the consent of the German authorities for those in custody to celebrate Jewish holidays, and sought additional classes and vocational training for prisoners.[92]

Reports from the Central Lockup uniformly draw a picture of the terrible conditions that prevailed in it. One report reads:

> The lack of ventilation, the impossibility of air circulation given the undisputable overpopulation creates conditions that may cause suffocation.
>
> Instances of carbon monoxide poisoning are constantly increasing. In addition, as a result of lack of space and compaction, contact and rubbing against each other causes widespread transmission of skin and infectious diseases. The absence of a dependable delivery of heating material prevents the steady functioning of the bath and disinfector. Insufficient nutrition (no more than four hundred to five hundred calories) furthers the physical degradation of the detainees.[93]

The result of these conditions was extremely high mortality. On March 22, 1942, Czerniaków wrote, "Four months later, the number increased to eighteen hundred prisoners."[94] The formal reasons, which Czerniaków writes about, were related to the fact that prisoners from Gęsia were still subject to the German Special Court. Each death had to be officially confirmed and recorded in the protocol; only after approval by the German authorities

FIGURE 17. Children imprisoned in the Central Lockup, mid-1942. Source: JHI, MŻIH E-2/8/2.

could a body be removed. As one officer wrote, when over time the problem of custody of the corpses in the Central Lockup exceeded the capabilities of its staff, the German authorities granted permission by phone to remove them: "And every morning in the Directorate of the service we heard as the duty officer 'checked in' with the German court prosecutor with a list of the dead in the Jewish lockup and recited on the phone the various names, sometimes five, sometimes eight, sometimes ten. The prosecutor listened to the litany of names with unquestioned seriousness as he gave permission for them to be buried. And so it went on for months."[95]

The situation in the lockup deteriorated when, in April 1942, the decision was made to transfer Roma, mainly people with German citizenship displaced from the Reich and deported to Warsaw, to the ghetto.[96] In April and June 1942, the Central Lockup took in several transports from outside of Warsaw, including from Łowicz, where about 190 Roma were arrested for "vagrancy."[97] According to Czerniaków, among those in the ghetto was the Roma king, Janusz Kwiek.[98] The situation of the Roma, who did not receive food packages from their families and had no acquaintances among the guards, was tragic. On June 16, Czerniaków received an order to release the Roma from the lockup. They were ordered to wear white armbands with a red letter Z (for *Zigeuner*, German for "Gypsy") and to remain in the ghetto, in the shelter at 10 Wałowa Street maintained by the Jewish Council.[99] According to the chairman's diary, Polish beggars were also detained in the Central Lockup, although there is no further information on this subject.[100]

The Central Lockup was subordinate to the Jewish Order Service; however, according to official information provided by *Gazeta Żydowska* on the day of its opening, the Blue Police were exercising supervision over it.[101] This supervision was more than just formal because both the Blue Police and representatives of the German administration regularly carried out inspections on Gęsia Street. Lockup director Leopold Lindenfeld's official pass to the Aryan side indicates that the German police directorate required him to "provide daily reports on the functioning of the lockup and to discuss a number of current cases concerning prisoners with various police authorities."[102]

Lindenfeld, a judge, the former head of the organizational and administrative department and a member of the Disciplinary Section of the Jewish Order Service, enjoyed a very good reputation in the ghetto. His first deputy was an official of the legal commission named Lewkowicz (first name unknown), who was later replaced by one Ignacy Blaupapier, considered one of the closest and most trusted associates of Commandant Szeryński. Blaupapier was later replaced by Izaak Rudniański.[103] The staff of the lockup was made up of members of the Jewish Order Service, the commandant of the men's and women's guards, and auxiliary staff. Administration of the lockup was supervised by a former captain of the Polish Army, Fryderyk Rose.[104]

Members of the Jewish Order Service assigned to lockup guard duty had special insignia—a number and the letter *A* (for the Arrestanstalt)—and were paid a fixed salary. We do not know how policemen were chosen for the platoon, or whether they had any training. In August 1941, women appeared among the lockup guard; they were not regular functionaries of the Jewish Order Service but were subject to the organizational regulations and uniform and disciplinary provisions applicable to the service.[105] Appointed as the commandant of the women's guard was a lawyer from Łódź, Sylwia Hurwicz, wife of Jewish Order Service officer, Izaak Hurwicz. According to the recollections of one officer, female guards also worked at the ghetto gates, where they searched women returning from forced labor.[106]

"I was happy that I was among Jews. A terrible life is also good," Chana Gorodecka wrote in her memoir. She had been caught during an attempt to cross the German-Soviet border and was held successively in the Pawiak, Daniłowiczowska, and finally Gęsia prisons.[107] For many who, like Gorodecka, were imprisoned earlier on the Aryan side, the replacement of German

FIGURE 18. Female guards in the Central Lockup, mid-1942. Source: JHI, MŻIH E-2/3/2.

or Ukrainian guards by Jews was a great relief. Yet, while some members of the Jewish Order Service selflessly helped the prisoners to keep in touch with family or even to escape,[108] many of the guards quickly became corrupt, led by the example of Ignacy Blaupapier. For a bribe to him, you could leave the lockup for a while and even get an early release. In August 1941, Ringelblum wrote that "the prison commander Blaupapier collaborates with him [the German commissioner of the prison, a Schmidt (first name unknown)]. With the consent of the commissioner, those who give a bribe are released quickly; others have to stay for long weeks."[109] Those who had money for bribes or acquaintances among lockup employees could easily get passes to go to the doctor, have a bath, or even visit family in the ghetto. Sometimes policemen assigned to guard prisoners during hospital tests escorted them to see family or friends and then escorted them back to the lockup.[110] Prisoners with connections among the staff had no difficulty receiving food parcels. The fact that the situation of prisoners depended on their wealth was also mentioned in a memorandum, probably prepared for the Judenrat, regarding the conditions prevailing in the Central Lockup:

> south facing cells, small, reserved for intellectuals, 15–20 people in a small room. Mostly members of the free professions and industrialists. Almost everyone, without exception, was detained on the "Aryan" side, where they were hiding. Their cases are waiting. They are in danger of

being sentenced to several months in prison. North facing rooms, formerly intended for 10–15 people with a small top window, filled with 100–120 people. The air is so bad that you cannot breathe, frequent fainting. Everyone is standing, children from the age of 8 and old men look like corpses. An impression of Dante's hell.[111]

On May 25, 1942, Menachem Mendel Kon, a member of the Underground Archive of the Warsaw Ghetto, visited the Central Lockup at the invitation of its administration. He was a well-known and influential social activist who later wrote his impressions of the visit for the archive.[112] Kon wrote that there were sixteen hundred people in the lockup at that time, including about five hundred children under the age of fifteen, the vast majority of whom were detained for trivial smuggling. The visit, led by Ignacy Blaupapier, begins with the men's section of the lockup. The description left by Kon is dramatic:

> The housing conditions are terrible, and for the most part where there should be from fifteen to twenty people, ninety to one hundred people were packed in. The air there is so poisonous that a significant percentage of prisoners die from poisoning. As we go from the cell to cell, we see terrifying scenes. People are emaciated, dry, with sunken, dark eyes—human skeletons, 90 percent corpses that despite the order of the commander have no strength to get up! Horror fills me when I see these living dead waving their hands; they are demanding something. Unfortunately, I cannot help them in anything. I ask what they want. Some fresh air, but we cannot give it.[113]

Only slightly better conditions prevail in the women's cells, where there are also children. Visiting the building ends at the death chamber where the sick prisoners are held: "The commandant opens the cell; such hell, such terrible suffering cannot be described. In a dark, dirty cell on dirty rags, there are six groaning, tangled bodies, I cannot recognize in any way whether these are people."

Regarding wealthier prisoners, Kon writes:

> We are going towards a small prison, which is located in the same yard. The aristocrats sit there—major smugglers, foreign currency dealers. Here no more than 8–10 prisoners are sitting in a cell. . . . I can see that they are eating white bread with butter, which they get straight from their homes. You can already notice a cheerier expression on faces; they have a chance of getting free for a big bribe here.[114]

The visit ends with a concert by juvenile prisoners:

> A 12-year-old boy, the conductor, goes out in front of the group and the
> children start singing Jewish songs with all their strength. They sing:
> "Our hope is not yet lost, we must be brave and joyful, the rabbi told us
> to be happy," etc. Unknowingly, tears appear in my eyes. I notice that
> the eyes of my guide are also damp.[115]

Kon's report drew a positive image of the lockup guards, who, it seemed
to him, were sincerely interested in the fate of prisoners, especially the children, and attempted to provide them with, among other things, extra time
in the open air. But, as Kon also writes, "prisoners are often beaten because
they do not respect the regime established for them." Information about the
violence of the Jewish Order Service guards against prisoners also appeared
in the underground press. One of the underground newspapers reported
during this period "on blacklisting, for inappropriate treatment of prisoners
[in] a lockup for Jews at Gęsia Street, members of the [Jewish] Order Service:
Rozin, Ber [and] Sznajder."[116]

While some of those imprisoned had committed crimes, there were
also bakers, owners of factories, foreign currency dealers, or major smugglers who, in their dealings, had entered into conflict with the Jewish Order
Service.[117] Most of the prisoners in Gęsia were, however, Jews detained for
participation in small-scale smuggling or for illegally staying on the Aryan
side,[118] many of them having been judged by the German courts and given
death sentences for crossing the borders of the ghetto. It seemed that these
judgments would not be carried out, but on November 12, 1941, Czerniaków
unexpectedly received information that a group of imprisoned Jews, including several women, would be shot. In spite of mediation attempts and the
pleading of the families to pardon them, on November 17, a firing squad consisting of Blue Policemen under the command of the German court prosecutor came to the lockup. Eight people, six women and two men, were shot:
Rywka Kligerman, Sala Pasztejn, Josek Pajkus, Luba Gac, Motek Fiszbaum,
Fajga Margules, Dwojra Rozenberg, and Chana Zajdenwach.[119] During a second execution, on December 15, fifteen people were shot.[120]

A woman who was in the Central Lockup at the time described the second
execution:

> Horrifying screams and cries were heard. They cried that they wanted
> to live. There were eight posts from the previous execution. A rabbi
> arrived and the convicts prayed with him for the last time. They were
> then executed in the presence of German police and the summary

court. Before the execution, Pinkiert's funeral wagon arrived. Too soon! The convicts were divided into two groups because there were only eight columns.

Four Jewish policemen tied a convict to a post, and the Polish police shot them with a machine gun. . . . The worst case was Mikanowska. With superhuman strength, she kept tearing away from the post, screaming for her child to be brought in so that she could breastfeed the child. She threatened the executioners, pleaded with them, begging them for pardon because she wanted to raise her child. Prisoners watched the execution from their windows. The women were especially shocked.

After all, they were watching their own fate! The screams of prisoners blended in with the cries of the convicts. The policemen rushed into the cells and, instead of calming the women, started beating them.[121]

The unexpected executions shocked both prisoners and the entire population of the ghetto. Afterward, one of the ghetto prisoners wrote to her family:

Now you have to try to get me out, because the court will be on Leszno Street, and a Jewish lawyer can defend. I also wrote today a decent letter to my brother so that he remembers you and me and you all try to get me out of here. . . . The more prisoners come, the less food they give. Believe me, writing this I am in tears because I know that you yourselves are going without, but what am I to do? If I want to stay alive, then I have to eat, because on days when I have no food I feel horribly ill, because I mean not only my life but I want to live for [my] children.[122]

For the first time, Jewish Order Service members were used as an auxiliary service during the execution of other Jews. Many wrote at that point that Szeryński tried not to participate in the executions, or maybe they just wanted to believe it. Even the highly skeptical Ringelblum wrote on November 22: "They tell us that Szeryński told the Polish police commander that he would carry out the sentence but would commit suicide fifteen minutes later. Others argue that Szeryński said that even if he was shot for not obeying an order, he would not, of course, carry it out."[123]

For many, these executions became a symbol of the final moral collapse of the Jewish police—and in hindsight came to be seen even as an initiation to their actions on the Umschlagplatz during Operation Reinhard. The underground periodicals in the ghetto stigmatized "Polish-Jewish blind performers of National Socialist law" carrying out "the bloody duty of Cain."[124]

The author of an article in *El-Al*, a publication of the left-Zionist youth organization *Ha-Shomer ha-Tsair*, wrote:

> The hands of Hitler's Jewish henchmen are soaked in blood, hands that so generously share their time with batons in the streets of the ghetto, which [sentenced] thousands of their confreres to labor camps—they attached condemned prisoners to the pillars. If at any time there was any doubt as to the [real] face and role of the Jewish police, now this illusion must have disappeared with the eloquence of facts. On the Jewish street the Jewish police fulfills the [f]unction of a proxy and an executor of the occupier's orders. It feeds on the body of exhausted Jewry, it inserts in its life the capital of brutal vulgarity and fascist "culture" with clubs and polished boots, and above all its own free will, just for the lust of evil profit, serving the occupier, helping him in fulfilling his criminal decrees.[125]

The executions were also widely commented upon on the Aryan side. Corp. Wiktor Załek from the Twentieth Police Precinct, who was the only one of the thirty-two-person Blue Police execution squad to volunteer, was condemned in the Polish Underground press.[126]

CHAPTER 4

Police in the Eyes of the Ghetto Population

Describing the first days of the Jewish police presence on the ghetto streets, Stanisław Gombiński wrote, "The Jewish population welcomed the appearance of the functionaries on the streets of the ghetto with a smile of kindness. Associated with this smile was a mixture of light irony: for every Jew a real policeman was still a Polish policeman."[1] The majority of descriptions of the policemen, even before the deportations, are, however, far from ironic.[2] The underground Jewish newspapers may have described the policemen as characters "from the land of Czerniaków's grotesque"[3] and ridiculed them, but they also portrayed them as a criminal organization, a real threat—seen in terms of both physical danger and the threat to the unity of the community. Despite being fully aware of the reality of ghetto life, the ghetto inhabitants saw the policemen as people with agency, who chose to carry out orders against the interest of other Jews. The majority of personal documents written in the ghetto by those who considered themselves to be victims of the overwhelming violence of the police saw the Jewish Order Service as a collection of smugglers, Gestapo informers, war profiteers, assimilated young attorneys, and converts headed by Józef Szeryński, with their prewar choices of assimilation, sometimes baptism, driving them out of Jewish society.

FIGURE 19. Policemen of the Jewish Order Service, probably in the Central Lockup with detainees, early 1942. Source: JHIA, ARG I 683-24.

Without a doubt, the principal and most sophisticated account of the actions of the Jewish Order Service created in the ghetto is that left behind by the members of the Ringelblum Archive, also known as the Underground Archive of the Warsaw Ghetto, gathered together by the underground group Oneg Shabbat. Using the research methods of the Jewish Research Institute (YIVO), the members of the team tried to document as completely as possible the Jewish experience during the war. Oneg Shabbat's founder, Emanuel Ringelblum, wrote that they sought the truth "however bitter it would be."[4] An essential element of this bitter reality of the ghetto was the existence of the Jewish Order Service—which was seen as a collaborationist organization and one that betrayed its own community.[5] Members of Oneg Shabbat not only described the actions of police functionaries in detail but also gave themselves the right to evaluate them morally. Even if they expressed understanding for its individual members, the Jewish Order Service, as a formation, was seen by members of Oneg Shabbat as one of the most extreme manifestations of the wartime collapse of values in the new reality of the occupation.

In spite of the growing criticism of the activities of the Jewish Order Service, its members remained part of the ghetto community—a fragment of the network of prewar family and social relationships transferred to the closed district. They were brothers, husbands, and sons; in the police was a cousin or the husband of a friend. The policemen participated in house committee meetings and in social gatherings. While there are no intimate diaries of ghetto policemen that could give us an indication as to how they acted in the shelter of their homes, their close family life and immediate surroundings could encourage policemen to become more involved in their everyday work in order to move up the ranks of the service. Even if their power was more limited than generally thought, members of the service were invaluable sources of information and support for their closest family circle and social network. They could warn them about forced-labor round-ups, protect them from having tenants forced upon them, or negotiate on behalf of the house committee with other members of the Jewish Order Service who were collecting various types of "contributions."[6] Those benefiting from such help were not only from the relatively wealthy or assimilated groups from which the officers were recruited. Even those most critical of the Jewish Order Service—Rachela Auerbach, Abraham Lewin, and even Emanuel Ringelblum himself—refer in their diaries to information gleaned from service members; and Ringelblum included two service members in his carefully selected archival team.[7] One officer wrote that despite the general hatred of the Jewish Order Service, "there was an exception in many thousands of houses: husband, father, brother, son, nephew, cousin, brother-in-law. 'This one does not allow vicious acts, he is different.'"[8] This distinction persisted throughout the ghetto's existence. Family members or close friends joining the service were described as the honorable exceptions. Others, even from the same social circles, from the moment they put on the cap, became alien—a part of the faceless, hostile, and hated collective of the Jewish police.

The foreignness of policemen, which in principle excluded them from the community, was manifest on several levels. The policemen were perceived as strangers because of their assimilation (understood here not as a neutral category but as a value-laden term of the political polemic)[9], and as such they were not considered to be real Jews. The policemen were strangers because the community declared their behavior offensive and unfit for someone who claimed to be part of it. Finally, policemen were strangers because they were part of the foreign authority imposed on the ghetto. A year after the ghetto was enclosed, in the autumn of 1941, a Jewish underground newspaper issued in the Warsaw Ghetto, *Neged Hazarem* (Against the Stream) published an article titled "Symptoms of Moral Corruption," in which the editors referred to the Jewish Order Service as members of the "Quisling family."[10]

Biographical Interpretation: Policemen as Non-Jews

The police stood on the border between the Jewish world and the Aryan side not only in guarding the ghetto wall but also in a symbolic sense. The *Gazeta Żydowska* of April 1, 1942, published a text titled, "The Duty of Service," which contained ten commandments to be followed by members of the ghetto authorities. The second commandment was "Know that you are the son of a Jewish nation, that you are just as Jewish as your brothers, that the same brotherly blood runs in our veins."[11] However, in wartime testimonies of ghetto inhabitants, a member of the Jewish Order Service is usually someone who is not considered a Jew anymore. In reports by religious or Zionist Jews, the police became a symbol of assimilation, understood here as a result of the conscious decision of individuals—an explicit denial of Jewish roots and separation from the Jewish nation and the Jewish collective.[12] Thus, members of the Jewish Order Service stopped being part of the community even before the ghetto was separated from the rest of the city. They were not "representatives of the people"—they were strangers.

The Jewish Order Service was considered an assimilationist institution by definition: it was founded by assimilated Jews and represented the defects ascribed to them, in particular a feeling of superiority and kinship within their social group and a negative attitude toward the Jewish masses, which they considered to be inferior. In this narrative, the police not only did not identify with Jews or feel empathy for them, but they also devalued them and treated them with hatred, the result of "assimilation complexes" (which can be seen as a variation on the concept of the Western, assimilated "self-hating Jew").[13] As one ghetto inhabitant explained, "Religious Jews had no contact with Poles and thus no inferiority complex. Socialists and Zionists, in turn, had a high sense of Jewish dignity that defended them against inferiority complexes."[14] These ghetto policemen's "inferiority complexes" were unloaded by the police on other Jews, however. In this narrative assimilation becomes the "ideological" preparation for violence that these men may be perpetrating against those they would consider more "Jewish" and thus inferior—that is, poorer, not educated in the Polish school system, and not playing a significant role in prewar Polish society. The poverty and chaos on the streets of the ghetto only reinforced these attitudes. Policemen were thus conditioned above all by their cultural belief system.

The issue that generated the most controversy was the very visible participation in the Jewish Order Service of baptized Jews. Józef Szeryński became their symbol, "a convert, for whom the misery and pain of the Jewish masses were always foreign. Surrounded by . . . a similar element, half and completely assimilated individuals."[15] The thread of conversion runs through all critical opinions about him. Szeryński personified not only the assimilated clique that assumed power over the alien or—in the extreme version—hated Jews, but it also became a symbol of the gradual seizure of power by converts.

Various rumors and anecdotes on the subject, which well reflect the prevailing mood, appear also in the wartime writings of highly assimilated ghetto inhabitants mistrustful of converts taking on prominent positions in the ghetto community. It was said, for example, that for a long time in the Jewish Order Service, it was impossible to find high-ranking officers who could be delegated for the reopening ceremony of synagogues, after they were allowed to function again in May 1941.[16] It was even rumored that the policemen who were supposed to keep order during the Masses celebrated in the two Catholic churches operating in the ghetto shouted, "Down with the Jews!"[17] The greatest controversy was caused by Szeryński himself, who became the subject of innumerable rumors connected with his Catholicism and the alleged antisemitism resulting from it. Marcel Reich, who himself came from an assimilated family and worked as a translator in the Judenrat, mentioned one of the rumors in his postwar testimony: Szeryński asked a certain policeman why he was unshaven, and when the policeman replied, "Today is a holiday"—meaning, a Jewish holiday—Szeryński replied with sarcasm, "Oh, this is your holiday again." In Reich's view, Szeryński ran the ghetto as if he were a commissar who was sent to work in the ghetto but who himself did not belong properly to the place and had nothing to do with it.[18] There were also rumors about his wife, who supposedly "did not want to go out into the street, so as not to rub elbows with Jews."[19]

While these rumors reflect well the inclination of the community to ostracize members of the Jewish Order Service as alien to the collective, in reality there were not many converts among the policemen, and not all functionaries came from strongly assimilated families. Although there is no doubt that there were officers in the service who were strongly polonized, this does not rule out the possibility that at the same time, like the majority of politically active Jews, they sympathized with Jewish parties before the war. The fact that as people educated in the Polish educational system they spoke only Polish and had a strong Polish cultural identity did not necessarily lead to the loss of their Jewish ethnic or religious consciousness.

Commenting on this phenomenon, Ezra Mendelsohn wrote, "The Polo-nisation they favored did come to pass, but it was not accompanied by a widespread acceptance of the integrationist ideology—Polish antisemitism saw to that."[20] Calel Perechodnik, a policeman from Otwock near Warsaw, spoke for many when he described his identity in his diary: "My brother and I belonged to Betar, a Zionist organization that propagated the idea of creating an independent Jewish state in Palestine. This did not interfere at all with my feelings as a good patriotic Pole. I adored Polish poetry, particularly that concerning the loss of independence—and particularly Mickiewicz. It really spoke to my heart because I connected it with the history of the Israelites. I assumed that Poles, so long oppressed by their enemies, would understand Jews and have compassion for us, and help in whatever way they could."[21] While few policemen had as idealistic a view of Polish-Jewish relations as Perechodnik, many may have shared his deep attachment to the Polish language and culture, which formed the backbone of their prewar education in the Polish educational system. To quote the historian Kamil Kijek: "In concrete terms, this process translated into the rising popularity of the Polish language as the daily vernacular of the Jews and the language of the Jewish press and literature (both Polish Jewish and Polish) used by Jews. This meant not only changing the relations between Jewish usage of the Polish, Yiddish, and Hebrew languages but also a profound change in the symbolic world and the ways of thinking and imagination of Polish Jews."[22]

The narrative portraying the policemen as a homogeneous group of assimilated Jews, however, allowed much of the ghetto population to view them as separate from the community of "real" Jews, who, therefore, would not bear the responsibility for their behavior. There were also those who perceived the disgraceful actions of the policemen as a manifestation of the fall of the entire community due to assimilation processes that began before the war. The reason for this fall was seen in the assimilation of the prewar Polish Jews (though in a limited way in comparison to similar processes in Western Europe).[23]

Exclusion from the Community

In the eyes of people locked behind the ghetto walls, the power of the policemen was based on two foundations: their violence and their material status. At the same time, this power led to their exclusion from the community. Those corrupted as a result of their rapid enrichment within the police were, according to accounts from the ghetto, wartime collaborators who were accepted into the service through patronage—most likely the influence of the Gestapo—and gilded youth, the children of swindlers who had enriched themselves in the ghetto. It was these policemen who were seen in the ghetto as associated with prostitution, dives, the infamous nightclub Arizona, and the cheap comedy shows in ghetto theaters. They belonged to the underworld of "smugglers, speculators, . . . boors and illiterates, snobs, gilded youth, and the sex-crazed," living by exploitation.[24] They were part of the system of oppression that ordinary people hopelessly attempted to confront in the ghetto. Their behavior symbolized moral decline, the dissolution of social ties, and the loss of sensitivity to the suffering of other Jews. An anonymous journalist wrote, "The heroes of modern times . . . well-fed young people with mocking faces, [in rickshaws] slouch more than they sit, shamelessly and impudently. They have, after all, accepted their sacrificial service to the Jewish people without any satisfaction and, God forbid, salary. That's why President Czerniaków gave them the monopoly of bribes and the legalization of disgusting blackmail and corruption, which they use in full and copious handfuls."[25]

The visible symbol of the moral failure of policemen was in their excessive consumption of food and alcohol. According to some accounts, the rank-and-file policemen drank most of all during their service duty, often bribed by custodians or representatives of the house committees with a bottle of vodka. The officers, on the other hand, drank ostentatiously, almost provocatively—in the midst of the misery that surrounded them, in bars and restaurants. They enjoyed substantial, heavy meals with alcohol.

The ostentatious consumption by Jewish Order Service members was seen as another act of arrogance—an attempt to humiliate those who could not afford copious meals, an elevation of themselves, and an underscoring of their distinctiveness. In this way, these policemen moved from the zone of those imprisoned in the ghetto to the zone reserved for the occupier and his collaborators. As policeman Stanisław Adler noted, "Complicity in the traffic in the contraband, although damaging and superfluous in some ways, and desirable and useful in others, badly corrupted the Jewish Order Service. Large uncontrolled incomes allowed many to lead debauched and corrupted lives. Against a background of universal impoverishment and misery, this contemptible conduct made a macabre impression and created a wall not only of antipathy, but of vehement hatred between them and the rest of the population."[26] To quote the Jewish underground press, policemen thus became the epitome of "an environment rampant in carpe diem . . . live while you can and consume while you can," a symbol of the new reality that grew within the walls of the ghetto.[27]

In the eyes of the ghetto population, the process of gradual moral corruption was to affect in particular young people who joined the ranks of the Jewish Order Service. Thus the service and its members were not only corrupted themselves, but they also corrupted the young, the backbone of the imagined postwar Jewish community. Judenrat employee Stefan Ernest wrote that the Jewish Order Service "brought up this part of Jewish youth in the spirit of true servility, blatant bootlicking in certain circumstances with the gendarmes, sanctioning, thanks to their power, abuses, all kinds of bribes and similar 'earnings,' to complete moral corruption, drunkenness, and hooliganism."[28]

The Jewish Order Service as an Element of Imposed Wartime Reality

In the spring of 1941, Stanisław Różycki, one of the members of the Ringelblum Archive, managed to reach Warsaw from Lwów and illegally entered the ghetto. He described his first moments there:

> The very act had a taste of some ritual, a ceremonial passage into the underworld, the rule of Hades, and this ritual was accompanied by uniformed representatives of Polish and Jewish authorities, appropriately "prepared." I pass through a breach in the wall and fall into the embrace of Jewish policemen, the trap door shuts behind me, I feel terrible, like a mouse in a trap, like a hero in a criminal movie, entering the underground, cellars or tomb, which suddenly closes behind him silently, moved invisibly. I shake off my first unpleasant feeling, pinch my hand and try to look realistically at the surroundings. I'm entering the street.[29]

In Różycki's works, the Jewish policemen are the key element of the "ritual of entry" to the ghetto.[30] Różycki and other diarists confront in their wartime writings what Alexandra Garbarini described as the fact that "the world was now fundamentally different, different in its suppositions as well as in the material circumstances to which [the diarists] were daily subjected. In and through their dairies, they responded to the staggering psychical and physical changes."[31] The police become the main element of the new reality: chaos and lawlessness, which completely devalued human dignity and even life. Policemen are not only another link in the chain of violence in the ghetto—they also even impose it. Quoting Różycki again: "Thieves and conmen are officially requested to pay ransom under threat of being handed over to the Blue Police or to the Gestapo. You can count neither on justice, nor courts, nor the 'order service' to actually keep order, nor on the public organs' protection of private property. What can one do?"[32]

Although the underground press published in the ghetto focused primarily on internal ideological discussions of the international situation and reports on the extermination of Jewish communities outside of Warsaw, articles on the social life in the ghetto and Jewish police activity aroused the greatest reactions. The image of the Jewish Order Service in the ghetto underground press of all political stripes can only be described as extremely negative. In its pages we do not find a category of "good policemen" or attempts to understand those who had to earn a living in this way. This message was strengthened by numerous reports of the brutal activities of the Jewish Order Service in ghettos outside of Warsaw.

In the ghetto underground press, there is no distinction between "our" and other policemen; the Jewish Order Service is rejected as a criminal organization, set up to obey German orders. Descriptions of the gross servility of some policemen, manifesting itself in the imitation of the German style of uniform or even a psychological identification with Germans, appear in many accounts of the ghetto. The outward marker of this identification was the fashionable high boots that distinguished the wearer, above all policemen and Gestapo collaborators, in the streets of the ghetto. As *Gazeta Żydowska* wrote in April 1942, "A police officer in half-boots is a half-officer; all the majesty of the officer is stuck in the uppers of his boots."[33] In March 1942, a Warsaw engraver advertised in *Gazeta Żydowska* "signet rings for the members of the Jewish Order Service, and covers for cigarette cases, miniatures of emblems and numbers."[34] Such insignia of power, similar to those of officers of the Thirteen or wealthy smugglers, meant that in the accounts of witnesses, police officers, even more than members of the Judenrat, began to take over the role of governing the ghetto.

Yet accusations against policemen of associating with the Germans had much stronger foundations than the wearing of high boots. The policemen's sternest critics accused them of internalizing German propaganda. One underground newspaper commented:

> There is also a Jewish police. It is a special chapter in the life of the Jewish district. It's not the police, not the civilian guard, rather an aping of the police. Such is a monster of war. The chief of the Jewish law enforcement service, the local "dictator"-"colonel" his "office" modeled on the "great" Adolf, only a slightly smaller desk, smaller room, the same stylish furniture, the carpet on the floor, and as many bells. Speeches and gestures following the example of the "Führer." He is not so bloodthirsty, but he often forgets that after all, all the fun in the war will end, and he will have to pass an examination of the conscience.[35]

The image of the Jewish Order Service was also very strongly influenced by its relations with the Polish Blue Police. Szeryński's friendly relationship with his colleagues from the Blue Police was widely commented on in the ghetto and the underground press. It was widely acknowledged that the strict subordination of the service to the Blue Police was not a consequence of German orders or legal regulations but rather was supposed to have resulted primarily from Szeryński's own initiative. The superintendent of the Jewish Order Service cultivated relationships with the Blue Police, maintaining social relations with its officers, in particular through dinners in ghetto restaurants and late-night drinking. "An unending flirtation with the commanding officers of the Polish [Blue] Police went on," Adler wrote. "There was no end of drinking bouts, which took place in Szeryński's apartment and in public places, causing general public outrage."[36] Czerniaków took note of the informal contacts between Szeryński and the Blue Police, remarking in his diary that Szeryński was the first to learn from sources in the Blue Police about roundups for deportations to be carried out in the ghetto.[37]

The Blue Police, with its minimal interest in investigating criminal matters, remained in the ghetto, according to many, only to participate in the smuggling and to coerce money from the Jews. This example went from the very top. According to the Polish Underground, Franciszek Przymusiński, the high-level officer who visited the ghetto most often, profited enormously

FIGURE 20. Adam Czerniaków (in bowler hat) with functionaries of the Jewish Order Service and the Polish Blue Police in the courtyard of the Jewish Council at 26/28 Grzybowska Street. Source: JHIA, ARG I 683-16.

from smuggling between the ghetto and the Aryan side. One of the contributors to the Ringelblum Archive wrote of the Blue Police:

> At every opportunity, [they] mercilessly and ruthlessly rob people of
> their last penny. Despite everything else, we have never known such
> moral corruption. They beat [Jews] whenever they get a chance, with
> a club, a fist, a foot, they spit, insult and, without any scruples, inform
> about fabricated crimes of Jews who do not want to or cannot pay a
> bribe. It is pointless to write about their exploits because it is also a
> well-known phenomenon.
>
> They are hated among the Poles as well. They are recruited either
> from former policemen, informers, and spies, or from the half-Poles
> from the Poznań District. Therefore, it is neither the place nor the
> time to write about their methods because it would not—to be
> honest—shed any light on Polish-Jewish relations, since Polish society
> also rejects them.[38]

According to Ringelblum, the Blue Police, apart from the ordinary daily
bribes, received a monthly payoff from merchants and businessmen active in
the ghetto.[39] Starting a business in the ghetto was also dependent on appro-
priately high bribes. Informers reported corruption among officers of the
Blue Police to the German authorities in the ghetto,[40] as did interrogators
and Jews in the prisons on the Aryan side.[41]

Similar information about corruption can be found in the reports of the
Polish Underground, examining, above all, abuses committed by the Jewish Order Service, especially those instances that occurred in cooperation
with the Blue Police and the Germans. A reference to this aspect of Jewish
police activity also appears in the Blue Police documents. They refer not
so much to the internal situation in the ghetto as to what was occurring
in the border area where Jews, Poles, and Germans met—above all, smuggling through the walls of the ghetto and related criminal activities.[42] Illegal profits of this type were made by almost all policemen working from
the ghetto's police stations, although this mainly concerned the officers
assigned to the ghetto in February 1942 in the Convoy Escort Unit.[43] As
the Polish Underground report noted, policemen in this unit did not take
their bread ration, not caring that it would go moldy, and when a drunk
policeman was stopped near the ghetto border, he had on him about five
hundred zlotys, which might lead one to conclude that the Blue Police did
not have it so bad materially.[44]

Because of the fear of typhus, the transfer of policemen from the police
stations in the ghetto to units located on the Aryan side was avoided; only

policemen from the ghetto were vaccinated against it.[45] The practice of not turning over staff at the police stations in the ghetto also contributed to an increase in corruption.

The image of the Blue Police declined even further after the death penalty was imposed for Jews found outside the ghetto. As one underground ghetto newspaper reported in January 1942, "It was found that nearly 80 percent of the Jews caught on the other side were handed over to the German authorities by the Polish [Blue] Police. Premeditated, deliberately, with a smirk of a well-accomplished duty, aware also that, after all, the people delivered into the hands of the German tormentors are crossing the border from life to death." The report went on to say that "even a German policeman sometimes shows more understanding and less meticulousness at the police station."[46] It should be added here that there are also accounts, though not many, of decent behavior on the part of Blue Police toward Jews—usually their prewar acquaintances,[47] whom the policemen assisted in making arrangements on the Aryan side or helped to leave the ghetto.[48]

Forms of Opposition

Such symbolic expulsion of policemen from the Jewish community was undoubtedly an attempt to moderate the fear that they increasingly provoked. In addition to fear, there was a desire for revenge. As early as March 1941, the inhabitants of the ghetto were informed through *Gazeta Żydowska* that "persons opposing the orders of the Jewish Order Service members, or in any way diminishing the authority of the Jewish security organs by their speech, are subject to maximum administrative punishments."[49] Attacks on policemen taking place in this period were, however, mainly the result of frustration by specific actions rather than a desire to manifest hatred of the police, as it would be during the period of deportations. On March 14, 1941, *Gazeta Żydowska* wrote about the case of Mojsie R., a resident of an apartment on Pawia Street who, despite a typhoid quarantine, tried to get out of the blockaded building: "When the [Jewish] Order Service policeman standing in front of the gate tried to stop him, the man threw himself at the policeman with a knife, wounding him badly on the shoulder. The injured policeman was transported to the TOZ [Towarzystwo Ochrony Zdrowia, Society for the Protection of Health] outpatient's dispensary. The man was escorted to the Fifth Polish [Blue] Police Precinct."[50]

Although during this period the underground Jewish press was not yet calling on the community to openly oppose the Jewish Order Service, it certainly called for a boycott of its activities. To quote one of the publications: "The low, disgusting swamp of Hitler's new order with its Jewish servants in the ghetto will not stifle us. We believe that the day of retribution is near."[51] Another publication, *Dos Fraye Vort* (the Free Word), hinted in May 1942 at planned postwar retribution, stating that "the names of these neophytes who use their position in such a disgraceful manner will be diligently registered."[52]

Outside the Ghetto

With newspapers from the Aryan side also distributed widely, though illegally, in the ghetto, its inhabitants must have been acutely aware of the portrayal of the Jewish Order Service outside the ghetto. It was in particular the most widely distributed newspaper there, the German-approved *Nowy Kurier Warszawski*, which used the service for propaganda purposes. Completely ignoring the realities of life in the ghetto, it presented the Jewish Order Service as the only force that could control—under the watchful eye of the Blue Police—the chaos in the district inhabited by the Jews. In January 1941, in an article illustrated with scenes from the ghetto streets, *Kurier* explained to its readers that "this task is quite difficult, because the unruly Jews, unaccustomed to any order, are crowded together and a temporary lack of attention to a functionary of the service is enough to create confusion. Thus, from morning till evening, there is shouting, and [there are] orders, and where these do not help, order is restored with the rubber truncheons with which the Jewish Order Service guards are provided."[53] *Kurier* also reprinted fragments from the crime section of *Gazeta Żydowska*, which it used to illustrate the claimed moral failure of the ghetto's inhabitants.[54]

Dariusz Libionka has observed that participation of the Jews in the persecution was often the dominant subject in the Polish Underground press as well.[55] While usually the Jewish Order Service was described in the context of divisions within the Jewish community and the oppression of the Jewish masses by Jewish "collaborators," this was not the only narrative. In the right-wing press, the attitude toward the Jewish Order Service was transferred to the entire ghetto community. This message intensified after the deportations from the ghetto began. The newspaper *Wielka Polska* (Great Poland), published by the National Party (Stronnictwo Narodowe) opined: "In these tragic moments, Jewish society revealed utter stupidity, resignation, and a complete lack of a sense of national solidarity. Every Jew pushed another Jew to his death, hoping that he would survive—counting on something to happen. Meanwhile, let others go to be slaughtered."[56]

CHAPTER 5

Policemen's Voices

In the spring of 1942, a year and a half after the sealing of the ghetto, a police officer described a scene he had witnessed during the sanitary quarantine of an apartment building:

> Immediately one of the tenants noticed me, it was my colleague, engineer H., "a young man from high society"—as we used to say before the war, a great gentleman with impeccable manners. He called me, I approached. He asked me, considering my rank, to release him at the gate, as he had an urgent matter in the city. He added that he explained all this to the [Jewish] Order Service officer at the gate, but that . . . (here H. uttered a few expletives) did not want to let him go. The expletives were spoken loudly, on purpose, so that not only I, but also the guard at the gate could hear them. By the way, the guard was another engineer, F., a technical director of a big enterprise in Łódź before the war.[1]

The policeman went on, writing that Mr. H. would not have thought to behave like this in front of a Polish Blue Policeman and "in other circumstances, when meeting me or Mr. F., he would surely be very polite."[2]

The author of the quoted account indicates two reasons why, in his opinion, the Jewish Order Service was hated during that period. The first originated in an exaggerated notion of the earnings of policemen. The second was more psychological, stemming from an inability to subordinate oneself to other Jews in higher positions previously reserved for Poles. He explains: "[People] could not believe . . . that some distant friend of theirs, their relative, a son or a son-in-law of their neighbor, was allowed to give them commands, mistreat them, push them around."[3] Such sentiments, writes the anonymous policeman, resulted in "gossip and slander against ghetto officials; undoubtedly there were abuses of power, and many of them, but rumor blew them up to unbelievable proportions. People whispered with some sadistic pleasure. . . . Tongues still turned like windmill blades, grinding truth and lies."[4]

The anonymous officer was correct in his statement that the behavior of service members was the subject of many (sometimes false) rumors.[5] However, he purposefully ignores or fails to note the fact that the main reason for the negative view of the Jewish Order Service members was their actual behavior and increasing zeal in carrying out German-imposed orders, their violence, and their corruption. This practice of claiming that opinions of police violence were exaggerated and that individual cases should not be seen as representative of the whole group would become a pillar of policemen's defense strategy after the war. Jewish policemen rationalized their behavior also by emphasizing the external pressure they were under. This was their way of maintaining a good opinion of themselves despite the hatred and contempt surrounding them.

Situational Factors: Living Conditions

By the time they joined the Jewish Order Service, Jewish policemen had lived in occupied Warsaw for over a year, and during that time they had experienced daily pauperization, anti-Jewish orders, and resettlements and brutality inflicted by Germans and, increasingly, by Poles. The large number of people willing to serve in the service not only during its formation but also throughout the existence of the ghetto testifies to the fact that in the period prior to the deportations, for the majority of policemen the positive aspects of membership outweighed the negative. After a year or two of professional inactivity, recruits finally had a job and a chance to leave their overcrowded apartments. Serving in the force also provided certain privileges: exemption from deportation to camps, free health care, protection against apartment requisition, and sometimes a pass enabling them to temporarily leave the ghetto.[6]

There was, however, an enormous gap between the financially privileged group of the police elite, who lived well from bribes and extortion, and other members of the Jewish Order Service. The situation of rank-and-file policemen was radically different. T. Witelson, who claimed to belong to a poorer group of policemen, wrote in a report for the Ringelblum Archive:

> For a year and a half or longer, we have been working [for free], our children are starving and freezing, we are literally dying from exhaustion and lack of vitamins and food, while our managers and commanders get salaries for themselves, and they tell us to survive on . . . air! . . . Even taking into account the manner in which recruitment has been carried out, one has to side with very numerous, completely pauperized, and ruined refugees, mainly intelligentsia, who are forced into unpaid heavy labor for the second year running, while heroic sacrifices and starvation are demanded from them. And who demands that? People who have everything and live better than before the war, people who have no right to condemn or judge others.[7]

Despite the tales circulating about the fortunes that policemen were accumulating at the expense of other Jews, in reality the rank-and-file policemen did not earn much from bribes. As reckoned by G., a policeman from the Fourth Precinct, every policeman in that section served at the three ghetto exits only four times a month. He described the earnings of policemen from "over-the-wall" trade as "minimal."[8] While policemen also took bribes during the sanitary blockades, these took place only during typhus outbreaks, so they did not provide regular income. Moreover, the money extorted by policemen was pooled and then divided according to a previously established system based on the official hierarchy. Even Leon Piżyc, deputy head of the First Precinct, which included the richest streets of the ghetto, reportedly complained to Szeryński that the policemen were arriving for duty weak from hunger and with holes in their shoes.[9]

We should also bear in mind that policemen supported their families using bribe money, and not only their wives and children, but also often other relatives of both spouses. Financial assistance was not the only form of support for relatives; policemen helped them in smuggling or in business, in avoiding payments of "contributions" to the Polish Blue Police or other members of the Jewish Order Service, or even by obtaining for them work connected to the service in some way—for example, cleaning police offices or canteens. Policemen's wives often worked as waitresses in cafés. Although there was a ghetto stereotype of a "wealthy policeman's wife," some wives worked as cleaners in private apartments, while their closest relatives died of starvation.[10] This information does not come exclusively from the relatives of police families. One woman who lived in the ghetto during the war noted in her memoirs a conversation with a friend, the wife of a policeman, who was in a dire financial situation and relied on her to sell her last belongings, which she carried out in a small case: "She had a small attaché case with things left she wanted to sell. She counted on the fact that she had three new bedding sheets for sale. Today she noticed that they had moth holes. She wanted to buy some potatoes and honey for her daughter, for the winter. But honey is out of the question now."[11]

As an attempt to regulate pay did not bring any results, both the Jewish administration and the authorities of the Jewish Order Service gave tacit permission to participate in bribery and extortion. As was the case with the Polish Blue Police, the leadership of the service also accepted the necessity for policemen to find additional income. Jerzy Lewiński, deputy head of the Third Precinct, testified after the war that he had worked in the Jewish Order Service for three to four hours a day and had earned additional money as the custodian of a building in which his brother had lived.[12] One of the police guards in the Central Lockup worked in a toy factory run by his family on the Aryan side, which he was able to get to from the ghetto on a regular basis thanks to his membership in the service.[13] Others worked in ghetto cultural institutions, with one policeman taking over management of a coffeehouse.[14] Yet the borderline between gaining material resources necessary for survival and trying to get rich was blurred, and it soon became difficult to draw a distinct line between the two. Taking advantage of the leniency of superiors toward such behavior, many policemen became involved in shady businesses cooperating with smugglers, underworld figures, and Gestapo collaborators. Senior officers also took advantage of their connections in the Jewish Council. In his memoirs, Stanisław Adler describes the relations of senior Jewish Order Service officers with the Zakład Zaopatrywania (Supply Department), which allocated to them the right to distribute to ghetto entrepreneurs (usually in exchange for a large bribe) the molasses necessary for the production of ersatz honey.[15]

The foundation for the spread of corruption among policemen was, therefore, open tolerance of such practices and even group pressure in this regard, which led to the development of specific patterns of bribery. Bribery also permeated the structure of the service itself, where one could purchase both a higher rank and a transfer to a more prosperous precinct. The most widely discussed case was that of Abram Solnik, a lawyer and a group leader in the Gmina Precinct, who as deputy platoon commander was collecting money from subordinate policemen for a large bribe, which was supposed to transfer the whole platoon to the Fourth Precinct, where profits from corruption were bigger.[16]

One employee of the sanitary brigades explained the slide into corruption: "Although I found myself in such material conditions that I did not feel compelled to earn something 'on the side,' I looked at my colleagues with a certain envy when they were bragging about their achievements with a smile on their faces, and I, exhausted more than anyone else, went home with my tail between my legs. Gradually, I became used to 'taking' money. The soaring prices made me aware of how much I needed."[17]

Regular policemen believed that their efforts and the risk to their health and life were disproportionate to those of the officers, and that they were therefore entitled to an income that would allow a lifestyle comparable to that of the officers. The sense of inequality in earnings was accompanied by a serious disintegration of prewar social relations. Rank-and-file service members with intelligentsia backgrounds struggled with police discipline and in particular with being subordinate to officers who behaved condescendingly and who had gained their positions not so much due to qualifications but rather through the support of the Blue Police or through acquaintances in the Judenrat. After a few months of service, T. Witelson wrote that "officers became so assertive, they got used to the rank that was given to them. They began to behave like real generals towards their subordinates, among whom there were many people with higher education, and even many actual army reserve officers."[18]

FIGURE 21. Jewish Order Service functionaries, First Precinct, mid-1941. Source: JHI, E-1/15/3.

A list of the addresses of residences of individual policemen, created in the first months of the operation, confirmed these differences. Out of thirty-three members of the Jewish Order Service command, twelve lived on Sienna Street. Adler, who himself lived there, wrote of it in his memoirs:

> [The street] was mainly inhabited by the "aristocracy" of the quarter. For these more prosperous people, that is those who still owned some moveable property or jewelry or had connections with hierarchy of the Jewish Council, better times had come. With the sealing of the ghetto, the rummaging of German soldiers, the SS and scoundrels working on their own account stopped. The plundering ceased and the unorganized theft of furniture became a rare occurrence. For the moment, the price of food had stopped rising. It is understandable, therefore, that we experienced a sense of relief in our part of the ghetto because living within an exclusively Jewish society, we were rid of the annoyance and degradation we had experienced in the Aryan Quarter, where we had been singled out by our arm bands, and drawn into conversation with people affected by anti-Jewish propaganda.[19]

Two high-ranking officers lived on each of the next most representative streets in the ghetto, Leszno, Chłodna, and Elektoralna, and on Grzybowski Square. One member of the Directorate of the Jewish Order Service and the head of the Central Lockup, Judge Leopold Lindenfeld, found an apartment in the parish of All Saints Church, inhabited by the social elite of converts in the ghetto. The situation in the Reserve command and the Gmina was very similar.

In the separate precincts, the differences were even bigger, with precinct commanders always living on the "better" streets of the ghetto, and rank-and-file on those considered, even by ghetto standards, impoverished. People who held managerial positions in the Jewish Order Service were thus clearly well connected and well off and could afford apartments in the most affluent apartment blocks.

Therefore, alongside the "we have to take bribes in order to survive" argument, which was used to rationalize bribery, another one appeared: "We take bribes because we work harder and we risk our lives more than officers who earn more than we do." In time, this competition among comrades included the use of violence against ghetto inhabitants.

Institutional Factors: Service Duties

Corruption and violence were also inscribed by the German authorities into the daily obligations of the Jewish Order Service. According to some policemen, this was aimed at creating a scapegoat—making the police the perpetrators on whom the Jews' hatred was to focus. According to others, the policy aimed to morally corrupt the entire Jewish community. The Germans acted according to the "divide and rule" principle, and they used the divisions in the ghetto as an instrument of social disintegration, with victims forced to play the role of persecutors. In a letter to Berlin dated November 24, 1941, Heinz Auerswald noted that "when conflicts occur in the ghetto, the Jewish population directs their discontentment primarily against the Jewish administration, not the German authorities."[20] The situation that Auerswald writes about is well documented in personal accounts. There is no doubt that Jewish policemen were often blamed for carrying out the orders of the German administrators of the ghetto, in particular roundups for forced labor. Their duties not only involved violence, but, just as important, this was a violence that was fully visible, one that could not be hidden from ghetto inhabitants. As one policeman wrote, the Jewish Order Service had "to perform dogcatcher-like service and get in return, as trophies, hatred and condemnation from the people." As a result, policemen often emphasized the need for accommodation and used the "lesser evil" argument, claiming that roundups carried out by Germans would be much worse for the population than those organized by the ghetto police.[21] Maria Zadziewicz, the wife of a Jewish Order Service physician, drew attention to this after the war:

> None of them acknowledged he was doing anything wrong. Each one thought it was a sacrifice on his part, as he risked his life, for example by the very fact that he remained constantly in the vicinity of the Germans. They were blamed by the Germans for many offenses they did not commit. Even those who beat others claimed that betraying their own character and hitting another person for the first time in their life was an act of heroism. And that you have to beat that person for preventive reasons: so that the [German] gendarme does not do it.[22]

Using this argument to explain the use of violence, policemen not only stressed the risk associated with refusing to follow orders but also sometimes even tried to paint their actions in a heroic light—their violence saved the ghetto from German intervention, thus serving a higher purpose. They portrayed their own violence as a lesser evil, even a preemptive Jewish self-defense against German violence.[23]

Similar arguments were used by *Gazeta Żydowska*. In October 1941, the newspaper drew attention to the "exceedingly violent behavior" of policemen. They attempted to explain it as the result of the difficult conditions of their service, a lack of understanding on the part of citizens of the official responsibility of Jewish Order Service members, and the need for "absolute obedience to existing regulations."[24] The same argument was further raised in the article "Police Brutality" published in June 1942.[25] In both texts, the newspaper called on those who felt unjustly treated by the police to make a formal complaint, "which will be the subject of a truly impartial inquiry, [and] inevitably bring about justice."

In documents created by the Jewish Order Service Directorate in this period, a clear message prevailed: Jewish civilians underestimated and did not understand the difficult duty that policemen performed for their good. This point was reinforced by the fact that from the first days of its existence, the Jewish Order Service was harassed by the German military police. This particularly affected policemen serving at the gates, as they were among the few people in the ghetto who had daily contact with the Germans who were rotated in to guard the ghetto: Battalions 304, 308, 61, and 53 of the Orpo.[26] By November 1940, a rumor had spread in the ghetto that fifty newly appointed policemen had decided to resign from the service after the "exercises" that Germans reportedly arranged for them in the center of Warsaw.[27] In February 1941, a contributor to the Ringelblum Archive wrote:

> There was a terrible incident involving a policeman from the Jewish Order Service. The Konarski School at Leszno is still open. It has always been a very antisemitic school. Students have passes and come to the ghetto for their classes. On the way home, they often mercilessly beat passing Jews. This was another such case; the students attacked the Jews with great cruelty. The Jews called the Jewish police, and immediately a large number of policemen from two stations appeared. They gave the attackers a good thrashing. Some fled to the [ghetto] border on Leszno Street; some stayed but could not defend themselves against the policemen. One of the attackers was beaten very severely. The students called the [German] gendarmes, who arrested one Jewish policeman and escorted him to Pawiak Prison. There they tortured him to death. There are rumors that the policeman's body was bitten by dogs. According to the Jewish police, the family did not receive any compensation from the Judenrat. The deceased left a widow and a family for whom the police collected some money so that at least they would have something.[28]

A few witness accounts mention the harassment suffered by members of the Jewish Order Service, and these were the only times when ghetto residents exhibited any sympathy or trace of kinship with the Jewish Order Service policemen.[29]

The policemen knew what was happening in the work camps, and they witnessed executions in the lockup on Gęsia Street. It seems that in the face of the division between "us" and "them," at least some came to terms with the tasks imposed upon them. They assumed, as Adler wrote, that "it was preferable to catch than to be caught."[30] It is, however, worth considering whether it was possible to extricate oneself from these duties (or at least ease one's way out of them) in the period before the deportations began and what were the factors, both formal and informal, including peer pressure. In the spring of 1941, Ringelblum wrote about rumors circulating in the ghetto that under public pressure a group of policemen had reportedly refused to participate in roundups. Some of them had even said that they would prefer to go to the camp themselves than continue to arrest people.[31] Similar information was provided by the underground press. Rumors or publicly known information about actual (yet sporadic) events testify rather to people's deep need to find something positive in their nightmarish situation—the need for a "good policeman" and some type of moral justification for service members' deeds.

This was wishful thinking born of a vague hope that even in that corrupt, brutal, egoistic group there were still some noble individuals. In their accounts and memoirs, the policemen demonstrate antipathy toward their superiors, yet there were not many cases of open defiance of orders. A policeman of the lowest rank, unless he was extremely well connected, could not choose the duties to which he was assigned. Those who refused to carry out orders would be in danger of expulsion from the service or even more severe punishment. An anonymous worker in the sanitary brigade wrote about an order from Dr. Edmund Kubliński, an epidemic control commissioner, who threatened the members of the Jewish Order Service with an immediate summary judgment if they released anyone from a building quarantine. The anonymous worker wrote that this was included in the orders of the Jewish Order Service (the orders in question have not survived). Furthermore, the well-informed Salomea Ostrowska, the director of the quarantine facility at 109 Leszno Street, wrote that it was said in the ghetto that if the police did not provide the right number of workers, they would be sent to the camps themselves.[32]

It is difficult to estimate to what extent the tasks delegated to the Jewish Order Service, especially those that involved violence, led to increasing moral disengagement and influenced the attitudes of policemen during the deportations. The term "moral disengagement" I understand, following James Waller, to mean "an active, but gradual, process of detachment by which some individuals or groups are placed outside the boundary in which moral values, rules, and considerations of fairness apply."[33] The fact that high-level officers increasingly resorted to violence themselves resulted in a consensus for violence in the entire formation, as was the case with corruption in its ranks.

We can assume that for some officers, over time, violent abuse had become not only routine and professionally acceptable behavior but also a way of emphasizing their status and power. To quote Wolfgang Sofsky: "Violence was also a demonstration of social belonging. 'Prominents' assured each other that they belonged to the same category. Violence set the social borders between the 'Prominents' and the people of the ghetto; it strengthened the sense of their privileged community and closed the circle to the outside."[34]

Closing of Ranks

The ghetto population's antipathy toward the Jewish Order Service was increasing, and the officers responded by closing their ranks and seeking acceptance within their own group, a phenomenon that Adler described as *"esprit de corps."*[35] Despite the upending of the social order caused by the chaos of war, the ghetto was also a place where new groups formed and governed by their own rules based on specific common experiences. The Jewish Order Service was one such organization, with its own group dynamics and clearly very strong binding factors. A female relative of one of the policemen described the phenomenon:

> He found among them many pre-war friends, and all their meetings inevitably ended in vodka-drinking, or supper in a restaurant, because there was always someone who wanted to get an additional star and was willing to entertain them and be seen in the company of "higher ranks" They exchanged jokes, discussed politics, local news, who was doing well at smuggling, and who was successful at the wall, and then told stories about the Germans. All policemen had permits to stay out at night after the curfew, and so their meetings lasted late into the night.[36]

How did this gradual development into an insular group affect policemen? In the accounts of their relatives, we often find descriptions of dual pressures: on the one hand, the family and the ghetto community, and on the other, fellow officers. Some responded to this conflict by choosing one of the sides, and it was usually easier to manifest their loyalty to the service,

FIGURE 22.   Jewish Order Service functionaries, Second Precinct, mid-1941. Source: JHI, E-1/16/3.

an organization that increasingly fulfilled one's need for power and status—in short, one that enhanced their self-esteem.[37] In her study of the Warsaw Ghetto, Barbara Engelking writes about the search for external and internal normality. In the case of policemen, external normality meant drinking with prewar colleagues or an individual office desk for which they were willing to participate in immoral activities. As I have already written, bars, cafés, and theaters, where the police were regulars, were a grey zone within the ghetto. This internal normality was an adaptation to the moral norms prevailing in the police ranks, which were introduced through professional socialization. This was accomplished not necessarily through individual policemen's use of violence but by their becoming accustomed to it and not reacting when others used it (the absence of reaction is not, however, tantamount to acceptance of violence). Engelking describes this attitude as "exhibited indifference."[38] This adaptation in time gave rise to a clearly present informal culture of cruelty that helped policemen cope with their daily duties. In addition, the policemen were convinced that their actions were morally justified. This explained, in their eyes, the need to suspend compassion toward individuals for the good of the community.

Service members also accepted police norms through language and ritualistic behavior, which constituted another important bonding factor. The latter included parades, roll calls of the fallen, and photo albums put together for internal use that turned policemen into soldiers on the battle front. In December 1940, an organizational anthem was composed. Throughout the existence of the Jewish Order Service, its leadership strove to strengthen the policemen's morale and their identification with the service, as well as to establish its hierarchical nature, using these methods. In the accounts of police officers, we find descriptions of various military-style ceremonies that aimed to build a sense of belonging to a respected group. Such events were usually accompanied by speeches from Szeryński, who, according to Adler, took his inspiration from Mussolini. In Adler's words: "These bursts of eloquence received ingratiating praise from his closest entourage of flatterers, while the rest were choking with laughter strongly tempered by fear."[39] One policeman described an April 1942 roll call in honor of the fallen, devoted to officers who had died while in the service, mainly victims of typhus:

> In the courtyard of the Judenrat, in the building at Grzybowska Street, two thousand Jewish Order Service officers formed a quadrangle, taking up the entire square in long ranks. At the appointed hour the following persons entered the square in the middle of the quadrangle: the chairman [Czerniaków], Colonel Reszczyński, Polish Blue Police Warsaw commander with his adjutant, Szeryński, and several [Blue Police] officers: Maj. [Mieczysław] Tarwid, Cpt. [Karol] Moniak, Dudziński, [Wacław] Kleczkowski, and [Władysław] Rodkiewicz. Lejkin reported to Lederman, and Lederman to Szeryński. . . . The entire ceremony made some impression: about two thousand people, in a tight formation, standing at attention, in complete silence, interrupted only by the words of the report and the reading of the list of the deceased and their superiors repeating every time: "Died in the line of duty."[40]

The roll call described above was not the only ceremony Szeryński organized in honor of the fallen policemen. According to reports by the Polish Underground, another one, ending with a sumptuous reception and the participation of Blue Policemen, was organized in November 1941.[41] Even if the policemen distanced themselves from this type of ceremony, it is difficult to assume that such symbolic recognition of fellowship did not affect them in any way. Above all, it justified their behavior as an act of martyrdom that prevented the suffering of the ghetto as a whole.

Despite all the shows of unity, it appears that moral corruption within the Jewish Order Service stemmed above all from the weakened authority and limited control of its command. The weakness was the result of constant personnel changes and internal intrigues. Initially, the Jewish Order Service command consisted of people whom Szeryński knew before the war, but with time included officers who had distinguished themselves in the structures of the ghetto service by exemplary fulfillment of their duties—often those who had some militaristic predispositions. They were the ones who voluntarily and most often took on duties requiring the use of violence, such as roundups for forced labor or quarantine blockades, and carried them out more aggressively than the wider community considered to be necessary. Their rise in power is proof that violence was rewarded and went hand in hand in the service with ambition and careerism.

Professional advancement was hence another strong motivation for violence, which became a mark of distinction. The most infamous new members of the Jewish Order Service command, who were known for brutality in the predeportation period, were Jakub Lejkin, who in May 1942 took over the position of head of the Jewish Order Service, and Mieczysław Szmerling, head of the Anti-epidemic Company, who became a key player during the deportation operation in the Warsaw Ghetto in the summer of 1942.

CHAPTER 6

Response to Violence

We cannot say whether, upon taking over the leadership, Józef Szeryński was aware of the pathological situation that had prevailed in the Guard of the Labor Battalion, which formed the backbone of the Jewish Order Service (see chapter 2). Yet, the first measures he undertook were aimed not at combating the omnipresent bribery, extortion, and violence but primarily at enforcing discipline among people who were not used to serving in a police organization. The daily orders issued between November 1940 and January 1941 reveal the disciplinary problems he had to face during this period.[1] On November 21, Szeryński ordered the platoon commanders to "see that the functionaries in their divisions were thoroughly informed about the time of meetings and beginning of duty and that they could not leave the Jewish district without authorization." On December 24, 1940, he reported, "There are multiplying cases of missing registration numbers, hats and clubs, and bands. I warn you that those guilty of losing these items will be subject to disciplinary accountability, regardless of the obligation to pay back the costs of the lost items." Policemen even had to be reminded of the need to maintain a proper appearance ("shaved, clean clothes and shoes, etc.") and to salute all senior officials, thus signaling obedience to authority. Police instructor Józef Prussak wrote in a pamphlet aimed at new recruits:

> Saluting is an act of duty and courtesy. Salute skillfully, carefully, willingly. When saluting, look into the eyes of the person whom you salute,

whether giving or receiving the salute. Always salute superiors equally regardless of their rank in the service. District, group, and section commanders have the right to a slight inclination of your head, always done with the same will and care. Remember that a careless salute leaves an impression of disrespect; [it] irritates, embitters, discourages, and it does not speak well of you.[2]

Another problem was absenteeism. On December 19, Szeryński carried out a review of the service, and on December 21, 1940, he reported the dismissal of twenty-five policemen from their positions and the next day a further thirty. On December 23, without giving any reason, all those who had been dismissed on December 21 and nine of those dismissed on December 22 were reinstated. On December 24, another seven were dismissed. Although *Gazeta Żydowska* reported at the time that "all unfit and undesirable elements have been eliminated (from the Jewish Order Service)," the actual changes in this period were trivial.[3] It is not known whether such demonstrations of dismissal from the service took place later as well.

Regarding criminal accountability, members of the Jewish Order Service, like other ghetto residents, were subject to the German judicial authorities. Within the Jewish Order Service, the judicial function was carried out by the Referat Porządkowo-Dyscyplinarny (Order and Disciplinary Section) under the leadership of Mieczysław Goldstein, later Henryk Nowogródzki.[4] Its activity can be seen as the most important step aimed at acquiring transparency in the activities of the service. The inspectorate also played an essential role in the disciplinary proceedings, with the task of monitoring the discipline as well as the behavior of policemen during and outside of working hours. It provided the policemen with suggestions and reminders and, in the event of a proven disciplinary offense, transferred cases to the Order and Disciplinary Section. In theory, individual functionaries could also address the Order and Disciplinary Section on their own, submitting complaints about the behavior of their superiors. We do not know how the system functioned in practice. Complaints were to be submitted to superior officers—in other words, to those who were the subject of the complaint, and they, along with their own statements, sent them to their superiors, who would eventually decide whether to refer the matter to the Referat Dyscyplinarny przy Komisji Prawnej Judenratu (Disciplinary Section at the Judenrat Legal Commission), which dealt with the misconduct of all employees of the Judenrat.[5]

According to police reports, the inspectorate and the Order and Disciplinary Section acted vigorously: in January 1941, 100 cases were submitted, 31

FIGURE 23. Members of the Disciplinary Section, mid 1941. Source: JHI, MŻIH E-1/11/3.

of which were transferred to the Disciplinary Section by the Judenrat. The section was then allowed to reprimand the functionary in question, reduce his rank, impose a fine, suspend him from duty for up to one year, or expel him from the service.[6]

Detailed information on the section's activities can be found in the weekly Jewish Order Service report to the commissioner for the Jewish Residential District in Warsaw, which recorded the number of disciplinary cases considered over the period of a week and the penalties imposed. In the period covered by the reports (June 1941 to July 1942), 996 disciplinary rulings were handed down. The number of cases considered during a week ranged from six (April 4 through April 10, 1942) to fifty-four (two weeks later). Additional information is provided by daily reports in which data on the number of persons summoned by the Disciplinary Section were posted. For example, in the second week of February 1942, the Disciplinary Section called about thirty witnesses and defendants per day, and only ten policemen were punished during that week. We may conclude from this that many witnesses were summoned for each case or, as Barbara Engelking and Jan Grabowski note in their study on crime in the ghetto, that the data concerned not only disciplinary matters but also criminal cases that would be resolved by the Order and Disciplinary Section of the Jewish Order Service. The inclusion of this information in official reports would suggest that the Germans realized that such offenses were tried in the ghetto.[7]

The authorities of the Jewish Order Service probably imitated the Blue Police and were attentive to preserving at least a semblance of the rule of law within its ranks. This was noticed and widely commented on in the ghetto, though, as one might suspect, hardly anyone had any precise information on the subject. On April 17, 1941, Emanuel Ringelblum noted that 750 policemen, out of a total of 1,700, had been disciplined by that date.[8] Some saw it as evidence of the progressive corruption of the Jewish Order Service, but according to others they may have contributed to improving its image. Commenting on the expulsion of three policemen accused of removing the clothing from the corpse of one of the victims of the mass executions of spring 1942, Rachel Auerbach wrote, "In addition to expulsion from the police the case was also passed to the judicial authorities before whom these individuals will face charges of theft and desecration of corpses. This must be noted for the rehabilitation of the Jewish Order Service command—i.e., to clear it of at least one of the allegations. It is viewed rather negatively in the eyes of Jewish society."[9]

Policemen were much less sympathetic to the work of the Disciplinary Section. In their testimonies we often find opinions that the section defended the interests of the group of officers around Szeryński; that it dealt sternly with minor offenses of rank-and-file members of the Jewish Order Service while ignoring those committed on a broad scale by their superiors. This was especially true with regard to investigations of fraud, which targeted small police bribes. One policeman, writing about the trials for accepting bribes, described the members of the section as patrons "who have several positions and a monthly income of one thousand to three thousand zlotys, because virtually the rule here is that the lawyers from the Disciplinary Section are at the same time commissioners of several apartment buildings and partners in several cafés, and besides, as 'officers' they receive three hundred to four hundred zlotys a month." He went on to say that "the better off 'officers' are, the more energy they will show in the fight against their defenseless and hungry subordinates. This is what their 'legal' and 'civic' consciences tells them."[10] The same opinions can also be found in other sources concerning the irrefutably privileged financial standing of the Disciplinary Section members who used their positions for further gain. One policeman wrote:

> If matters were related to smuggling—one had to turn a blind eye, being officially an officer who is meant to combat smuggling but silently

acknowledging the necessity of the existing smuggling and smugglers; if the cases concerned certain acts that, according to the letter of the law constituted offenses but in light of the realities resulting from the poverty and disease—even the reception of some donation—then it was necessary to proceed according to the circumstances. If the cases concerned certain people, by virtue of their various inviolable contacts, one had to maneuver carefully or avoid them.[11]

All these attempts to introduce order were thus dramatically inadequate when compared to the scale of the fraud committed by the Jewish Order Service. What is more, they contributed significantly to the deepening of divisions within its ranks.

The policemen did not limit themselves to criticizing the formation in which they served. They also attempted to address the problems. At least several memorandums were addressed to Czerniaków regarding irregularities in the Jewish Order Service. One of them, an undated memo from a group of policemen, was deposited in the Underground Archive of the Warsaw Ghetto by Zygmunt Millet.[12] This group called on Szeryński to clearly define the tasks of the service and its powers, related primarily to the use of force by policemen. Other suggestions were to carry out vetting at the service aimed at "removing individuals who are morally tarnished or disqualified in terms of skills and abilities, who have been nevertheless accepted into the Jewish Order Service in the organizational period due to the rush resulting from practical circumstances," reducing the number of service members and further complementing the composition of the service "to include people from different spheres of society, so that representatives of the working class can be incorporated."

The authors of the memorandum also demanded that police officers be paid, "which is the only guarantee of absolute integrity and independence of the Jewish Order Service policemen, and which makes it possible to demand their unconditional dedication to their duty, by providing also full moral title to require their obedience and apply the most severe disciplinary measures."

Increased control over the activity of the service was to be exercised by extending the competence of the Disciplinary Section. The authors of the memo wrote, "Only by implementing the postulates described above can the Jewish Order Service be healed, as it has become broken and morally corrupt over such a short time, losing from day to day its reputation and public trust, and, consequently, preventing good and honest people from remaining in its ranks, unless this state of affairs changes drastically."[13]

The only visible result of these initiatives was the issue of an *instruk-cja służbowa* (duty manual, in part almost identical to the demands of the memos)[14] and the establishment of the Komisja Kwalifikacyjna (Qualification Commission), the purpose of which was to verify the Jewish Order Service in terms of the moral integrity of its members. From the beginning, the leadership of the service feared that Szeryński would use the commission to remove inconvenient policemen. One policeman predicted that the commission would be a body with "unlimited authority": "using its own sources of information, it [will] be allowed to dismiss a policeman from his position in the Jewish Order Service, without questioning him, without examining witnesses, deliberating in secret and without an adversarial hearing; in a word— an extraordinary commission to conduct a purge, without any procedural restrictions."[15] In a diary entry from June 12, 1942, Adam Czerniaków notes that it was, however, the chairman of the Judenrat who ultimately decided to remove over a hundred policemen from the service.[16] According to one policeman, due to the tense situation in the ghetto at the time of the decision, these policemen were only suspended, and their removal from the list never occurred.[17]

The ghetto authorities also attempted to resolve the problems within the service by providing the policemen with tolerable living conditions. The first effort in this direction was the establishment in April 1941 of the Order Service Fund, maintained from fixed contributions of businesses and household committees, which was to constitute the source of salaries for policemen who were not employed by the Judenrat.[18] However, tax revenues in the ghetto, which was rapidly becoming impoverished, did not allow for regular payouts but only for small payments granted once every few months.[19]

A similar step was the establishment of the Samopomoc Funkcjonariuszy Służby Porządkowej (Mutual Assistance for Functionaries of the Order Services).[20] This body, ultimately under the name of Sekcja Pomocy Rzeczowej dla Funkcjonariuszy (Section of Material Assistance for Order Service Functionaries, or SEPOR), was created within Section III (economic) of the Jewish Order Service. SEPOR's task was to allocate the additional food quotas granted by the Judenrat or purchased on the open market, which were then distributed on the basis of food ration cards. It also supported sick policemen and convalescents and provided assistance to the families of policemen who had died.

Despite the lofty objectives of its creators, abuses and corruption also took place in SEPOR. Higher officers of SEPOR were accused of appropriating food supplies that were supposed to go to poor policemen, seizing SEPOR

FIGURE 24. Staff members of SEPOR, mid 1941. Source: JHI, MŻIH E-1/17/5.

funds and setting up companies and factories, which then sold their products to SEPOR at inflated prices.[21] Some claimed that the rank-and-file police-men got only the products that their superiors did not want—beetroot, stale sausages, and sour cabbage distributed in large quantities. Meanwhile, the leaders of the Jewish Order Service used SEPOR funds to pay for sumptuous dinners with the Blue Police.[22]

The policemen benefited more from special police kitchens, established in June 1941 from the police tax money. As *Gazeta Żydowska* reported, you could eat nourishing and tasty soups there for seventy groszes;[23] Czerniaków wrote that it was half a liter of soup with beans, a bit of meat, and dump-lings. It is doubtful that the soup presented to the chairman of the Juden-rat and the high officials accompanying him during the inauguration of the kitchen was the same soup that was to be given daily to rank-and-file police-men.[24] At the end of 1941, a support fund for families of policemen who had died was organized. The everyday life of rank-and-file policemen was also significantly improved by the precinct heads' efforts to share fairly the income from bribes and smuggling or the food quotas (especially for bread) that business owners in the area were forced to provide.[25]

The involvement of the Judenrat in improving the life of the members of the Jewish Order Service stemmed from the links between the two institu-tions. Despite the discrepancy in the formal division of power and everyday-life practicalities, there are no grounds to believe that Szeryński tried in any way or wanted to become independent of the Judenrat, and he did not seek to strengthen his position at the expense of Czerniaków's authority. Nonetheless, the bad opinion of the service adversely affected the image of the Judenrat, especially when policemen committed offenses while enforcing tasks assigned to them by the Judenrat. In October 1941, Czerniaków described a few policemen who, after a housing matter was resolved in a manner not to their liking, beat up Mojżesz Fogel, the head of the Judenrat's Housing Office.[26] The Judenrat was also forced to intervene (probably on the night of January 5, 1942) after the service's arrest of the chairmen of some apartment block house committees, who were responsible for the arrears of the residents' municipal contribution. This case aroused enormous indignation. As Judenrat councilor Szmuel Winter wrote in a letter to Czerniaków, it only heightened the ghetto residents' dislike of the Judenrat.[27] As a result, Czerniaków demanded that the Jewish Order Service not undertake such procedures without his permission.[28]

Attempts to heal the Jewish Order Service were not forceful and probably were made too late to build understanding and trust between it and the ghetto populations. It did not help that the campaign to improve the service's image was carried out through the widely despised *Gazeta Żydowska*, which, in its own words, was aimed at informing the Jews "about Jewish problems in the spirit we [Jews] desire."[29] This task was carried out in a specific way: through building a community of readers around their shared responsibility for life in the ghetto. *Gazeta Żydowska* struggled to counteract "instigators of the manipulation of public opinion,"[30] and in many articles it expressed hope that "society will also show understanding for the weighty tasks of the Jewish Order Service members and will meticulously obey all their orders, issued in the interest of society, to which they sacrifice themselves and are often devoted to serving. During its relatively short period of existence, the Jewish Order Service has shown in various areas of social work that it is truly a civic institution."[31] The newspaper claimed that the existence of the Jewish Order Service was a manifestation of a new self-government, and that subordination to it was in the interest of the ghetto community, since it was an opportunity to "show that we are able to rule on our own and be subordinate to the authorities. . . . Remember also that the present times are quite different from the past."[32] At the same time the police were to be included in the system of traditional internal Jewish power, and *Gazeta Żydowska* even suggested that it was the successor of *Straż Religijna przy Dozorze Bożniczym* (Religious Guard at the Synagogue).[33]

We may assume that for many ghetto inhabitants, *Gazeta Żydowska* was far from convincing. On the contrary—it identified the Jewish Order Service even more strongly with the German administration and the worst practices of the Jewish leadership. Commentators often drew attention here to the history of antagonism between the politically involved Jewish masses and the prewar Jewish community associated mainly with bourgeois assimilated and Orthodox Jewish circles. Ringelblum wrote in June 1942, "The same is repeated, which we have read about in the history of the Jews, namely: the Jewish *kehilla* [local communal Jewish structure] with its apparatus always exploited the Jewish masses more than the Christian magistrate his subordinates."[34]

Yet the complete failure of both the Judenrat and Szeryński to alter the general view of policemen clearly shows that the actions of the Jewish Order Service were at that point well out of their control.

CHAPTER 7

Spring 1942

On May 22, 1942, Rachela Auerbach wrote in her diary, "About midday a rumor spread that 'something' would be happening tonight. The entire Jewish police force was placed on high alert. Mobilization of the entire force, two thousand people. And many different versions of what was happening. So, a 'roundup' of young people to camps. . . . Or is it just a trick? Maybe this was 'finally' 'it' or rather 'that,' as in Lublin, Zamość, Łódź, etc. And what can we do? Where to sleep? And if it is not done by address, but by apartment block, and you can fall out of the frying pan into the fire?"[1] On the same day, Rabbi Shimon Huberband noted, "All night we could hear the heavy boots of Jewish policemen brutally striking the pavements of the Warsaw Ghetto."[2]

Toward the end of 1941, along with the refugees and letters arriving in Warsaw, information about the mass murder of the Jewish population in the eastern parts of occupied Poland began to reach the ghetto. At the end of October, the underground Jewish press had alarmed its readers with news about the massacre of Vilnius Jews in Ponary. The first vague information about the extermination center in Chełmno appeared during the winter. In early April 1942 came news of the expulsion of Jews from the Lublin region and the Galicia District (Distrikt Galizien). It soon became clear that they had been sent to their deaths in the newly established Bełżec death camp. With increasingly worrying information coming in, the Jews of Warsaw were beginning to fear for their own community, which to that point had seemed too strong and populous to be affected by mass violence.

In the spring of 1942, preparations for Operation Reinhard began in the Warsaw Ghetto as elsewhere. Gestapo officers were increasingly seen in the streets of the ghetto. The German administration introduced additional forceful measures aimed at the separation of the ghetto from the rest of Warsaw, and Jews who were residing illegally on the Aryan side were more aggressively hunted down. Almost every day people came across corpses left at the doorways of buildings at Orla Street, brought by night from the Gestapo lockup on Szucha Avenue.[3] As before in other ghettos, so now in the Warsaw Ghetto the Germans began to survey the attitude of the population and search out possible resistance leaders.

On April 17, Sipo and SD officers ordered several Jewish Order Service policemen to appear in front of Pawiak Prison. What happened later that night was described by Judenrat clerk Stefan Ernest: "From eleven o'clock in the evening until dawn, one could hear the drone of motorcycles and sounds of shootings. A pogrom was beginning. It was said the next day that hundreds of victims, taken from their beds and packed into trucks were finished off a few hundred meters away, often only several dozen meters from the doorways of their homes."[4]

That night the German police murdered fifty-two Jews chosen from among the Gestapo collaborators but also some individuals who had played a significant role in the social life of the ghetto. Again, Jewish policemen were ordered to perform auxiliary activities, such as assisting in bringing victims out of flats and removing their bodies from the streets.[5] The next morning, Czerniaków recommended that the Directorate of the Jewish Order Service calm the population of the ghetto.[6]

The operation aimed at the ghetto elite also struck the Jewish Order Service. On May 1, Józef Szeryński was arrested. "Er kommt nicht wieder" (He will not return), associates were reported to have heard over the phone when they asked about his prolonged absence after a meeting at the German criminal police office. Szeryński's arrest shook the service, and the news immediately spread throughout the ghetto.[7] The formal basis for the arrest, according to information provided to Czerniaków by Karl Brandt, was the accusation that he gave his wife's fur coat to a Blue Police officer for safekeeping, which violated the December 1941 ban on Jews owning furs.[8] Brandt claimed that Szeryński had been denounced by a Jew who had personal conflicts with the Polish Blue Policeman who stored the fur coat. This information cannot be confirmed. It should be noted, however, that Szeryński avoided the death penalty required by the regulations.[9] Still, Czerniaków's attempt to

mediate for Szeryński's release with the head of the SS and the police in
the Warsaw District, Arpad Wigand, was unsuccessful. The intervention of
the Blue Police also failed.[10] Despite Czerniaków's efforts to have him sent
to the Central Lockup on Gęsia, on May 6 Szeryński was placed in Pawiak
Prison and remained there until the beginning of the deportations. The Blue
Policeman who stored the fur, arrested at the same time as Szeryński, was
released after eleven days.[11]

Czerniaków wrote that Szeryński, haggard, unshaven, and dirty, was
escorted to Pawiak through the main streets of the ghetto, Leszno, Karmelicka, and Dzielna, by a Blue Policeman. Jewish policemen looked on as
Szeryński was led through ghetto and their gaze, one of them wrote, "was
devoid of respect or even sympathy."[12] The same was reported by an anonymous Gestapo informer from the ghetto: "Although his arrest caused a sen-
sation, because it involved a senior official of the ghetto, it did not arouse
particular feelings of compassion. It is difficult to avoid the impression that
Szeryński was not only disliked by his closest colleagues, but even hated.
It was even rumored that in the evening many of his colleagues 'celebrated'
the event in the bars."[13]

Despite the amount of gossip on the topic circulating in the ghetto, there
is little information about Szeryński's time in prison. According to Czerniaków's notes, Szeryński's salary was stopped on May 8, but his wife, at the
order of Auerswald, received help from the Judenrat's social welfare apparatus.[14] On May 13, Czerniaków was informed that Auerswald did not agree
to release Szeryński, and if he were released, he could at best get the post
of adviser (*Berater*) in the Jewish Order Service, not commander.[15] It was not
until a month after his arrest that Czerniaków was allowed to deliver parcels
to him, which was the basic source of food for prisoners.[16]

Following Szeryński's arrest, it was necessary to designate his successor,
someone who would enjoy the common trust and take responsibility for the
functioning of the Jewish Order Service at such a difficult moment.[17] The
deaths of Leon Berenson in April 1941 and of Maksymilian Schönbach in
February 1942 ruled out two obvious candidates. Various candidacies immediately became the subject of rumors and tenders, with some of those interested in taking up this position (among them Marian Händel) making visits
to the German authorities.[18] However, as a well-known Gestapo collaborator, Händel did not have much of a chance of taking the post. Finally, on
May 5, 1942, Jakub Lejkin, the head of the Department of Service and Training, became acting commander.[19] On that day, Czerniaków communicated
the decision during the officers' briefing and, as he wrote, he recommended
"peace, discipline and submission to the orders of the new commander."[20]

The next day, in the early afternoon, Czerniaków introduced Lejkin at a meeting at the Blue Police headquarters.[21]

Lejkin, a graduate of the Officer Cadet School in Jarocin, had been promoted in the organization of the Jewish Order Service not only thanks to his effectiveness in personnel matters but also because of his efficiency in carrying out roundups for labor camps. Undoubtedly, this effectiveness was appreciated, since he was entrusted with the command of the important disinfection operation at Krochmalna Street.[22] A year earlier, one of the collaborators of the Ghetto Underground Archive described him this way:

> Speaking of the [Jewish] Order Service, it is impossible to skip one of the senior officers who, although allegedly not involved in any bribe organisation or cooperative, should nevertheless find a place in the glorious annals of the [Jewish] Order Service. Mr. Lejkin, a lawyer from Warsaw, one of the leading figures of the [Jewish] Order Service, was so diligent in carrying out his duty to provide slaves (and also candidates for envoys to a better world) for the Germans that in one night he dragged 1,600 Jews out of beds or basements, and personally delivered them alive to the Collegium, whence they were sent to concentration camps. The superior of this conscientious policeman, Colonel Szeryński, found proper appreciation for the zeal of his subordinate and gave him a star with an appropriate acknowledgement in the daily orders. Regardless of this, Szeryński reported his accomplishment to the supreme authority in the district, Mr. Czerniaków, who also properly appreciated Mr. Lejkin's heroic deeds and gave him an award in the amount of 300 zlotys in cash. It was a rare event in the history: virtue was handsomely rewarded.[23]

Despite Lejkin's reputation for dutifully carrying out German orders, there is no reason to think that he was chosen by the occupying authorities. On the contrary, according to Czerniaków, the choice was initially opposed by Brandt, who had reservations—about the short stature of the new commander.[24]

An extract from the daily reports from the refugee shelter published in the underground press shows that even in the atmosphere of danger that prevailed in the ghetto in the spring of 1942, policemen carried out their tasks as usual: from the beginning of April to the beginning of May, they visited that particular shelter several times.[25] On April 2 and April 8, policemen intervened in the case of wood stolen from an attic and escorted refugees infected with typhus into quarantine. On April 17, they escorted more groups of refugees and guarded a floor of the building that was under quarantine.

FIGURE 25. Jewish Order Service functionaries, Third Precinct, mid-1941. Source: JHI, MŻIH E-1/17/9.

On April 18, they organized a roundup and managed to send thirty refugees to forced-labor camps. They carried out another roundup on the night of April 20–21. That same night they participated in the registration of refugees who volunteered to go to a camp. On April 27, the police sought a refugee, Zelig L., to send him to the camp, but it turned out that he had been there for a long time already. In the next sweep, on May 1, twenty people were taken to a camp from a refugee center. On May 10, they intervened in the case of the missing son of one of the refugees.

Likewise, reports of the commander of the Jewish Order Service from this period contain no information about fundamental changes in the daily tasks of the police. There was, however, a clear increase in the number of people detained in the ghetto by the service from the beginning of April to mid-June. In the first week of June, 771 people were detained for crimes against public order, while a year earlier, in the summer of 1941, up to 180 people a week had been detained.[26] The reports also noted an increase in the number of previously sporadic acts of resistance against the authorities: from the beginning of May 1942, over twenty acts of resistance a week; in the first week of June, already thirty-five. It is difficult to say whether this marked the tightening of police activities resulting from direct orders of the Germans or whether Lejkin and the leadership were trying, on their own initiative, to meet the expectations of the German authorities.

The increase in the number of acts of resistance in May and June 1942 was probably related to the next wave of roundups to labor camps. These looked different from those carried out in the spring of 1941. People were taken from their homes, most often at night, according to compiled lists of names. But now the ghetto was better prepared. As Auerbach wrote:

> The roundup in the apartment blocks lasted until two fifteen in the morning. Policemen patrolled in units of six. Wherever they went, the houses had been forewarned and prepared thanks to the gossip circulating in the morning. Usually the doorway was opened by a woman, the caretaker's wife, who, after making sure that it was only the Jewish police, shouted in the agreed way. . . . Groups of women were keeping vigil in the courtyard. Usually only women were seen anywhere in the apartments. But when it became known what and who was being looked for, the representatives of the male gender suddenly appeared among them as if they had been playing cards. Except that one of them had a white mark on his back from hiding in crawlspaces behind walls. Another of the men had his head covered in a spider's web.[27]

According to police officers' reports, the introduction of a list of names to some extent reduced bribery, but another problem arose. Often when those whose names were on the lists were hiding, other people were taken in their place. When the Jewish Order Service policemen were still unable to collect the required number of workers, prisoners from the Central Lockup were taken straight from their cells and led to the collection points without any luggage. One such instance was described in a note for the Ringelblum Archive by an employee of the lockup:

> On March 25, 1942, at nine thirty-five, two noncommissioned officers from the Sonderdienst, a few *junaks* and several policemen from the Schutzpolizei arrived at the office of the Central Lockup. One of the noncommissioned officers demanded in a categorical tone that sixteen persons should be brought to the office within five minutes. At the same time, he showed an authorizing letter from the commissioner for the Jewish Residential District [i.e., Heinz Auerswald] whereby those people were to be handed over to the Polizeifuhrer and the SS. . . .
> In the absence of clear instructions, the persons named arrived at the office without belongings. Bringing them to the office as ordered took five to seven minutes. The noncommissioned officer, noticing that they had arrived at the office with no belongings said that if we did not care for them, he would not take care of them either. After preparing the

relevant receipts, which were signed by the commandant of the transport, the above-mentioned persons were escorted from the lockup. At the last minute, each prisoner was able to get a kilogram of bread.[28]

With every day the atmosphere of terror in the ghetto thickened. The roundups were seen as a preamble to deportation. In the beginning of June, reports from Sobibór and the first information about the construction of the Treblinka extermination camp began to reach the ghetto.[29]

Roundups organized at that time, referred to by one policeman as "small-game hunting," were aimed at catching child beggars who were out on the ghetto streets. For a few days, the children were held on the premises of a former cinema on Leszno Street, and then they were transported to boarding houses run by the Department of Social Welfare.[30] This operation, although carried out on Auerswald's orders, in the eyes of the ghetto nullified all of the Jewish Order Service's past achievements on behalf of children, including the creation and, to a large extent, the funding of the children's holding centers. One policeman wrote about "the sight of [Jewish] Order Service policemen hunting children, the sight of the boys and girls fighting and crying, the sight of many dozens crowded together, stretching out their hands through the bars, asking for bread."[31] Stanisław Gombiński noted with bitterness, "What is happening to them, who will feed them, who will wash them,

FIGURE 26. Jewish Order Service functionaries, Fifth Precinct, mid-1941. Source: JHI, MŻIH E-1/19/4.

clothe them, look after them? It doesn't matter. This is not the point. The ugly sight disappears from the streets—the problem is solved."[32]

Probably in response to such sentiment, *Gazeta Żydowska* reminded its readers of the "social-civic" nature of the work of policemen, including their participation in the care of children, and called for "understanding of the tasks and duties of the [Jewish] Order Service" and a joint effort "for the good and for the benefit of the Jewish District."[33]

In May and June 1942, Jewish Order Service members took part in one more assignment—preparing scenes for a propaganda film to be made by the Germans in the ghetto. The police received instructions to search for apartments that could be used to illustrate the luxurious life of the ghetto elite and to find and gather healthy and wealthy passersby who, posed on a dance floor and at a café bar, would create a backdrop for footage of beggars and Orthodox Jews. These directed scenes were to illustrate the social inequalities in the ghetto.[34]

Jewish Order Service functionaries forced by the Germans into the role of persecutors were also often the victims of persecutions. In the spring of 1942, the number of reported deaths among policemen increased significantly. The cause was not typhus, because the epidemic had already been eradicated, or the number of arrests by the SD. In April, the deaths of four policemen and the arrest of eight were reported; in May, four deaths and

FIGURE 27. Jewish Order Service functionaries, Fifth Precinct, mid-1941. Source: JHI, MŻIH E-1/19/3.

seven arrests; in June and the first week of July, seven policemen died, and twenty-six were arrested.[35] Jechiel Górny wrote on June 20, "This morning a Jewish policeman went from Nowolipie to the corner of Smocza. He met a Blue Policeman he knew near Smocza; they both stood and were talking freely. A moment later a car with Germans arrived from Żelazna. They stopped, called the Jewish policeman over and, without a word of explanation, shot him on the spot. Leaving the dead body, they went on along Nowolipie."[36] The most exposed to violence were again the most visible: policemen serving at the gates and walls of the ghetto.

In connection with the preparations for Operation Reinhard, the Germans made great efforts to strengthen the isolation of the ghetto. In May 1942, they intensified their fight against smuggling. More and more smugglers and Jewish policemen were killed near the walls, and at the beginning of June, a rumor spread about plans to completely cut the ghetto off from the Aryan side. According to gossip circulating in the ghetto, five hundred additional policemen were to be employed for this purpose,[37] and as some claimed later, Jewish Order Service policemen were to be punished by death for any smuggling taking place.[38] It became evident that the rumor was not completely unfounded. More smugglers were getting killed at the ghetto walls and in formal executions, in which, some of the reports suggest, Jewish Order Service functionaries participated as an auxiliary service.[39]

On June 30, 1942, inhabitants of the ghetto learned about the planned execution of 110 Jews accused of resisting German orders, among them ten policemen involved in smuggling. Adam Czerniaków found out about it only when he received the order to print a poster announcing that the execution was to be carried out. "The courtyard [of the Judenrat building] is black. Panic in the entire district," he wrote at the time.[40] The decision to execute the policemen was particularly commented on, with ghetto inhabitants seeing it as evidence of a tightening of German policy toward the Jewish administration. The tension was heightened by the fact that the underground press had reported on similar events in other ghettos, such as Mława, where on June 4 twelve Jewish policemen were hanged for smuggling.[41] The chaos of information in the ghetto can be traced in testimonies, which provide varying reports on the circumstances of the arrest of the ten policemen. Some said that several (from one to four) policemen were taken from among those who did not appear at the roll call that day, and the rest—here again various numbers are given—were drawn randomly, taken from among those serving by the walls or from the patrols in the area.[42] Someone else wrote that nine policemen were detained, and the tenth person designated for execution was the convoy guard.[43] According to others, policemen who could not be located were replaced by anyone accidentally found in the Jewish Order Service offices. Czerniaków wrote in his diary that three of the men were detained on the street in the place of others who had "vanished."[44] Finally, according to the postwar testimony of German policemen, victims among police officers were chosen on the basis of the opinions of German guards posted at the ghetto walls.[45] Czerniaków, clearly concerned by the fate of the Jewish Order Service members, tried to intervene, again to no avail. On the morning of July 2, the defendants were taken from the Central Lockup in three parties to the Warsaw suburb of Babice, where they were shot.[46] After the execution, Auerswald demanded a list of service members from the Judenrat for the purpose of conducting verification.[47]

The shooting of the policemen in Babice did not significantly change the attitude of the ghetto's residents regarding the Jewish Order Service. In almost all accounts describing the murders, there is a very clear demarcation of one hundred martyrs and ten policemen. On July 2, when posters informing the population of the execution appeared on the streets, Górny wrote in his diary, "A simple Jew who does not understand the 'small print' only catches that ten Jewish policemen were killed; no one knows why, he doesn't question anything, just shouts, "Damn them! They got what they deserved! Yesterday they wanted 150 zlotys from my son—he gave them nothing at all."[48]

On July 20, Jakub Lejkin announced by megaphone, by order of Czerniaków, that all rumors about an impending deportation operation were unfounded.[49]

CHAPTER 8

Umschlagplatz

On the morning of July 22, 1942, Jakub Lejkin, as the acting commander of the Jewish Order Service, was summoned to the Judenrat building. There, together with Chairman Adam Czerniaków and several representatives of the Judenrat, he was informed of deportation plans for the General Government. SS Sturmbannführer Hermann Höfle, the head of Operation Reinhard in Warsaw, read out the order for displacement of Jews from the ghetto.[1] The order stipulated that the Jewish Order Service was to serve as the executive organ of the Judenrat responsible for carrying out the deportations.[2]

At the same time, a car arrived at the building of the Directorate of the Jewish Order Service at 17 Ogrodowa Street. SS Hauptsturmführer Hofman and SS Untersturmführer Karl Brandt, surrounded by SS guards, got out. Later, an anonymous policeman described the scene:

> In the Directorate of the [Jewish] Order Service there has been a stir; it was known only that a council meeting was taking place—nothing more. Lejkin and Stanisław Czapliński (the only two who, due to their functions and visits to Aleja Szucha, knew Brandt) were not there; they had not returned from the Council. . . . Hofman and Brandt went up to the first floor, into the Secretariat. . . . Brandt told Gombiński that starting the next day, the Sonderkommando der Sicherheitspolizei [Security

Police Task Force] would officially take over the office and that, therefore, both rooms and the desks standing in them were to be cleared and prepared for them.[3]

A few hours later, posters with information about the "resettlement" appeared on the streets of the ghetto. The next day, Adam Czerniaków committed suicide.

Thus, the regular daily service of the Jewish Order Service came to an end. From July 23, morning briefings were not held in the precincts but at the headquarters of the service's Directorate and were led by Jakub Lejkin. It was most likely on the first day of Operation Reinhard that Józef Szeryński returned to the position of the head of the Jewish Order Service. According to one former policeman, he was released from prison at the explicit request of Lejkin; according to another, as a result of Karl Brandt's intervention.[4] On the same day, Gestapo collaborator Józef Ehrlich became the deputy head of the service, nominated for that post on the direct orders of SS Hauptsturmführer Hermann Worthoff from the Lublin Gestapo.[5] Szeryński did not regain the position he had held before his arrest, however. Although he remained the head of the Jewish Order Service, now it was Lejkin who technically managed it and Mieczysław Szmerling who managed the operations at the Umschlagplatz, where residents of the Warsaw Ghetto were taken before being transported to Treblinka. Following Czerniaków's death, the post of the chairman of the Judenrat was filled by his deputy, Mieczysław Lichtenbaum, but these three policemen became the highest Jewish authorities in the ghetto.[6] Of course, the real power during the deportations was exercised by the leadership of Operation Reinhard in Warsaw (headquartered at 103 Żelazna Street) and SS and Gestapo officers at the headquarters of the Jewish Order Service. An anonymous informant for the Ringelblum Archive reported on the basis of information obtained from policemen:

They came to the Directorate of the [Jewish] Order Service several times a day. There, they issued orders related to the deportation for the current day or the next (depending on the time of the visit). Their appearance at the Directorate of the [Jewish] Order Service caused great nervousness. Whispers were heard everywhere: "Quiet, you know who is in the building." They were in a separate room on the first floor, where Marceli Czapliński and his brother Stanisław were present. Nobody [else] dared to enter this room.[7]

Aside from those employed in the offices, the daily duties of all other functionaries of the Jewish Order Service from that time consisted only of assisting in the deportations. On the first day of the operation, July 22, the policemen were to bring two thousand people directly to the Umschlagplatz before four in the afternoon; according to the deportation order, "a contingent could be drawn from the general population."[8] As the first to be displaced, the Directorate of the Jewish Order Service designated the residents of a "refugee town" located at the Umschlagplatz, at 3, 9, and 12 Dzika Street, which housed twelve hundred people. The complex included a children's shelter for two hundred children and one for sixty girls and boys aged fourteen to eighteen. According to a witness, this operation began at one o'clock in the afternoon under the command of group leader Seweryn Spotkowski,[9] a lawyer from Warsaw and former head of the Jewish Order Service teaching staff, who not long before had taken over the management of the Gmina Precinct. Spotkowski already had experience in such operations; in April 1941, he had commanded the blockade of buildings during roundups to labor camps. A witness the roundup of July 22, 1942, wrote:

> No one from the house was released. In addition, the double cordon of the [Jewish] Order Service led from 3 Dzika to the Umschlagplatz. The people from the building had only one option: straight into the wagons. The [Jewish] Order Service urged and hurried them. People did not put up any resistance. They were often deportees [from other localities]; they agreed to be deported again. But the children and young people in the shelter reacted differently, especially young people who, after much torment and many misadventures, had received a few days before, a clean bed, new clothing, were in extreme despair. The shelter managers made every effort to get Spotkowski to release them and leave them in peace. Spotkowski agreed to displace these institutions only at the very end, but he would not agree to a full release. . . . Of the fifteen hundred residents, about fifteen remained on the site—several people because they hid, and a few because they showed their papers proving that they worked in the factory workshops.[10]

A few hundred prisoners from Gęsia Street were later joined to the group of deportees from Dzika Street. According to witnesses, these were led into custody in front of despairing family members. Beggars, including children who gathered on the street, were also taken.[11] Leon Najberg, who observed this scene, wrote in his memoir,

> The [Jewish] Order Service took all the beggar children sitting on the edge of the sidewalks and in the gutters and loaded them on trucks hauled by horses. . . . In the ghetto, news of a children's roundup

spread like lightning. The cry of mothers looking for their children echoed through the walls of the apartments. People shut themselves up in apartments. Mothers threatened and cursed the Jewish Order Service. The service did not give any explanation as to why they were after children. It was thought that this was a roundup of beggar children, to take them to the Jewish prison.[12]

From that day on, the Jewish Order Service was to bring six thousand people to the Umschlagplatz every day. The addresses of the apartments designated for deportation were given to Lejkin the previous evening. First to be taken were young people from boarding schools and refugees from the shelters; apart from that, members of the Jewish Order Service were ordered to carry out the first blockade of apartment blocks on Miła, Zamenhofa, and Muranowska Streets.[13] According to service members, during this period about twenty to thirty policemen under the command of an officer took part in the blockades of the apartment buildings. Stanisław Gombiński, who watched the first deportations from the office of the Directorate of the Jewish Order Service, wrote, "A dozen or so policemen are scattered along the marked section of the street. In addition, there are others, standing one at the gate of each apartment block. The gates are closed. . . . The unit enters the first apartment and with loud cries makes all the inhabitants go down to the courtyard, leaving the apartments open. A few order policemen enter the stairwells, check that no one has stayed in the apartments; they drive out the 'slackers.'"[14]

Those who did not have employment certificates were transported to the Umschlagplatz. Those who were not loaded immediately into wagons waited for their turn in an evacuated hospital building. The few who were found to be fit for work went to the quarantine area at 109 Leszno Street, where a transit camp (*Dulag*) was established for persons to be sent to forced labor.

With the announcement of the deportations and the suicide of Czerniaków, the ghetto was seized with panic, but even after the first deportation from Dzika and Gęsia Streets, many people still held on to the illusionary hope that the deportations would be only a continuation of the June operations against beggars, that they would concern only the "nonproductive elements," and that they would proceed according to the rules specified in the order.[15] One service member commented bitterly, "As long as the policemen prowl the alleys of poverty, as long as the operation stays far from the center, quite different assessments and different opinions are heard. But when the *Aktion* was approaching Leszno and Chłodna Streets, and there was no end in sight, when more and more people were taken . . . then the mood changed, people started to think differently."[16]

And indeed, on the third day of the operation, on July 24, Abraham Lewin described in his diary "the savagery of the police during the roundup, the murderous brutality. They drag girls from rickshaws, empty out flats, and leave property strewn everywhere. A pogrom and a killing the likes of which has never been seen."[17]

Apart from escorting deportees, members of the Jewish Order Service also took over the twenty-four-hour watch at the Umschlagplatz, assisted by employees delegated from the Jewish Council and Emergency Service officers, whose red-ringed caps, as Ringelblum wrote, "were covered with the red blood stains of the Jewish masses."[18] Henryk Makower (whose position as a police doctor protected him from deportation) wrote that the employees of the Jewish Council also took part in roundups on the streets. In his memoirs he describes a group of civilians leaving Ogrodowa Street in the morning led by Jewish Order Service policemen: "[The policemen] walked in the middle of the street in the form of a wide-open V, with the open angle facing the direction of movement. Individual elements of this letter were connected by batons, so that you could not get out, the rest of the catchers walked along the street, along the pavements, stopped passers-by, and checked their papers."[19]

Mieczysław Szmerling, who supervised the Umschlagplatz during the day, was promoted from deputy district commander to district commander.[20] Szmerling was already known for his aggression and brutality and had faced the disciplinary commission for beating detainees.[21] There is no doubt that during the deportations he made full use of the experience acquired from the roundups for the camps and the sanitary blockades. During the deportations his name became a symbol of the often mindless, impulse-ridden cruelty of the Jewish Order Service. While many attempted to justify Szeryński's behavior during the deportations, none of the former policemen later attempted even to partially explain Szmerling's. He was uniformly described as a bribe taker who made a great deal of money from the tragedy of the ghetto and a sadist who freed no one on the square—not even for the highest bribe or even when ordered by German officials and soldiers.[22] The night manager of the Umschlagplatz was Salomon Kosman, a former deputy head of the Labor Battalion. A team of "loaders," led by Deputy District Commander Mieczysław Brzeziński, loaded people into wagons and counted, probably not very accurately, the number deported on a given day.[23] The result was written in chalk on each of the wagons.

Figure 28. The Anti-epidemic Company. First from the left, Mieczysław Szmerling, mid-1941. Source: JHI, MŻIH E-1/14/1.

On July 29, the Operation Reinhard squad took over the roundups. Until then it had been only intermittently involved.[24] Greater direct involvement of the Germans in the deportation operation did not mean, however, the complete elimination of the Jewish police from it. On the same day, an announcement signed by Józef Szeryński appeared on the ghetto walls; it stated that every person who volunteered for deportation before July 31 would receive three kilograms of bread and one kilogram of marmalade.[25] The police were also still involved in blockades. According to a report by members of the Jewish underground, groups organizing blockades consisted of ten to twenty SS men in cars or rickshaws, fifty to one hundred Ukrainians, Lithuanians, and Latvians, and 250 to 350 Jewish policemen.[26] The ratio of members of each formation was dependent on the size of the area being blockaded; during this period many apartments buildings or even whole streets were blockaded at the same time. The author of a document from the Ringelblum Archive, drawn up on the basis of police officers' reports, states that the blockade groups included fifteen to twenty Germans, about forty Ukrainians, and sixty to eighty members of the Jewish Order Service.[27] The deportations directly supervised by the Germans were much more brutal. In many buildings they did not accept documents exempting people from deportation, and all the residents were taken straight to the Umschlagplatz or murdered on the spot. On July 30, Abraham Lewin wrote, "From five in the morning we hear through the window the whistles of Jewish policemen and the movement and the running of Jews looking for refuge. Opposite my window, in Nowy Zjazd Street, a policeman chases a young woman and catches her. Her cries and screams are heart-breaking."[28] In the eyes of many, Jewish policemen were becoming a greater threat than even the most brutal Germans because they were more familiar with the topography of the ghetto and able to find the hiding places of Jews.[29]

In the first week of August, a particularly dark chapter in Warsaw Ghetto history, deportations from the orphanages began. From August 4 to 6, members of the Jewish Order Service brought to the Umschlagplatz children from the boys' facility at 7 Twarda Street, the girls' shelter at 28 Śliska Street, and from Janusz Korczak's orphanage.[30] On August 7, twelve hundred children were removed from the Children's Home at 14 Wolność Street and a few hundred from the CENTOS boarding school at 18 Mylna Street. At the same time, the nightmare of daily blockades and roundups continued. Beginning probably in mid-August, every policeman was required to bring five people a day to the Umschlagplatz. Policemen looking for "heads," as they were known, were capable of anything. Surviving ghetto inhabitants exchanged tales of children taken from the streets and courtyards where they played, policemen delivering their own family members and friends to the Umschlagplatz, and of the price for buying "heads" from their colleagues who proved more successful at catching. Halina Birenbaum described in her memoirs the streets of the ghetto after the announcement of this order:

> In alarm, we rushed to the window. Crowds of Jewish police, armed with batons and bludgeons, were invading Leszno Street. Like a herd of wild, famished animals provoked by the smell of blood, howling and yelling, they run into the gateways of the apartment blocks. . . .
>
> We fled to the attic which had no roof, but was shrouded in helpful darkness. We lay on the floor, side by side. We could hear the police yelling and smashing down doors; sounds of struggling, coarse oaths and scuffling on the staircase. The police traded the people they captured with one another; a man who succeeded in catching more victims sold his "surplus" to a less resourceful colleague.[31]

From then on, policemen were called "dachshunds" because they were able to enter the smallest of holes, pulling their victims out of wardrobes, hidden rooms, lockers, shelters, and basements. In the August heat, every day more than ten thousand people were packed together in the Umschlagplatz. Witnesses described people fainting and trampled in the pressure of so many bodies, children choking, Ukrainians firing at the crowd, and the bestiality of Szmerling, who oversaw and supervised the Umschlagplatz.[32]

On August 19, the Operation Reinhard staff moved to ghettos in the suburbs of Warsaw. According to gossip circulating in Warsaw (though not confirmed elsewhere), the Jewish Order Service was to organize the deportations there.[33] From August 19 to 24, there were breaks in deportations caused by the reorganization of Treblinka, where new gas chambers were being built.

The participation of the Jewish Order Service in the deportations provoked horror. This was what historian Natalia Aleksiun calls "intimate violence"—that perpetrated by those from within one's closest circle of trust.[34] There was, however, also hope that, as before the deportations, life and freedom could be bought from the policemen. People swapped information about friends and relatives who managed to get out of the Umschlagplatz by paying a Jewish policeman. In the first days of the blockades, when the German control was not yet so rigorous, it was possible to buy oneself out of the roundup, as had been the case earlier during the roundups to camps and antityphus blockades. As Chaim Kapłan wrote, the banknote could still at that point replace documents, although the price for freedom increased every day.[35]

Policemen usually demanded cash, although jewelry and other valuables, even a silk umbrella, are also mentioned in the memoirs as a price paid for release from the roundup.[36] Jewish policemen also made money on the Umschlagplatz in a different way. Alone among the ghetto residents, they received large amounts of bread, which they sold at exorbitant prices. And for the right payment, they agreed to deliver a letter to the family or, in the other direction, packages from the family in the ghetto.[37] Finally, as Emanuel Ringelblum wrote in his journal, the police sexually abused women who were being held for transportation. Tellingly, Ringelblum condemned both policemen and the women who paid for their freedom in this way.[38]

Another element of the police participation in the *Aktion* was looting. The property left by the expelled Jews was looted by members of the Jewish Order Service and also often by the Blue Policemen. According to the order on deportation, the service was to secure property and then transfer it to storage; its appropriation was punished by death. Yet on the third day of the deportations, Abraham Lewin wrote that "the police are carrying out elegant furniture from the homes of those who have been driven out."[39] A year after the deportations, Henryk Rudnicki recalled: "When checking the apartments, the closed doors were broken down with axes and picks. During this inspection, not a few valuable things went into the pockets of the members of the [Jewish] Order Service, although it no longer mattered to the people who had been deported, but there were those who returned, and there were those who saw with their own eyes from their hiding places members of the [Jewish] Order Service filling their pockets with their possessions."[40]

Paradoxically, the corruption of Jewish policemen gave some hope that there would be someone among them who could still be bribed: maybe it would be a prewar colleague or a neighbor's son, someone whose conscience would not allow the deportation of old friends. Even when they were blockading the apartments, when they became "dachshunds," policemen were still Jewish boys. One survivor of the ghetto recalled after the war: "When the Jewish police were forcing people from their apartments, searching for people who did not work and had no work certificates, two came to my apartment. One of them was my high school classmate. I stopped him at the entrance and said that I had hidden my mother in the bathroom. I asked him to pretend that he did not see her and that he would not allow his colleague to search. 'Well, well, this and that. . . .' So I gave him money and he did not see my mother."[41]

Desperate people would stand all night at the door of the apartment of their neighbor, a policeman, pleading for the release of their family members from the Umschlagplatz. Emanuel Ringelblum described the dinners that house committees organized for policemen who carried out blockades in a restrained manner.[42] He and his family saved themselves during the blockade thanks to the help of a policeman's wife.[43]

Thus, alongside tales of police brutality, stories about the honorable behavior of some policemen circulated in the ghetto, giving people at least some hope. On July 29, Lewin wrote about eight policemen who were said to have committed suicide in the first week of the operation.[44] Many remember the names of policemen murdered for helping other Jews, among them one Kapłański, a member of the Zionist organization HeHalutz, shot for rescuing people from the Umschlagplatz.[45] Some policemen (their number cannot be established) decided to "throw away their hat"—that is, leave the Jewish Order Service (with all the consequences that entailed) during the operation. Such a dramatic decision was described (probably during the operation or immediately afterward) by Władysław Szlengel in the poem "Farewell to the Cap":

The horror of those days, fever of fear and blood,
out there, outside the bars looking on, the real living breathing world,
and here: blue police caps, and here: cellars—traps . . . and the service,
    busy chaps,

and a cordon, an *Ausweis* [identification card], a workshop, and Szmerling, Lejkin, Kac,
and Többens, Schilling, and the square, and cash, gold, coins . . .
and blood, tears, diamonds . . . and chaos, and night savagery, and
  whips, and rickshaws,
and shots fired, the crowds, the rush, and buttstocks, batons, rods . . .
and sweat, clatter, and cry,

and the struggle, struggle for life . . . and hopeless days,
and caps . . . the Police Service caps. SUPERVISOR, SIR I beg to report,
that I've worn this cap—thank you, no more . . . enough, thank you.
  It's all good and swell,
but it can go on without me just as well. The city died and the heart died,
and everything will fade away, just like life,
I take off my armband, I hand over the number, thank you, I'm leaving,
  leaving the ranks—no . . . I bear no grudge, there's no ill will,
that's the way it had it to be,

I don't know what's true, what's right what's the duty anymore,
I go my own way, the end, that's all.[46]

Szlengel's poem is the only surviving text that can be considered to have
been written by a Jewish Order Service member "there and then," during
the period of the deportations, although there is no evidence suggesting that
Szlengel directly participated in the roundups.

Even though policemen and their wives and children were not subject
to deportation, most of them needed to find a safe place of employment
or shelter for other family members and often organized at the same time
their transfer to the Aryan side.[47] But even the best-connected people could
become victims of the chaos prevailing during the deportations. Salomon
Kasman's mother described her release from the Umschlagplatz:

I survived the whole horror of selection. Once during the selection,
I went in with my daughter-in-law to the gate of the building, and
we were not taken because we were the close family of a policeman.
That's why I managed to avoid the Umschlagplatz. . . . [When I was
caught,] despite the fact that I was still shouting that I was Kasman's
mother, they drove me with everyone to the platform. Just one policeman came in, I shouted to him, 'I'm Kasman's mother!' I grasped him
with both hands and went with him. On the other side, an officer took
care of me. . . . Meanwhile my son brought a release form for me."[48]

On August 6, policemen received the order to move with their wives and children to the so-called police block, a separate building located between Karmelicka, Nowolipki, and Dzielna Streets. Mina Tomkiewicz, a resident of the block, wrote:

> Movement started in the house at five in the morning, when the policemen went out to start their tours of duty. Through a loudspeaker they announced new orders and rotations for the whole day. "Attention all personnel! The Third Section to meet at the corner of . . . Attention! Attention!" There were loud conversations and the stomping of heavy boots. . . . Doors were slammed, instructions about lunch shouted from a balcony by a lady in a nightdress and her hair curlers. Then there was an hour or two of silence. Afterwards the policemen's families spilled out. Around seven or eight the normal life of the day began in the courtyard of the block.[49]

Just like the other blocks in the ghetto, where people were housed according to the place of employment, the police block was fenced off with barbed wire. Another resident of the block, Samuel Puterman, wrote in his memoir that the block was strictly isolated and positioned in front of the gate were "men of trust," members of the Jewish Order Service who were making sure that no unauthorized person entered the building. If one of the policemen wanted to bring in a family member, he had to get a valid pass for two hours at the headquarters of the Jewish Order Service.[50] Inspections were carried out on regular basis by the residents themselves; they checked that no one kept people outside of their immediate family in their apartment, as this endangered other inhabitants of the building.[51] Janina Bauman lived with her mother in the police apartment block. She wrote:

> There were four or five families of doctors serving in the Jewish police crammed into the same seedy flat, with their children, bedding, pans and suitcases; rude quarrelsome and restless. Alas, without a man to take care of us, we were immediately put in the worst room which everyone else had to go through on their way to and from the loo.
>
> Not that it really mattered. After the horror of the past days and nights, we felt somewhat relieved. Some strange mechanism made us believe that we were safe there. For the time being at least. The same mechanism made us indifferent towards what was still going on outside the police block, towards the plight of the tens of thousands of human beings driven daily to the Umschlagplatz, then to the trains. Every day we heard hair-rising stories about the Umschlagplatz from

eyewitnesses: from policemen who were doing the job, or from people who had been helped to escape in return for money or out of pity.[52]

This "strange mechanism of self-defense" was also described in the memoirs of Janina David, who was twelve years old during the deportation operation. She wrote:

> The raids continued but in our apartment block, full of policemen and other "essential" workers, we felt comparatively safe. There were always policemen around—which to me was a reassuring sight—and father looked in on us several times a day. . . . There were dozens of children of my age milling around the vast courtyard. None of us was allowed to leave the apartment building. The weather was splendid. We still heard occasional shooting, screams and passing lorries, but our flat was in the side wing from which the street was not visible, and I had firmly shut my mind to all that went on outside.[53]

For many, the police block became a symbol of the Jewish Order Service members' complete breaking of ties with other Jews. Safeguarding their families from the horrors of the *Aktion*, the policemen did not share the fate of their community. With the nightmare of the deportations going on around them, they seemed to lead a normal, safe life: some ghetto inhabitants recalled seeing policemen's wives sunbathing on deck chairs in front of the apartment block, waiting for the return of husbands, who were carrying out blockades.[54] In nearby Otwock Ghetto, local Jewish policeman Calel Perechodnik wrote about rumors reaching him from Warsaw: "The police take over entire rows of apartment buildings encompassing four city blocks and let it be known that they live there now with their families and that no one has the right to enter there. They take over apartments of strangers after telling the people to get out, ordering them to leave all their possessions behind. They themselves hoard in these apartments extensive wealth. They drink, rob, and fulfil the orders of the Germans."[55]

From the beginning of the deportations, people attempted to attack the policemen during the blockades and on the way to the Umschlagplatz.[56] Reports from the deportations are filled with descriptions of individual resistance attempts, always directed at policemen. Henryk Rudnicki wrote, "During the blockades, there was a daily struggle between the catchers and the caught: men did not let themselves be dragged onto the omnibuses, which were to take them to the Umschlagplatz—there were bloody fights. Women scratched the faces of the catchers, children scratched and bit the hands of policemen from the [Jewish] Order Service."[57] Perhaps the most dramatic are descriptions of parents trying to wrench children out of the hands of the policemen. An anonymous ghetto inhabitant recalled immediately after the war: "I shall not forget the shriek of a little girl in a green coat, perhaps six years old, who was begging the policeman through her tears: 'I know that you are kind man, don't take me, my mummy has gone out for a minute. She'll be back soon and I won't be here, don't take me,' but the lament of the little girl, which might have moved the heart of a monster, did not move the policeman. He carried out his duties in cold blood. Two hours later I saw a distracted woman running in the middle of the road in the direction of the square. She was shrieking despairingly, 'My child—where's my child?'"[58]

On August 20, Israel Kanał, a former policeman, and a member of the Jewish underground, shot Józef Szeryński on the doorstep of his apartment at 10 Nowolipki Street. Although Szeryński was only slightly wounded and after a few days of convalescence returned to daily work, the attack was enthusiastically received. Ten days after the attempted assassination, Jehoszua Perle commented on it in his diary, "Khurbn Varshe" (The destruction of Warsaw): "For this 'beautiful' work, the murdering of the entire Jewish community in Warsaw, a just hand (bless this hand) sent him a bullet in the head. Unfortunately, the shooter aimed badly so the bullet did not put the despicable convert in his place. He has not dropped dead yet."[59]

The attempted assassination of Szeryński, the first armed act of the Jewish underground, was definitely a turning point for the ghetto community—it showed that resistance was possible.[60] After the attack, during the night, members of the ghetto armed underground—the Jewish Fighting Organization—carried out the first act of sabotage, setting fire to German ammunition stores.[61]

After a break in the deportations, the blockades and selections in large workshops were resumed on August 24. They were carried out much more easily and required fewer forces than before: the workshops were already fenced in. The police had only to block the entrances and transport the workers provided by the managers and the guards (*Werkshutz*) of the workshops to the Umschlagplatz.[62] On the night of September 5–6, the Judenrat, on the orders of the German authorities, posted notices calling on everyone in the large ghetto to appear by ten o'clock the next morning in the area between Smocza, Gęsia, Zamenhofa, and Szczęśliwa Streets and Parysowski Square with food supplies for two days and drinking vessels. Particular groups of the population had congregation points there, depending on their type and place of employment. Remaining outside this area after the set deadline was punishable by death. This registration, known as "the Cauldron," lasted two days, after which some people were sent back to their workplaces and their apartment blocks, and others to the Umschlagplatz. Gombiński wrote:

> The Umschlag is so similar to hell during the whole period of displacement; in these six days, during the period of the Cauldron, it resembles the last, lowest circles of Hades. Thousands of men, women, children, crying, tumult, noise, cries, prayers. September 9 and 10—Wednesday and Thursday—this is the New Year. A dozen or so Ukrainians, always drunk, on guard, they rob, rob people, take away what they have. Shooting can still be heard; corpses lie in the outer courtyard and at the back of the building. A loaf of bread—five hundred zlotys; a glass of water—twenty-five zlotys. There is no longer even brutality, savagery—but some sort of a kind of order, the order of Szmerling. He and his unit are still on duty there, but there is nothing to say to the loaders with Brzezinski in charge standing next to the wagons. Train after train leaves. It is almost impossible to get any more people out from the Umschlagplatz.[63]

The policemen shared the fate of the ghetto. Henryk Makower, who, as a police doctor, lived in the apartment block of the Jewish Order Service, remembered the first night of the Cauldron: "At the time when sleep is the deepest, around two, in the yard there were whistles. Is this an unexpected roundup, at this time?! After a while, our anxiety takes on firmer shapes. . . . We got dressed very quickly, and we all went to Wołyńska Street. Together with us were our neighbors; everyone had a backpack, a suitcase or some sort of box. . . . We entered the first free home—no. 3—where on the second floor we found an empty apartment. Dirt, feathers, broken junk."[64]

Janina Bauman, walking with her mother in the same column to the designated collection point on the odd-numbered side of Wołyńska Street, described the "scathing glances" that accompanied their journey through the ghetto. For the first time, she wrote, the policemen and their families ceased to be untouchable.[65] "You had to see how these 'heroes' looked being chased along with the other wretches. They were scared dogs, pathetic, dirty— not dogs in principle, but nits that crawl on all fours, hiding in attics and basements—in apartments previously plundered by them," wrote Yehoshua Perle at the time.[66] Later on, Bauman wrote about their new lodgings:

> The former inhabitants of the dreadful apartment houses [at Wołyńska] must have been deported long ago. All the doors of the flats stood ajar showing sickening pictures of devastation and filth. The newcomers were driven in by the Jewish policemen on duty, and settled down on

the floor next to each other. We entered one of the sordid flats and sat on the floor, our backs propped, luckily, against the wall. People kept flooding in. Women moaned loudly, children cried. In a matter of seconds, the room was tightly packed. From a policeman attending to his own family crammed next to us, we heard that our stay at Wołyńska Street might last several hours or several days.[67]

During the Cauldron, the police received five hundred "life numbers," which provided an exemption from the requirement to report to the Umschlagplatz (of which about half were for policemen, others for their families and auxiliary staff)—that is, one quarter of the pool allocated to the Judenrat.[68] A commission consisting of four officers was to decide who would receive the numbers. Throughout this time, Szeryński and the Czapliński brothers were kept at Ogrodowa Street as hostages.[69] Jakub Lejkin handed out the numbers to the policemen lined up along Wołyńska Street. Samuel Puterman, who was present when numbers were assigned, wrote, "A voice shouted nonstop to the policemen with the life numbers. Policemen snuck away in the direction of Zamenhofa Street. Lejkin went down the middle of the street and was attacked constantly from the sides of the street by policemen, begging for life numbers for wives, for children. Lejkin swung his baton, as if at a pack of dogs. The policemen took the hits, but they did not cease begging for life numbers."[70]

Those policemen who did not receive life numbers were to become laborers. About thirty of them were immediately sent to the Ostbahn railway workshop in the Praga neighborhood, and the next day around fifty, with their wives and children, were billeted at the city streetcar depot at Młynarska Street. The others who did not manage to escape were divided into two groups and housed in apartments on Lubeckiego and Ostrowska Streets. The group from Lubeckiego, who were hoping to work in the Lublin District, were sent to Treblinka with their families.[71] On September 21, a blockade of the so-called police apartment block in Ostrowska Street was put in place. The last group of policemen deprived of their ranks lived there, and the children and wives of other former policemen were hiding there as well. They were all led to the Umschlagplatz, from which the women and children were sent to Treblinka, and the men, later, to Majdanek.[72]

As Abraham Lewin wrote in his journal on September 23, "the Jews who watched this scene [the taking of the policemen to the Umschlagplatz] felt a definite satisfaction. This is the reward for their brutal acts against the Jews of Warsaw."[73]

FIGURE 29. Jewish Order Service functionaries, First Precinct, mid-1941. Source: JHI, MŻIH, E-1/15/5.

The policemen exempted from deportations were placed in a block on Nowolipki Street. As Henryk Makower writes, along with them were many children whose parents managed to keep their families together.[74] However, it was much more difficult to help more distant family members. Makower, who had a number for himself and his wife, lost his mother, his sister with her husband and daughter, as well as his brother and sister-in-law in the deportation operation. On returning from Wołyńska Street after an unsuccessful attempt to save his family from the Umschlagplatz, he wrote:

> At home, I threw myself like a log on the couch. I do not remember how long I lay there, distraught and blank. Finally, around five in the evening, I dragged myself off the couch to go to the Umschlagplatz. Every few dozen steps guards were posted as before. I was let into Wołyńska Street for a few things; I couldn't get into the Umschlag. . . . If I had tried hard enough to go all the way, maybe I could have gotten there, but I was frightened. I realized and accepted that it wasn't allowed and that they didn't recommend it. I will not forgive this cowardice until the end of my life. I cannot explain it. I do not understand it. All I know is that all my relatives were waiting for me—they believed in the help that I would bring to them—and I failed them.[75]

During the deportations, the earlier hostility toward Jewish Order Service members turned into hatred. They were completely excluded from the community and doubly so—on one side by the Germans who exempted them from the deportations and equally by the community as those who had acted against them. The Jewish policemen's demeanor defined the boundless and terrible cruelty of the deportations. The people of the ghetto talked about their unprecedented brutality toward children, the sick, and the elderly, the rabbi whom they took when he was officiating at the wedding of his brother, and those who dragged their own family members to the Umschlagplatz—these stories fueled the hatred. Later, they wrote about the madness of the Jewish police, running amok in the violence in which they themselves were to be immersed. Yehoshua Perle recalled:

> You had to see what happened to the Jewish police. They must have gone mad. Because even the greatest criminals do not show such ferocity, such cruelty. No cries and screams will help here. Mothers kiss the bandit's feet and want to save their children. But the bandits themselves do not know what is happening to them. They take patients out of beds, children from cradles. Everything leads to the carts. He speeds, rushes, beats mercilessly.[76]

In the behavior of the Jewish policemen, a cold calculation was seen. They were accused of servility toward the Germans, going beyond the duties imposed on them.[77] Policemen who went to loot had no fear of the Germans—they did it out of greed. It was said that some of them carried out their tasks with greater zeal than the Germans and even that Germans sometimes defended Jews against Jewish policemen's brutality.[78] Policemen commanding the deportations tried to become just like the Germans: their polished jackboots and their whips revealed this. After the deportations, Ringelblum noted in his diary that the Jewish police committed crimes that the Polish Blue Police did not commit. Further evidence of the policemen's complete exclusion from their society is the Jewish underground's unequivocally negative assessment of their behavior. The authors of the report "The Liquidation of Jewish Warsaw," addressed to the Polish government-in-exile in London and the Allied governments, wrote:

> To illustrate the organizational diligence, the following facts are enough. On the first day of the action, the nursery and boarding school dormitory at 3 Dzika Street (corner of Stawki Street) were emptied of about 150 refugee children and young people. The ghetto police did this "work" even though there was no official order from the German authorities. (In the first period of "resettlement," the institution for the care of children and young people had not yet been liquidated). It was typical of the [Jewish] Order Service policemen's procedures to force

the victims with violence—older women, children, the sick—onto carts, using fists and rubber truncheons. Around the blockaded apartment blocks, and there were several dozen of them a day, a permanent reserve of carts for transport—carts boarded up on all sides. Victims both resisting and resigned were loaded onto these carts and wagons. The order of the day was that mothers were to be separated from their children, children from parents, wife from husband.[79]

Testimonies written during the deportation operation and immediately after it are without a doubt the most shocking accounts from the Warsaw Ghetto—evidence of suffering created immediately after the death of loved ones and at the same time an indictment of the Jewish policemen. The destruction described in the final fragments of Emanuel Ringelblum's notes and in the works and poems of Yehoshua Perle and Icchak Kacenelson had the face of a Jewish policeman.

CHAPTER 9

After Resettlement

"Sometimes it seems to me that it's a fairy tale—the assertion by the medical world that the heart is a chamber of delicate membranes that cannot stand suffering or emotion and that they burst causing death"—wrote Calel Perechodnik, a Jewish policeman from the Otwock Ghetto, after the deportations. During the deportations he helped deliver his own wife and daughter to the transport to Treblinka. "Today, I would advise those who construct fighter planes to build them out of heart membranes. They will certainly not burst and will outlast the most enduring steel."[1] On September 24, 1942, the "deportation action" in the Warsaw Ghetto was officially completed.

The organized relocation to the newly designated Jewish district, the so-called residual ghetto, ended on September 27. At that point, there were about 70,000 Jews still living in the ghetto, with about 265,000 having been deported in the summer. This was no longer a closed quarter but rather an archipelago of fenced-off, isolated, guarded islands with workshops and buildings to house its workers. There was a ban on any unauthorized movement. The Jewish Order Service was entrusted with supervision over the implementation of the related orders—it was to patrol the area of the displaced ghetto and regulate traffic in the new district, as well as escort groups of workers to their workplaces. According to an order from the German authorities, the Jewish Order Service was also to post a guard at the outlets of the sewers in the "large ghetto," officially in order to prevent illegal trade.[2] The commander of the Jewish Order Service was appointed commissioner of a "Week of Cleanliness," from January 3 to January 9, 1943.[3] Six policemen, including Marceli Czapliński, were delegated for auxiliary service to the headquarters of the SS Management Board (Befehlstelle) for the ghetto at 103 Żelazna Street, where Gerhard Mende and Karl Brandt were now located. Ber Warm, who served at Żelazna Street from October 1942, recalled that policemen delegated to the Befehstelle dealt with administrative work and were also on duty in the lockup. When Jews who were caught on the Aryan side were brought to the ghetto, this is where they were kept—in the darkness of the basement cellars of the neighboring building.[4] Żelazna Street was a safe hiding place for the policemen when the ghetto was torn apart by the deportations, and as lockup guards, referred to as "Brandt's men," they could move about the ghetto fairly easily.[5]

Within the new borders of the ghetto, policemen were moved to the buildings at 30–40 Zamenhofa Street, and the new headquarters of the service was located at 4 Gęsia Street. According to the news bulletin published by Oneg Shabbat at the end of December 1942, 240 policemen were serving at the time in the Warsaw Ghetto.[6] While Józef Szeryński was still commander of the service, with Jakub Lejkin his deputy, Szeryński's friends wrote that after the August assassination attempt he broke down mentally and became withdrawn.

Despite the semblance of normality in Judenrat reports after September 1942, there was no return to the reality that existed before the deportations. With the strengthening of the Jewish underground in the ghetto, the number of acts of resistance against policemen increased.

According to Emanuel Ringelblum, representatives of the Jewish Underground met at that point with members of the Judenrat to discuss their mutual relations. The discussion focused in particular on the participation of the Jewish Order Service in the deportations and, according to Ringelblum, the underground ruled out any future cooperation with its members.[7]

On October 29, 1942, a member of the Jewish Fighting Organization, Eliasz Różański, shot and killed Jakub Lejkin, who was returning home after his shift, and injured Stanisław Czapliński, who was accompanying him. Henryk Rudnicki described the attack a year later as "perhaps the most sensational incident of those days,"[8] and the Jewish Fighting Organization proclaimed on flyers put up in the ghetto the carrying out of its death sentence on Lejkin and announced that "further repressive measures will be applied with all ruthlessness."[9] Satisfying the widespread desire for revenge was the underground's best way to establish itself in the ghetto's collective consciousness and legitimize its authority, as well as ensure the security of underground operations. As historian David Engel notes, the Jewish Fighting Organization's actions were aimed not only at revenge but also at intimidating policemen. Attacking them was a preventive act because the policemen were perceived not only as guilty of moral betrayal but also as zealous helpers of the Germans, without whom deportation would have been much more difficult.[10] Jechiel Górny, a member of the Jewish Fighting Organization, wrote in November 1942:

> Today, three months after those first days, when we know for sure where more than a quarter of a million Jews went, when news is still coming about resistance, about Jewish policemen in some cities and towns who refused to take part in the actions (most recently in Sandomierz), it is possible to assess how wretched was the behavior of the Jewish police in Warsaw—the largest Jewish city in Europe.
>
> Maybe on the streets of Warsaw there would have been tens of thousands of people killed, maybe in Warsaw all deported Jews would have dropped dead (on the spot), but it is certain that this would have stopped and weakened the "resettlement action" both in the General Government and in other countries. And instead of a million victims in Treblinka, the number of victims in Warsaw would have amounted to one hundred to two hundred thousand Jews in the worst case. But the energy with which the Warsaw Jewish police performed the job enabled the Germans to utilize only around 150 people for the entire operation.[11]

On November 29, 1942, three members of the underground assassinated the Gestapo agent and head of the Judenrat Economic Department, Israel First; shortly thereafter Mieczysław Brzeziński, a Jewish Order Service officer and the commander of the "loaders" in the Umschlagplatz and Marian Händel's adjutant, Jerzy Furstenberg, were shot in separate incidents by fighters of the Jewish Fighting Organization and the Zionist-Revisionist Jewish Military Union (Żydowski Związek Wojskowy).[12] In January 1943, in the Hallman workshop on Nowolipki Street, the Jewish Fighting Organization carried out further attacks on former policemen (one being doused with hydrochloric acid).[13] Policemen sent to the camps were also victims of violence, with some murdered on the way to or immediately after arrival in Treblinka.[14] These deaths aroused panic among the police, especially since no one expected the

German authorities to react to these attacks. Władysław Szlengel master-fully captured the feeling in the service at the time in his poem "Zahlen bitte" (Please pay):

> Four officers sat
> in a dive, in the police district their drunken heads swayed, bottles
>   rolled around their feet. Spirit and vodka flowed,
> shots were paid by the load
>
> and each officer, drunk as a lord, sat at the table, overjoyed,
> told tales of his deeds, countless deeds, indeed,
> and one spoke about the methods—and the other about the loot—
> and the third policeman shrieked, "Bartender, vodka for the officers,
>   quick!" At a corner table, in the shadows concealed,
> someone sat somberly over a meal, and he listened to the feast, curi-
>   ously, dipping his bread in a bitter coffee.
> While those four yelled on,
>
> "Vodka, beer, goose leg, schnitzel!" and the old man looked from the
>   side and drank his bitter coffee in the dark,
> and he gazed at them fiercely, greedily, as if trying to remember every
>   detail,
> and then he tapped a glass with his finger and said, "You will have to
>   pay. . . ."
> The officers jumped to their feet mute, frenzied terror fell upon them,
> and they tried to see through the darkness, to see the one sitting in the
>   corner. . . .
> A glass fell to the floor,
> the company fell quiet, dismayed,
> and the whisper loomed over the table, a memento:
> "You will have to pay. . . ."[15]

The attacks immediately triggered a wave of rumors about the strength of the underground and the debasement of the hated policemen. It was said, for example, that Lejkin's body was dug up after burial and thrown into a pile of rubbish and dung.[16] In the ghetto there was also talk of the persecution of Jewish policemen employed in the workshops on the Aryan side, which, it was hoped, was a sign of the solidarity of Polish workers with the sufferers in the ghetto. Emanuel Ringelblum wrote, "Former Jewish policemen who worked in the tram depot are constantly oppressed by Polish workers. Even German soldiers persecute them in Rembertów. . . . I know the facts that for-mer policemen from a certain institution wear caps up to the gate, because they respect the caps in the ghetto. Out of the ghetto, they take them off because they are afraid of the Polish population, who hate the Jewish Order Service for what they did during the deportations."[17] This impression was confirmed by one of the ghetto inhabitants, who noted that the Polish workers in the forced-labor outpost where he worked "hated the Jewish Order Service as much as we did."[18]

Despite the hatred surrounding them, some members of the Jewish Order Service still benefited from their privileged position. This was especially true of those who moved on to other positions, often profiting from the knowledge and experience they gained during their service. Former policemen who worked as factory guards did particularly well, according to reports and recollections, in the "new stabilization." They created a new financial elite in the new reality and, as reported in a December 1942 Oneg Shabbat bulletin, were transferred to the Aryan side, "serving the German leadership and continuing the 'traditions' of the ghetto police."[19]

Janina David, who together with her parents and two other police families, moved to the apartment block occupied by Werterfassung employees in autumn 1942, wrote in her memoir, "My father was still able to leave the ghetto, escorting lorries with bricks or rubble, and still smuggling food. . . . Fresh milk, butter, cheese and even eggs arrived in father's pockets every day."[20] Soon afterward, David's father used his acquaintances at the ghetto gates to take her to the Aryan side, where she survived the rest of the war in hiding.

In January, during the second deportation operation (known as the "January action"), Jewish policemen no longer participated directly in the organization of the deportations. Instead, groups of several to a dozen or so policemen were used only as intelligence agents and as human shields protecting the Germans against Jewish insurgents.[21] The other policemen hid where they could.

On January 23, the day after the end of the January campaign, Józef Szeryński committed suicide. Henryk Makower, who was summoned to him, wrote, "There were a lot of people there. My colleague Brewda was preparing an injection, Mrs. Szeryński was crying quietly, Jasia, their daughter, was lying in bed and praying. The colonel was lying on the bed in navy-blue [Jewish] Order Service pants and in an unbuttoned shirt. Red-blue, he had a swollen face, he was unconscious, only occasionally mumbled some unintelligible words, he breathed heavily at intervals. He had taken potassium cyanide that was prepared just in case."[22]

Szeryński's death was widely read as a sign of divine justice. It understandably aroused great elation in the ghetto, but also anxiety. Czerniaków's suicide immediately came to mind, and people began to wonder: what could

Szeryński have known about the future of the ghetto? As his close friend Stanisław Gombiński wrote a year later, "Those who knew Szeryński better think differently. But their opinion does not matter to the public: the general public is far from objective judgments. This task will remain for the future; nowadays the general public still thinks in terms of the moment it has lived through and is living through. The people must have an object of hatred, a visible symbol of evil."[23] Szeryński's wife and daughter fled the ghetto without delay.

Following the January deportation operation, the Jewish Order Service Directorate was moved to the Judenrat Building at 19 Zamenhofa Street. Leon Piżyc, Szeryński's deputy after Lejkin's death, headed the service, while Herman Kac who before the deportations was deputy district commander in the Service and Training Unit of the Jewish Order Service, became his deputy. A Judenrat communiqué from January 1943 reported that the staff of the Jewish Order Service comprised seventy-two men and ten women. According to the memoirs of an officer who resigned from the Jewish Order Service during the January operation (although we do not know whether he was still in the ghetto at that time or knew about it from the reports), during this time reductions in police personnel were completely different from those in previous periods. Many of the policemen resigned from the service, some of them got out of the ghetto, and others took jobs as guards in workshops or in the Werterfassung. Fifty policemen went to work at an outpost in the Praga neighborhood.[24]

The remaining policemen were to have regular day and night duties and were assigned to protect workshops and warehouses. The report also carried information about the dissolution of the Central Lockup.[25] Henryk Makower recalled this period: "I was in the Directorate of the Jewish Order Service, where Piżyc currently has replaced the commander, Lejkin. Silence, eyes lowered. From time to time, someone from the leadership is shot by an unknown assailant, one in the hand, another in the back."[26] A February report contained the standard assurance that the Jewish Order Service performed the duties entrusted to it by the supervisory authorities and by the Judenrat. It also summarily informs the German authorities that the Gmina unit had been transferred to the Werkshutz.[27]

Although the Jewish police during this period played just a marginal role, rumors about them continued. They spoke of the role played by Warsaw Ghetto policemen in labor camps and on the Aryan side, where, it was claimed, they worked for the Gestapo, reporting on Jews who were hiding outside the ghetto. Information about executions in the ghetto also reached the Aryan side and was commented on in the Polish Underground press.

The Polish Underground was interested in particular in the executions of Gestapo agents who may have also been active on the Aryan side.[28]

On April 19, 1943, the Jewish Order Service was ordered to appear at the ghetto gate on Nalewki Street. Just as during the January action, the policemen were now to be used as a human shield against possible resistance fighters. These policemen were supposed to be in the first groups under fire from Jewish insurgents.[29] Describing the first day of what came to be known as the Warsaw Ghetto Uprising, Ber Warm, who was assigned to guard the emptied houses against looting by the Blue Police, noted, "The street [Zamenhofa] was empty—only individual SS-men were on guard at each gate. From Miła Street, an SS unit went out in the direction of the Umschlagplatz. Smaller units came out of one gate and entered the next. In some of them there were two Jewish Order Service members, also with axes in their hands."[30]

During that month, most of the policemen of the Jewish Order Service shared the fate of the remaining Jews. Marian Berland, who was then in the ghetto, described a group of former policemen he met then at the Umschlagplatz. They were waiting for deportation to what they believed would be the labor camp in Trawniki:

[At the Umschlagplatz] these people feel at home. They know all the tricks, how to manipulate the Ukrainians. They know every corner in the buildings like their own pocket. . . . These people, like Germans, are deprived of all feelings. To save their miserable life, they are ready to kill and turn the world upside down. And today, when they have nothing to say, they are imprisoned here like rats in a cage but have not completely lost the swagger and confidence in themselves. After all, they cannot be treated as equals with other mortals. After all, they have something to boast about to the Germans. Did they not serve them well during the first and the largest displacement? Everything is as under the military here. They keep order. They have even posted a guard by the door so that no stranger will enter.[31]

At the end of April, the several dozen policemen remaining in the ghetto, among them Leon Piżyc, were executed near Pawiak Prison.[32] "In this way, the majority of the executioners of the Warsaw Jews—the officers of the degenerate and corrupt Jewish police—died along with their families," Ringelblum wrote in his journal.[33]

Former policemen who managed to leave the ghetto for the Aryan side shared the fate of the Warsaw Jews hiding there. The wartime accounts of policemen speak of hiding in Warsaw or in the countryside, the 1944 Warsaw Uprising, and camps. Samuel Puterman left the ghetto in December 1942 and together with his wife Irena hid on the Aryan side. After the Warsaw Uprising, he was first sent to Sachsenhausen, then deported to Oranienburg. Gombiński also hid in Warsaw, and after the uprising he went through the transit camps in Ożarów and Pruszków. Stanisław Adler survived in hiding in Anin near Warsaw. Ber Warm probably died during the 1944 Warsaw Uprising. Everyone mentioned here began to write down their recollections while still in hiding, more or less consciously preparing for the courts waiting for them after the war. The majority of ghetto inhabitants at that point shared the view of Jechiel Górny, who wrote on November 5, 1942, "Unfortunately, right now we can only accuse; we can only nurture hatred in our hearts for those who, largely if not entirely, helped to implement the Nazis devil's plan: the extermination of European Jews."[34]

CHAPTER 10

The Courts

The discussion of justice and revenge that began in the Warsaw Ghetto continued in the chaos of the postwar reconstruction of Jewish life both in Poland and abroad. Jewish newspapers, political parties, and social organizations were flooded with denunciations from those who considered themselves to be the victims of policemen and their families, as well as from those who opposed the participation in public life of people suspected of collaboration and pursued their stigmatization. Their authors sought justice and in the Jewish organizations rebuilt after the war saw a chance of obtaining it. The collaboration debate was cautious and limited due to the growing antisemitism in postwar Poland, yet already in 1946 the Honor Court of the Central Committee of Jews in Poland had begun its mission to "cleanse Jewish society of people who in one way or another cooperated with the Nazi authorities during the occupation, unmasking those traitors of the Jewish people who have tens and hundreds of thousands of victims on their conscience. Those traitors consider themselves or want to be considered as decent people and want to try to play a role in the life of our society."[1] A large part of the cases examined by the Honor Court concerned Jewish policemen from Warsaw, especially lawyers who had returned to legal practice and thus were visible to a broader public.[2]

In the justification of the first verdict issued in the case of a former police-man from the Cracow Ghetto, the Honor Court clearly stressed the moral aspect of the proceedings:

> The blow inflicted by a Jew against an abused Jew was more painful than the blow of a German, because he inflicted moral pain. . . . An individual who in the most tragic period of the Jewish people, in the period when they were condemned to total extermination and when their best sons fought not for life but for a death worthy of a man, this individual who allows himself to commit national treason and enters into the service of the enemy and in this position persecutes his own brothers should be considered outside the Jewish community.[3]

The court did not consider the responsibility of the Jewish Order Service as an institution. Instead, each policeman was tried individually, and in each case the accused was held responsible for the deeds he committed. As historian Gabriel Finder has noted, the Honor Court in Poland, despite the pressure it was subjected to, remained cautious in its sentencing. Its goal was not revenge but preservation of social unity.[4] Of the thirty-one files in the archives of the Honor Court referring to past residents of the Warsaw Ghetto, twenty-three refer to former policemen. Two of these cases ended in trials; the others were discontinued due to lack of evidence, the accused's departure from the country, or his death. Both of the cases that went to trial concerned former police functionaries who had profited substantially from their service. Szapsl Rotholc was sentenced to the suspension of his membership in the Jewish community for two years. In its finding, the court stated:

> The Jewish law-enforcement service, popularly called the Jewish police, disgraced itself with its base cooperation with the invader and aided the invader in the extermination of Jews in the Warsaw Ghetto. . . . The testimonies of witnesses and experts together confirm that the major-ity of Jewish policemen behaved in the performance of their duties based on the model and performance of the German police, display-ing brutality and sadism. This applies above all to those members of the Jewish police who, after September 5, 1942, after the reduction in human resources, remained in their positions. The very fact that dur-ing the [deportation] actions each policeman was obliged to deliver to the Umschlagplatz a certain number of people proves that the police-men who remained on duty after September 5, 1942, performed their duty and in doing so participated in the extermination action against the Jewish people.[5]

Abram Wolfowicz was punished with a warning because the court established that he did not carry out Jewish Order Service duties and that he "used his cap" (used his position) to help others. Both Rotholc and Wolfowicz appealed their verdicts. Both were acquitted.

From the postwar perspective, the main issue in assessing the behavior of police functionaries was to determine to what extent they acted under duress and whether they could have evaded the service. Opinions on this subject were extremely varied. Jerzy Lewiński recalled after the war that in late July and early August 1942, at least two hundred functionaries were active in the Jewish Order Service. Other former policemen reported a higher number. Karol Peczenik claimed that six hundred to eight hundred policemen came to Ogrodowa Street to the Jewish Order Service collection point and half of them did not carry out their duties.[6] According to Gombiński, six hundred to seven hundred policemen participated in the deportations to begin with, and ten days later only about a hundred were left.[7] Hersz Wasser does not give any numbers in the cautiously written expert opinion he prepared immediately after the war. He claimed that senior officers could theoretically evade the line service: "This type of behavior was possible, given that the entire reality of that time was subject to constant fluctuations and changes. The continuous reduction and diminishment of the area of the ghetto was accompanied by chaos and disorder, which made it possible to not carry out the German commands."[8]

Although the court cited Wasser's expert opinion in the verdicts, it found that membership in the Jewish Order Service itself was not perceived as reprehensible. Among the persons against whom the proceedings were suspended were functionaries who remained in service structures even until January 1943 but who were able to prove that they did not take an active part in the *Aktion*. Activities in the administrative structures, as the dismissal of Jerzy Lewiński, Stanisław Gombiński and Henryk Nowogródzki's cases demonstrates, were considered separate from what happened at the Umschlagplatz or during the blockades of apartment buildings.

As this debate was taking place in Poland, honor courts were appointed in all major Jewish displaced persons (DP) camps in Austria, Germany, and Italy. In the immediate postwar years Polish Jews—those liberated abroad and those who had escaped postwar Poland—constituted the majority of DPs. In addition to regulating daily camp life, these courts considered and dealt with issues of collaboration, thus meeting social needs and attempting to prevent a wave of mob violence in the camps. In DP camps, unlike in Poland, former members of the Jewish Order Service were not required to submit applications for rehabilitation.

FIGURE 30. Jewish Order Service functionaries, First Precinct, mid-1941. Source: JHI, MŻIH, E-1/15/6.

In his essays on perpetrators of the Holocaust, Raul Hilberg names five methods of rationalization through which perpetrators justified their individual activities. The first, which he refers to as "the oldest, the simplest, and therefore the most effective," was the doctrine of superior orders that had to be obeyed. The second underlined "duty" and separated it from the personal feelings of the perpetrator. The third was a claim that one's actions, unlike those of one's fellows, were not criminal. The fourth diminished one's importance to that of a cog in the machinery of destruction, and the fifth underlined the combative reality of nature.[9] It was the fourth method that was most often used by the policemen. In December 1942, Emanuel Ringelblum wrote, "Every policeman I talk to now is 'as innocent as a lamb.' He never took part in the action because he was assigned to this or that institution. At best, he was the one who saved people from the Umschlagplatz. Others caught people—he did not."[10]

The same was true of the postwar trials. Defending themselves against accusations, former policemen claimed that they did not take part in the deportation operations because they had withdrawn from police work before the deportations commenced, or were working in administrative positions only. Those, however, who admitted to participating in the deportations usually claimed that their zeal was for show only and in fact their only purpose was to help others. Attorney Jerzy Lewiński, an administrative employee in the Third Precinct, for example, supposedly provided policemen with a blank certificate confirming that they had carried out an order to bring a contingent to the Umschlagplatz.[11] Many policemen managed to have their words confirmed by the testimonies of people they had helped or even saved, although they were usually within their circle of family or friends. Very often, in the policemen's testimony, there was also a mention of cooperation with the Polish Socialist or Communist undergrounds—the policemen were supposed to have mediated in the smuggling of arms and the distribution of Polish Underground newspapers in the ghetto. They made this claim in order to portray themselves as part of the new Communist regime's narrative of postwar Poland.

The policemen also tried to convince the court that they were just cogs in the Jewish Order Service's machine, they had no control over its activities, and therefore they could not be held responsible. However, in his memoirs deposited after the war in the Jewish Historical Institute, Gombiński voiced what none of the former Jewish Order Service policemen, including himself, dared to say in front of the onlookers gathered in the court's public gallery:

> Whose order should we disobey? The Jewish Council's? Did it give a sign, or was there any reaction or protest on its part? Or, finally, Engineer Czerniaków, the President of the Council, when he decided to end his life—a "better" moment probably could not have been chosen—if he had even said something, written something, left any last testament. That we should not have been obeying the orders of the Jewish Council. So, who were we to obey? Society? And where was it, where were the political parties, where were those who pretended always to the role of the leaders of society? They were silent. Not a single sign or word from them.[12]

Not all former policemen who survived the Holocaust stood before a court after the war. In the registers of survivors, we find at least a dozen or so names of people who can also be found on the first list of members of the Jewish Order Service and against whom no investigations have ever been carried out. We do not know how many of them left Poland immediately after the war to live abroad under an assumed name.[13] Others, cleared by the courts, stayed in Poland, where some worked in their prewar professions and in the public sphere. Gombiński, who in 1949 went with his family to Paris, was until the end of his professional life a lawyer involved in matters of war settlements. Szapsel Rotholc in 1948 went with his son to Montreal, where he became a furrier. Jerzy Lewiński worked as a prosecutor in, among others, the trials of Hans Biebów, the administrator of the Łódź Ghetto, and

Walter Pelzhausen, commander of the Radogoszcz Prison. After the war, Stanisław Adler was a member of the advisory committee of the Lublin Provisional Government and later deputy director of the legal department in the Provisional Government of National Unity. He committed suicide after the Kielce pogrom in July 1946.

Like other survivors, police officers also left records of their wartime experiences. Among them are the extensive memoirs of an anonymous policeman (probably another draft of Gombiński's memoir) and the postwar "fictionalized reportage" from the Warsaw Ghetto by the painter Samuel Puterman.[14] There is also the very important testimony of Szapsel Rotholc, dealing mainly with the organization of smuggling.[15] The memoirs of Stanisław Adler were deposited in the Yad Vashem Archives.[16] In the archives of the Ghetto Fighters House, there are memoirs and reports written by former policemen when they were in hiding on the Aryan side, collected by the Jewish underground.[17] While often very detailed, none of them goes deeply into the psyche of its author. In all cases, as Jacek Leociak wrote about the diary of Samuel Puterman, "the reporter remains deeply hidden behind the represented world."[18] Unlike Calel Perechodnik from the Otwock Ghetto, none of the Warsaw Ghetto policemen confessed to any wrongdoing in their diaries, nor did they ask for forgiveness.[19] Their testimonies, while invaluable as factual sources painting often extremely detailed collective portraits of members of the service, remain primarily exercises in self-preservation, constantly keeping readers at a distance. Additionally, these memoirs were written during the war or in the immediate postwar years, after which almost all the policemen fell silent.[20]

Among the interviews conducted in the 1990s for the Institute for Visual History and Education of the Shoah Foundation there are several from former policemen from the Warsaw Ghetto, but none of them was asked about his activities in the Jewish Order Service. Perhaps the questioners did not want to touch upon a topic that seemed sensitive, or perhaps they did not understand the seriousness of the problem. Descriptions of the daily life of Warsaw Ghetto policemen can be found only in the memoirs of their family members, but in none of these testimonies are the policemen the main topic.

The silence of the policemen was also forced on them by their environment. Despite the passage of time, Jewish policemen are still looked upon as they were in the first postwar years—as foreigners, more as oppressors than victims. The image of the ghetto policeman, preserved in the memories of many, has no bright side to it. If anything, it seems—and here my findings fully follow those of Christopher Browning—the violence committed by the policemen was described in greater detail in later testimonies than in those written immediately after the war.[21]

After the war, the accounts of how Jewish policemen had conducted themselves in the Jewish ghetto were unknown in the wider non-Jewish community. In accordance with the decision of the Central Committee of Jews in Poland, any discussion in the Polish-language Jewish press on verdicts by the Honor Court given in matters of collaboration was limited.[22] Also not published were the ghetto diaries of policemen. Browning wrote about "communal" memories that cannot be passed on to anyone outside of the immediate circle of survivors because "there is a kind of tacit consensus that these are memories of events and behavior that outsiders might not understand and that hence dissemination could be potentially embarrassing or hurtful to certain members of the community."[23] For many of the survivors, the attitude of the Jewish Order Service during the deportations belonged and still belongs to this category of experiences. Even in Israel, after the debate instigated by the trials of policemen and prisoner-functionaries (*kapos*) in the first half of the 1950s came to a close, the topic of the Jewish police almost disappeared from the public domain, which at that time was dominated by the heroic history of the uprisings in the ghettos and camps.[24] Raul Hilberg's observation about the Nuremberg trials can also be applied to the trials of former policemen: these judgments did not contribute to a better understanding of the history of the war but only to the conclusion of unfinished business.[25]

This chapter has not been closed, however. The image of Jewish policemen as traitors to their people, deserving of stigmatization, was strengthened with the publication of the earliest Holocaust survivor memoirs and the results of scholarly research on communal life in the ghettos. These memoirs and scholarly studies, as Noe Grüss wrote, were likewise building a "knowledge-monument."[26] In testimonies submitted immediately after the war, most of the survivors focused on the most shocking and drastic events and not on everyday life. So, there are policemen carrying out roundups but no policemen directing traffic, there are bribes but no inspectors of refuse in the streets. The policemen became a symbol of repression so quickly that there never was, it seems, time to understand them.

In the earliest research on the history of the ghettos, the Jewish Order Service was not seen as an element of "Jewish" social life.[27] It was an institution imposed on the ghetto that embodied collaboration between the Judenrat and the Germans. In historical studies produced in Poland in the early 1950s, the service was presented as a tool of oppression and terror in the hands of a Jewish bourgeoisie loyal to the Judenrat and the occupation authorities.

The presentation of the Jewish Order Service as a part of the class struggle was, of course, in keeping with the historical narrative that was in force there at the time, but it also facilitated the settling of accounts from the past. It was another step on the way to the symbolic purification of a Jewish community trying to rebuild itself in postwar Poland. The subject of the Jewish Order Service, as well as other aspects of Jewish life during the Holocaust, was dealt with in this period by historians associated with the Jewish Historical Institute and rarely entered wider circulation.

The discussion begun in the 1960s around the books of Raul Hilberg and Hannah Arendt, which led to the inclusion in Holocaust research of the internal dynamics of Jewish social life and to the resulting effort to understand the policy of accommodation and the adaptation of the Jewish Councils and Jewish administration during the Holocaust, touched on the Jewish Order Service only to a small extent.[28] Yet, even after this debate died down, in the much more sensitive work of Isaiah Trunk, the police, although shown in a much more nuanced way, were still a foreign body on the streets of the ghetto—a product of "destructive German nihilism."[29] It was not until the 1990s that work on the history of the Jewish Order Service began to appear that did not attempt to assess the morality or the ethics of the policemen's behavior.[30] A special role was played by studies of the service in the Kaunas (Kovno) Ghetto, where the activity was very well documented, thanks to the well-preserved underground archive of the local police.[31]

In Poland, the controversy around the Jewish Order Service was particularly visible in publications appearing as a result of the March 1968 antisemitic campaign. At that time, "Jewish collaborators" and "Jewish Gestapo" filling cattle wagons with passive Jewish masses were contrasted with the collective attitude of Poles, "a nation without quislings."[32] Symbolizing the "dark side of the victims," the Jewish police were used to fully justify the passivity of Poles during the Holocaust.[33] In a competition of suffering and in minimizing the Jewish tragedy, the Jewish police play an important role in antisemitic publications to this day.

Conclusion

Jechiel Górny wrote in November 1942:

> The Jewish police will perhaps try to justify: "We had to," "We received orders to deliver such and such a number of Jews a day," "The authorities threatened us with death." For a moment I will place myself on their side. I say that orders must be carried out when you are a "disciplined" soldier, even in the service of the enemy, when the lives of two thousand Jewish policemen are of a higher value than the life of the whole community. Is the behavior of the Jewish police during the action justified? No. And I think that there will not be a single Jew who would justify or try to defend the participation of the Jewish police in the "resettlement action." In stronger words, "I accuse" may be the answer to their conduct.[1]

Regardless of their composition, responsibilities, and relations with the Judenrat, Blue Police, or German authorities, Jewish Order Service formations in the ghettos of the General Government almost always displayed increasing violence and corruption, leading eventually to their forced participation in the deportations from the ghettos. As such, they were held coresponsible for the destruction of their community. In the case of Warsaw, the process of the corruption of the service clearly started with its formation in the autumn of 1940. Yet should we link the endemic corruption and growing violence of the Jewish Order Service with its actions on the Umschlagplatz? Who was responsible for the role that the service played in the history of the Warsaw Ghetto?

For many of those who have described the actions of the Jewish Order Service, the Jewish policemen were very far from what Primo Levi later described as the "grey zone."[2] Their story was transmitted as uniformly black. If they were spoken of, it was as a means of exacting revenge in the name of those who perished, of recording their names as perpetrators rather than as a means of understanding their behavior. While their actions on the Umschlagplatz, their predeportation violence, and their corruption were blotted out in many postwar memoirs, there is no doubt that even wartime writings, created in the ghetto before the deportations, are an almost uniform act of accusation against the ghetto policemen.

In his seminal essay on the grey zone of victim actions during the Holocaust, Levi wrote, "The harsher the oppression, the more widespread among the oppressed is the willingness, with all its infinite nuances and motivations, to collaborate: terror, ideological seduction, servile imitation of the victor, myopic desire for any power whatsoever, even though ridiculously circumscribed in space and time, cowardice, and, finally, lucid calculation aimed at eluding the imposed orders and order."[3] Among those who served in the Jewish Order Service, there were both rich and poor and those who feared the roundups for the labor camps and those for whom it was a way of doing business. There were those who found in it a career and those who fulfilled their duties in as limited a way as possible, treating the service only as a way of ensuring the survival of their family. Some underwent transformation in the ghetto, changing from ordinary people to perpetrators of extreme violence and corruption. These were people such as Meczysław Szmerling, who can be accurately viewed as having had a predisposition to violence that found an outlet in the service. The vast majority, however, seen as passively following orders, reacted in a way that would preserve their self-interest. They could not choose the responsibilities that were given to them; they could, however, choose the way they assessed and fulfilled them.

The policemen who appeared on July 22, 1942, at the command office on Ogrodowa Street had only one goal—to save themselves and their relatives. At the Umschlagplatz, the policemen ceased to be lawyers, assimilators, or players—they became people who had a chance to save themselves and their families at the cost of the lives of others. In describing the labor camp in Starachowice, Christopher Browning wrote that "Nazi power placed Jews in a 'less than zero-sum game' in which they had some agency or choice, but all choices caused harm to many and no choice guaranteed saving the life of

FIGURE 31.   Ghetto gate at Grzybowski Square, circa end of 1941. Source: JHIA, ARG I 683-37.

anyone."[4] In this situation, the life of those family members who remained alive became the highest imperative. For a short time, the functionaries of the Jewish Order Service were given the chance to save themselves, their wives, and their children, and many were ready to pay any price for it. Part of that price was rejection by the community, both at that point and for many years after. Those who survived were usually burdened with the stigma of "ghetto policeman" for the rest of their lives.

Postwar honor courts, assessing policemen individually, found the key to the examination of the service members that was often lost to later researchers. The most important objective was to show the diversity of the attitudes and their individual motivations; this applied to policemen both in the Warsaw Ghetto and in other ghettos. Their actions were above all else the result of the German policy aimed at the demoralization of the Jewish Order Service but also of the wartime reality: the brutality of everyday life in the ghetto and the shifting of acceptable behavioral boundaries. Finally, their choices were motivated by a search for normalcy and a pursuit of stability in their lives, which to a minimal degree was provided by membership in the Jewish Order Service. Based primarily on the work of Emanuel Ringelblum and his team, we can now say that the study of the police is largely a study of adaptation. As Raul Hilberg wrote, it is self-preservation through the pursuit of stability, "the craving for the familiar, the habitual, the normal," that should be seen as providing "an explanation of how these groups managed to go on—the perpetrators with their ever more drastic activities, the victims with their progressive deprivations, the bystanders with the increasing ambiguity and ambivalence of their positions."[5] In the end, all "strategies of survival" were futile; those who did survive ascribed it more often than not to luck or chance rather than to conscious choices. The service became a tool and, finally, with the destruction of the Warsaw Ghetto, a victim itself of the Holocaust. Perhaps by conducting more broadly focused research on the functioning of the service in other ghettos, including smaller towns, we will be able to find material allowing us to determine whether there was a network of connections between formations of this kind in the General Government. Exploring the ways in which the model of the functioning of the Warsaw Jewish Order Service was duplicated in other ghettos would increase the possibility of answering the question of the role of the Jewish Order Service in German anti-Jewish policy in occupied Poland and in the implementation of the Holocaust.

Appendix 1

Sanitation Instructions for Precinct Patrolmen

The precinct patrolmen duties in the area of maintaining order and cleanliness of streets (pavements and streets), squares, houses, and yards involve strict compliance with all applicable orders, in particular those regarding:

1) cleaning the streets every morning and keeping them clean throughout the day (in case of particularly low temperatures and black ice, roadways and sidewalks are to be sprinkled with sand or ash),

2) ban on ventilation (hanging out clothes), scuffing and vacuuming of bedding, clothes, etc. in stairwells, windows, and balconies, both internal and external, and the order to equip every property, inhabited or intended as people's permanent dwelling place, with carpet-beating and ventilation equipment,

3) keeping clean and daily washing, with water, permanent parking places for carriages, platforms, carts, etc.

4) daily, thorough tidying of gates, vestibules, courtyards, courtyards and staircases, as well as descents to basements and cellars, as well as places intended for garbage and waste disposal in all buildings subject to precinct patrolmen supervision,

5) washing staircases at least once a week,

6) maintaining proper cleanliness of the toilets, so they are fit for use, thoroughly cleaned and washed with water at least once a day and well illuminated from twilight to 9:00 p.m.,

7) garbage cans in an accessible place, provided with movable, easy-to-open, but tightly fitting covers, emptied regularly,

8) placing spittoons with water in staircases of buildings higher than one story,

9) prohibiting placement of cans with rubbish or leftovers in staircases,

10) making sure tenants keep their horses, cattle, and swine in stables or pigsties specially adapted for this purpose,

11) registration of incidents of animal deaths at the appropriate Polish Police station,

12) regular cleaning of cesspits in unsewered houses,

13) enforcing the ban on pumping sewage water from unsewered houses into the street storm-drain inlets.

In case of any deficiencies in the maintenance of order and cleanliness, one should:

1) in minor cases, resort to a warning,

2) in more serious cases or in case of persistent noncompliance with the regulations, draw up a protocol and submit it along with a report to the PrecinctCommand.

JHIA, ARG I 272 (I/787/2), trans. Krzysztof Heymer

APPENDIX 2

Official Instruction for the Order Service

CHAIRMAN OF THE JEWISH COUNCIL IN WARSAW,
THE BOARD OF THE JEWISH DISTRICT IN WARSAW, THE COMMAND OF THE ORDER
SERVICE

Annex to item 1 of Order No. 128, issued 21st May, 1942

OFFICIAL REGULATIONS OF THE ORDER SERVICE

1. General service guidelines

Membership in the Order Service imposes obligations that only an individual with specific moral and physical qualifications can meet. This service requires self-denial, civil courage, and self-restraint.

The main guideline for the member of the Order Service should be the principle that they perform their service for the benefit of all the inhabitants of the district, with special consideration and care toward the unfortunate, suffering, and poor. When carrying out all tasks, one should remember the social nature of the service. Meticulous compliance with the authorities' orders protects the population against the severe consequences of disobedience.

2. General principles of on-duty conduct

Every Order Service functionary should submit to commands and orders of his superiors, be compliant with his colleagues, polite to outsiders, and at the same time energetic, efficient, and zealous in the performance of his duties

The nature and tasks of the Order Service require that its functionaries act calmly and prudently. The quick decision-making should be founded upon cool-headed consideration. The diligent implementation of official duties consists not only in the performance of tasks arising directly from the order of one's superior but also in strict compliance with the provisions of the official instructions.

3. Off-duty conduct

An Order Service functionary is required to exhibit impeccable behavior off duty. An Order Service functionary should behave in such manner as to be a role model for the population. A disgraceful lifestyle shall result in disciplinary or procedural measures. Visiting suspect premises, unless in direct connection with one's professional duties, drunkenness, gambling, etc., maintaining relationships with persons of ill repute are prohibited.

Visiting places of entertainment wearing the Order Service insignia is forbidden, except for cases in direct connection with one's professional duties. It is not allowed to incur any debts from subordinates and persons with whom one comes in contact only because of one's official rank (business owners, persons who apply for providing supplies to Order Service, members of house committees).

4. Attitude toward the public

The tactful and courteous treatment of every citizen is an essential requirement while performing the service. Each inquirer wants and must see an Order Service functionary as his guardian. Inappropriate behavior of a particular functionary reflects negatively on the public's attitude to the entire Order Service.

A functionary, when asked on the street by a passer-by, is obliged to salute, then politely provide information as accurately as possible, and conclude the conversation with a proper bow. Well-mannered and polite treatment of members of the public must also be strictly observed in all Order Service offices.

5. Attitude towards colleagues and superiors

An Order Service functionary should always be ready to help other functionaries should they find themselves in need, address higher-ranking officers with adherence to prescribed official forms, and communicate politely with lower-ranking and inexperienced functionaries.

All signs of jealousy, servility, and exaltation are symptoms of a perverted character and should not be tolerated.

An Order Service functionary offended by the behavior of another functionary should report the fact to his supervisor, who will further examine the case in either regular or disciplinary mode. Providing gifts and so-called treating superiors to any benefits by the group or individual functionaries is prohibited. A gift is understood as any item that has exchangeable monetary value.

6. Proceeding through official channels

When dealing with any request, both verbal and in writing, the functionary is obliged to proceed through official channels, meaning that a request is directed to one's direct superiors, who in turn are obliged to send them along according to their character. Exceptions to this requirement can be made only on the basis of a specific regulation or special order.

7. Submission of verbal reports

A verbal report to functionary's supervisor or to the Jewish Council councilor should be expressed clearly, in natural voice, using the phrases "I report" or "I inform." When submitting a report, stand in front of your superior for three steps in basic stance, salute, and state his rank or title preceded by the word "Sir" and your own rank and name.

If a lower-ranking Order Service functionary arrives on a duty-related purpose in the premises where his superior is present, he should take off his hat at the entrance and report at the door as above, stating the purpose of his arrival.

Hold your cap horizontally, with the visor pointing forward, in your right hand, freely lowered. When contacting another Order Service functionary in the company of a higher-ranking officer, you should first ask the latter to address the lower-ranking colleague.

When a supervisor visits a unit, only the commander of the given unit or his deputy may report to the supervisor. Other functionaries—e.g., regular members of the Order Service on their posts, lecturers during classes, etc.— do not report and do not submit reports. Their name, rank, and type of duties fulfilled are communicated to the visiting person by the commander of the visited unit.

The exception is the duty functionary who reports verbally to each visiting person of a higher rank or function than the commander of the unit present on site. Bicycle patrol functionaries get off their bicycles when reporting to superiors (this provision does not apply during patrol service).

8. Confidentiality measures

An Order Service functionary is forbidden to reveal official messages and to use any of the information obtained during performing his service. In particular, the Order Service functionary should keep silent about all private information that he has obtained in course of the service and about all matters that, whether by command of his superiors or due to their confidential nature, should be kept secret.

9. Ban on battering—conditions of using batons

Battering citizens, especially detainees, is prohibited. The use of a rubber baton is only permitted as a last resort, after having exhausted all means of persuasion and after having issued two verbal warnings. In such cases, the blow may only be directed to the hands or back. Beating on the head is forbidden in any case, unless it is a measure of defending oneself against an armed attacker. An Order Service functionary should report every instance of using a rubber baton, both by making a proper entry in the official register and by submitting a report to his immediate supervisor, providing the background of the incident and the justification for the measure taken.

10. Attitude toward representatives of other authorities

When an on-duty Order Service functionary encounters officials of the Jewish authorities and the council, an functionary should behave tactfully and provide appropriate assistance upon request.

11. Complaints

Complaints about a direct or indirect supervisor that contain a request to hold the person accountable for regular, disciplinary, or criminal offenses shall be filed in the manner provided for in the provisions on Order Service functionary's regular and disciplinary liability. Complaints that do not contain such a request should be lodged with the immediate supervisor, who will immediately order to enter the complaint in the official journal and even—at the request of the complainant—will issue a confirmation of receipt.

Complaints may be lodged at the earliest after twenty-four hours and at the latest within seven days of the incident that was the reason for the complaint.

The supervising officer should immediately, within three days of the date of notification, send the complaint to the supervisor, attaching his description of the case. The complaint is settled by the direct superior.

The supervising officer to whom a complaint has been filed may neither settle it nor influence the withdrawal of this complaint. The complainant receives a written decision from the person entitled to settle the complaint, with confirmation of receipt, whereby the decision is subject to further appeal, within seven days, to the direct higher authority. Lack of response within three weeks of the day of lodging the complaint entitles the complainant to send a report to the supervisor of the functionary who received the original complaint.

It is permissible to make a complaint directly, verbally or in writing, to any supervisor during the inspection. Such case should be highlighted in the inspection report: "Requests and complaints."

When an functionary requests to submit the report to a superior officer, the direct commander shall be obliged to take this request into account.

Reckless or clearly groundless filing of complaints and disregard of the official proceedings entails responsibility and, in more severe cases, disciplinary action.

12. Illness

An Order Service functionary who, due to illness, cannot fulfill his duties should immediately notify his superior and, if the illness lasts longer than twenty-four hours, provide a medical notification. Malingering will be treated as unauthorized absence from duty.

13. Leave of absence

Commanders of Order Service executive units have the right to grant their subordinates special compassionate leaves for up to three days.

In other cases and for longer periods of time, a leave is granted by the head of the Order Service.

14. Praise and distinction

Distinguishing an Order Service functionary for special merit can take place only in exceptional cases and take form of a) a praise, b) a cash prize, or (c) promotion to a higher rank. Granting a reward to an Order Service functionary from funds placed at the disposal of the command by a private person does not in itself constitute a basis for including this distinction in the service inventory. On the other hand, the fact that a cash prize has been awarded from the funds of the Order Service command designated specifically for this purpose should be included in the service inventory.

The praise should be announced in an order from the command of the Order Service along with a concise presentation of functionary's courage, prudence, or presence of mind. Only praise granted in the order shall be included in the service inventory.

Commanders of executive units are only authorized to express their recognition verbally and to submit applications. Only the head commander of the Order Service can decide about giving the praise. It is forbidden to accept any awards directly from the beneficiary.

Persons or institutions wishing to reward an Order Service functionary for any act should apply directly to the Order Service command, which will decide about the acceptance of the prize or its distribution among individual functionaries.

15. Functionary's appearance and on-duty conduct

An Order Service functionary on duty should be clean-shaven, cleanly dressed, wearing the prescribed armbands (the regular armband and the service one with appropriate distinctions) and the service number visibly on the clothing, placed on the left chest, as well as have the service cap, a rubber baton, a whistle, service register, and writing accessories.

An Order Service functionary should avoid any behavior that could expose him to malicious remarks, slander, or ridicule by the public.

The attitude of the Order Service member should always be exemplary and his gait calm and deliberate so that he can be aware of everything that happens around him.

Smoking tobacco is forbidden while on street patrol duty or when entering official premises and private apartments. Walking arm in arm with anyone, sitting or lying at one's station, leading dogs without a special order, any unnatural and exaggerated behavior, unnecessary whistling or humming, raising one's voice, and conducting nonofficial conversations with other functionaries are prohibited. It is also unacceptable to push or touch the clients when admitting them inside official premises, organizing queues, etc.

16. Service register

Each junior functionary of the Order Service should carry a service register with him, where he enters, verbatim, the content of the order pertaining to him from the Station's Book before starting duty and during the shift should enter official results, including the time of departure and return to the office and the duration of each phase of daily service and rest, as well as significant events and incidents in which he intervened while off duty.

In particular, the following information must be entered:

a) amendments to official orders that occurred after leaving the district,
b) all official results during the functionary's duty or official intervention,
c) data required to file a report for violation of legal provisions,
d) information about persons and criminal acts that can be used as material for filing the report.

Entries in the register should be made immediately, at the site of the incident, succinctly, and concisely. It is unacceptable to make entries that are not closely related to the service. It is not allowed to enter confidential data. Such data should be submitted by an Order Service functionary to his supervisor in the form of a verbal or written report.

17. Staying in public premises

Entering public premises without a duty-related need while on duty is absolutely unacceptable. The following must be regarded as a professional reason for entering:

a) performing actions on public premises required for the execution of an order,
b) an intervention on the call of third parties or as a result of the functionary's own observation that the situation on the premises requires his presence.

Each time after ending daily duty, a report to the superior should be made about the intervention as well as a note in the service register. If an off-duty Order Service functionary finds himself on public premises where quarrels occur in his presence, he should immediately identify himself as a member of the service and take appropriate steps.

18. Rallies

The Order Service functionary should always arrive to a meeting on time, without deficiencies or inaccuracies in external appearance (shaved, combed, clean, cap, number, service armband).

The briefing before and after duty is carried out by the head of unit or a duty functionary.

19. Awareness of field relations

Awareness of field relations includes the size of the precinct, patrol schedule and division, duration of each patrol, the boundaries of the service precinct, the boundaries of the Jewish district in the region with special regard to exit points, ruins, walls, and fences along the border, communication conditions, flats and hideouts of dangerous persons and suspects, hospitals, refugee gathering points, government offices, offices, locations of hydrants, etc.

20. Awareness of personal relations

Awareness of personal relations includes, first and foremost, the knowledge of people who, by virtue of their office and type of service, often come into contact with the Order Service, knowledge of people in prominent social positions in the Jewish quarter, knowledge of people who have various connections within the population and who can therefore provide various testimonies (rabbis, teachers, doctors, midwives), knowledge of people under police supervision or released from prisons, tramps, beggars, and prostitutes.

21. Order Service functionary' basic duties

While performing his duties, an Order Service functionary should always bear in mind the following duties:

Vigilance:

1. Always be alert and attentive; avoid tardiness and talkativeness.

Politeness:

2. Always be tactful and polite to people asking for information.

Urgency:

3. Never delay in providing assistance to anyone requesting it, provided that such assistance entitles the functionary to leave the place of service.

Complaints:

4. If anyone makes a complaint about the Order Service, the functionary should ask the complainant to direct it to the precinct management or the Order Service command, where a record will be written down. If the complainant refuses to do so, the functionary will only enter the name and address of the applicant and all the details of the complaint into the service register and then submit a report.

Using the whistle:

5. A whistle should be used when a need for assistance arises, namely:

   a) Three short whistle sounds during a pursuit—at the sound of a whistle, all Order Service functionaries check if the suspect is in their proximity, and if that is the case, they join the pursuit.
   b) Long whistle sounds, when the person sounding the alarm needs immediate assistance on the spot—in this case all functionaries within the whistle's range should head toward the sound.

Cooperation in crime detection:

6. One of the main tasks of Order Service is to ensure public order and prevent crime, as well as to assist in crime detection. If a crime occurs, steps must be taken to ensure that its traces are not destroyed, especially that objects that serve as evidence or that can lead to the offender or to their trace are not touched or removed.

22. Daytime service

During the daytime rounds, one should:

- walk on the pavement along the road (by the cobblestones),
- provide polite and accurate responses to public inquiries,
- provide help to anyone in need,
- make sure that traffic on the road and pavement is not impeded,
- in order to prevent crime, especially theft, one should watch carefully what is happening around oneself,
- suppress any disorder and, if necessary, stop the culprit,
- report to one's supervisor about any offenses in order to be able to bring those responsible to justice,
- upon request, provide assistance in removing persons who break the law on private property or persons causing unrest in public places,
- record in a service register and report about all incidents and accidents, explosions, instances of people fainting in the streets, being bitten by dogs, and any other incident where liability may be established,
- pay attention to all public property in the streets or near streets, note any damage; persons who intentionally damage such objects should be detained,
- if any building poses a risk of collapsing due to its current condition, one should stop nearby in order to warn pedestrians (at the same time, the house administration and precinct command should be notified),
- immediately report any dangerous damage to the road or pavement,
- if traffic on the street is halted for any reason, it should be regulated immediately,
- if an item is placed in such a manner that they may tempt a thief, the owner must be immediately alerted,
- if the sewer inlets on the street are not right or are blocked by an animal carcass, waste, or scattered garbage, these facts should be noted and immediately reported about to the patrol commander, or reported directly to the precinct,
- if the street is in a dangerous condition due to slippery surface, it is necessary to immediately order sprinkling it with sand or ash,
- if an Order Service functionary identifies an instance of animal abuse (e.g., overloaded cart, horses unfit for work), he will take the steps he will consider necessary (stopping the cart, taking the horse unfit for work to the precinct command, writing down the names and addresses of drivers in order to file a report).

23. Nighttime service

During the nighttime rounds, one should:

a) walk on the pavement in such a way as to be able to check whether the doors and gates are closed,
b) when starting one's shift at dusk or early morning, first of all check that all doors, windows, shutters, basement locks, ladders, etc. within the round radius are properly secured. If the person on duty finds that something is wrong (e.g., a light that was usually on is off or another way around, or it is brighter than usual, suspicious murmurs or noises are heard), he should try to determine the cause and, if necessary, warn the owner. Such incident should be written down and reported to the manager. If the thieves are nearby, one should hold them down, and if it turns that help is needed, one should keep an eye on them until help arrives,
c) special attention should be paid inside burned-down ruins, galleries with access to upper windows, wealthier stores, etc.,
d) check shop shutters carefully to see if they are secure,
e) during doing the rounds, all interviews ordered by the superior should be carried out.

24. Service at permanent posts

During serving at permanent posts one should:

a) provide assistance to those who need it, in particular to people who want to cross the street during busy traffic,
b) pay attention to passers-by with regard to the descriptions of wanted persons; if a pickpocket or other suspicious person gets on a tram or an omnibus, the functionary should immediately and confidentially inform the conductor, warn other passengers, and watch the suspect,
c) make note of all events and report on any incidents,
d) if traffic is stopped, regulate it, even if it is not the post's duty,
e) if it is necessary to leave the permanent post, one should immediately note in the service register the time and reason for leaving and, immediately after returning, note the time of return to the post,
f) during cold weather, one can patrol within one hundred meters of the post but should always keep it in sight and always be on alert, so as to be always visible from the post.

25. Traffic regulation

Duty at the traffic regulation posts requires awareness, attention, and tact, in particular:

    a) one should not stop vehicles close to each other but give a signal to stop in advance and then calmly walk to the middle of the street and spread one's arms,
    b) names and addresses should be recorded and all cases of persons driving in a manner that poses danger to the public and who are not following commands should be reported,
    c) priority should be given to military and police vehicles, fire brigades, and ambulances.

26. Duty at exit and border points

Order Service functionaries at the exit points and the boundaries of the Jewish district serve alongside officers of the German and Polish police according to the instructions received from the authorities. Order Service functionaries should be at these posts at a distance of at least ten meters from the border line, inside the Jewish district.

27. Forms of interventions

In the event of a violation of law by a Jew, an Order Service functionary may:

    a) give the offender a warning,
    b) impose a mandatory fine,
    c) file a report,
    d) stop the suspect.

Regarding a), a warning should be used in cases of minor regular offenses, when there is a reasonable suspicion that the perpetrator acted in good faith and that there is no need to take further steps. However, when an offense becomes more severe or was repeated, or when a perpetrator does not comply with the Order Service functionary command, the name of the perpetrator should be noted and a report should be filed at the end of day's service.

Regarding b) and c), in the cases provided for in the instruction on immediate penalties, a penalty ticket should be imposed, and if a perpetrator refuses to accept it, the functionary has to establish the identity of the perpetrator and file a report. If it is impossible to establish the identity (no identity card or other documents), one should bring the perpetrator to the headquarters of the nearest precinct.

Regarding d), every person has the right to detain a criminal caught in the act or immediately after it, during a pursuit. In particular, Order Service functionaries should detain and escort the suspect to the proper jurisdiction, along with a report on the alleged offense, if:

a) there is a reasonable risk that he will go into hiding,
b) when a person is suspected of committing a crime,
c) when a person has no permanent residence or specific means of subsistence in the General Government or person's identity cannot be established.

An Order Service functionary may detain a person caught in an unlawful act, because of fear that the perpetrator will go into hiding:

a) if the person is unknown, cannot be identified, or identity cannot be established otherwise,
b) if the person has no permanent residence or specific means of subsistence in the General Government,
c) is under police supervision or is a habitual offender, a repeat offender, or a professional criminal,
d) if it is only through detention that the effects of a crime or attempt at a crime can be prevented,
e) if the person has not paid the immediate penalty ticket.

28. Detention

When arresting a suspect, an Order Service functionary should use the formula "You are detained in the name of the law" and list the reason for the arrest. Detention is tantamount to using force. However, one shall not use excessive force, more that is necessary to prevent the detainee from escaping. Under no circumstances should one be harsh toward a detainee or use abusive language. An act of detention should be carried out as discreetly as possible so as not to attract the attention of the public. Do not talk to the detainee. The functionary should immediately take items that could be used for assault or defense away from the detainee.

Escorting the detainee should be carried out as follows:

a) the Order Service functionary should walk on the detainee's left side and keep an eye on the person in transit,

b) choose, if possible, side streets so as not to attract the attention of pedestrians,

c) make sure that the detainee does not dispose of items in his possession and does not communicate with anyone,

d) the detained person should be taken straight away to the destination, with no stops along the way (e.g., from the place of detention to the headquarters of the appropriate precinct),

e) brawlers and the sick should be driven to their destination (insofar as possible in the company of two other functionaries), while making sure that the detained person does not escape.

Order Service functionaries who have detained a suspect are forbidden to notify his family about that fact, unless such ordinance is issued by the precinct command.

29. Fires

In the event of a fire, an Order Service functionary will save the lives and property of people endangered by the incident and in particular should:

a) call the fire brigade immediately,

b) alert residents who are in danger,

c) notify the Jewish Order Service precinct administration and the Polish Police Department about the fire,

d) empty the road and pavement in the vicinity of the fire from vehicles and people in order to facilitate the arrival and operation of firemen,

e) protect endangered property against looting (however, one should not hinder access of officials, workers of the gasworks and power plant, as well as insurance companies' agents possessing appropriate identity documents),

f) upon arrival of the fire brigade, strictly follow the instructions of a commander of the unit.

When saving the lives and property of people, the following guidelines should be followed:

a) avoid, if possible, opening doors and windows,
b) enter smoke-filled rooms on all fours, with a wet handkerchief in one's mouth,
c) people on fire should be placed on the ground and covered with woolen, possibly thick cover,
d) if fat or kerosene is burning, extinguish it with either sand, soil, or ash rather than water,
e) burning net curtains should be torn off and crumpled (in order to stifle the flames).

30. Accidents

If an accident occurs, one has to:

a) take care of the injured persons (give them first aid, remove them from the street to a gate or a shop, call an ambulance or doctor, make sure that the patient is not robbed, and take his valuable items with the witnesses present and retain the valuable items),
b) collect all the material related to the accident (determine the causes of the accident, identify responsible party, determine which witnesses corroborate the relevant facts).

31. Providing assistance

An Order Service functionary, regardless of whether he is on or off duty, should rush to every call for help to its source, determine the reason for the call, and provide assistance. If the call was made maliciously or arbitrarily, a report should be filed to bring the person responsible to liability under Art. 20 of the Offenses Law.

32. Damage to real estate and installations

An Order Service functionary should report any visible deficiencies and damages to houses, shop windows, and gates that he notices and order removal of items that threaten safety or that impede street traffic.

In the event of a water pipe rupture, gas leakage, etc., an Order Service functionary should warn the public, notify the relevant authority of the accident, and, if necessary, order street closure.

33. Electrical wires

If an electric wire snaps and falls to the ground, the area should be fenced off-limits to the public, and the precinct management and the tramway management or power plant management should be notified of the accident. If the wire fell on a person or animal, one should carefully remove the wire with a wooden object in such a way that one does not directly touch the cable or the injured body.

34. Lost and found items

A report about found items should be filed, and it has to include surname, first name, and address of the finder and the list of found items or found documents. If someone has found a lost item, it should be taken away from him, the name of the finder should be noted, and if the finder refuses to give the item up, escort the finder to the precinct command.

Items found along with the finding report should be sent to the Lost and Found Office at the Gmina Precinct. If an alleged owner of an item appears, it should not be handed over to the person until he proves, without doubt, that it belongs to him.

35. Lost children

Lost children should be taken back to their families. Only when it is completely impossible to identify the child's relatives should the child be brought to the precinct detention centers.

36. Drunks

Drunk persons who cannot be left on their own due to the state they are in should in principle be walked to their apartments or, if an address is unknown, to the precinct command until they sober up. If a drunk behaves violently, the functionary is advised to find outside witnesses in order to avoid allegations of violent handling of the drunken person.

Any person who, while intoxicated as a result of consumption of alcoholic beverages, causes a public scandal by his behavior and any person who remains in such intoxicated state in a public place, regardless of their behavior, is liable to a penalty. In such cases appropriate reports should be filed.

37. Corpses

If a person is found dead on the street, an Order Service functionary is obliged to notify the command of the nearest precinct, which will in turn issue appropriate order to secure or remove the corpse.

38. Sanitation supervision

In sanitary-related matters, the Sanitary and Order Regulations are in force, the content of which should be known to any Order Service functionary.

39. Assistance service

An Order Service functionary performs the assistance service on the orders of the commander of the executive unit or in the cases provided for in the commands of the Order Service commander. The official task is to enable the organs he assists to perform their official duties, remove obstacles, and overcome resistance.

Dz. I R. ORG. KSP. 1.VI.[19]42. 3000 [copies]

JHIA, ARG I 251, trans. Krzysztof Heymer

NOTES

Introduction

1. Yad Vashem Archive (YVA), O.33 / 129, 15.

2. United States Holocaust Memorial Museum (USHMM), 1992.262.1, Warsaw Ghetto R1.

3. The Archive of the Jewish Historical Institute (JHIA) in Warsaw holds two such albums: *Służba Porządkowa w Warszawie 1940–1941: Album podarowany przez funkcjonariuszy SP insp. Marianowi Handlowi* (Jewish Order Service in Warsaw 1940–1941: Album presented by the Jewish Order Service functionaries to Inspector Marian Handel) and *Gęsia 24: Areszt Centralny; Album podarowany Franciszkowi Przymusińskiemu* (Gęsia 24: Central Detention; Album presented to Fraciszek Przymusiński).

4. See JHIA, ARG I 683 (I / 1222), collections of photographs from the Warsaw Ghetto.

5. Emanuel Ringelblum (1900–44) was a historian, teacher, and social activist. Before the war, he joined the Yiddish Scientific Institute (YIVO) in what was then Wilno, Poland, as a researcher in its Historical Section, and was active in the Poale-Zion Left. In the ghetto, he was a member of the board of the organization Jewish Social Self-Help and a founder of the Underground Archive of the Warsaw Ghetto. He was shot in the ruins of the ghetto in March 1943. On Ringelblum, see Samuel Kassow, *Who Will Write Our History? Emanuel Ringelblum, the Warsaw Ghetto, and the Oyneg Shabes Archive* (Bloomington: Indiana University Press, 2007).

1. Establishment of the Jewish Order Service

1. Ludwig Leist (1891–1967)—prewar clerk; from March 1940 until July 31, 1941, the mayor of occupied Warsaw. Adam Czerniaków (1880–1942)—engineer, social activist. On October 4, 1939, he became the chairman of the Warsaw Judenrat. On July 23, 1942, Czerniaków committed suicide in the Jewish Council Building.

2. For more on the Labor Battalion and the Security Guard, see JHIA, ARG I 241 (I / 28), "Labor Battalion, General Report for 1940."

3. JHIA, ARG II 46 (II / 127), Chairman of the Jewish Council in Warsaw A[dam] Czerniaków, memorandum titled "Die neuen Aufgaben der Jüdischen Gemeinde in Warschau und die Lage der jüdischen Bevölkerung," March 26, 1940.

4. State Archive in Warsaw, Archiwum Państwowe w Warszawie (APW), Przewodniczący Rady Żydowskiej w Warszawie (PRŻ), RG 11, "9, 10, 11 Weekly Report of the Chairman of the Jewish Council: Report on the Activities of the Jewish Religious Community in Warsaw for the Period 12.6–4.7.1940."

5. Stanisław Gombiński, *Wspomnienia policjanta z warszawskiego getta*, ed. M. Janczewska (Warsaw: Centrum Badań nad Zagładą Żydów, 2010), 159.

6. APW, PRŻ, RG 13, "15, 16, 17 Weekly Report of the Chairman of the Jewish Council: Report on the Activities of the Jewish Religious Community in Warsaw for the Period 26.7–15.8.1940."

7. Beginning in the spring of 1940, rumors circulated in Warsaw regarding the creation of a type of Jewish police force, similar to the one in the ghetto of Łódź (renamed Litzmannstadt), which was to be a first step toward the establishment of the ghetto. Due to the proximity of the two cities and the number of Jewish escapees from Łódź in Warsaw, it was widely known that the so-called Ordnungsdienst (Order Service) was established in Litzmannstadt at the end of February 1940, two weeks after the regulation was announced to establish a ghetto there, and two months before it was cut off from the rest of the city (April 30). On the Ordnugsdienst in Łódź ghetto, see Andrea Löw, "Ordnungsdienst im Ghetto Litzmannstadt," in *Fenomen getta łódzkiego 1940–1944*, ed. P. Samuś, W. Puś (Łódź: Wydawnictwo Uniwersytetu Łódzkiego, 2006), 155–67.

8. Emanuel Ringelblum, letter dated March 29, 1940, *Pisma z getta warszawskiego*, ed. J. Nalewajko-Kulikov, trans. Adam Rutkowski et al., Archiwum Ringebluma: Konspiracyjne Archiwum Getta Warszawy 29 (Warsaw: Żydowski Instytut Historyczny, 2018), 88. This and other documents from the Ringelblum Archive are quoted from the full scholarly edition of the Underground Archive of the Warsaw Ghetto published by the Jewish Historical Institute in Warsaw. All volumes are available in Polish at cbj.jhi.pl. The series is currently being translated into English.

9. Order by Hans Frank dated September 20, 1940, on limits on free choice of a place of living in the General Government, in *Dziennik Rozporządzeń dla Generalnego Gubernatorstwa* [Journal of ordinances for the General Government], 288.

10. Instructions by Heydrich on policy and operations concerning Jews in occupied territories, September 21, 1939, in *Documents on the Holocaust, Selected Sources on the Destruction of the Jews of Germany and Austria, Poland and the Soviet Union*, ed. Y. Arad, Y. Gutman, and A. Margolit (Jerusalem: Yad Vashem, 1981), 173–78.

11. Order by Hans Frank on establishing the Jewish Councils, in *Eksterminacja Żydów na Ziemiach polskich w okresie okupacji hitlerowskiej: zbiór dokumentów*, ed. T. Berenstein, A. Eisenbach, and A. Rutkowski (Warsaw: Żydowski Instytut Historyczny, 1957), 73–74.

12. Order by Fischer on the Establishment of a Ghetto in Warsaw, October 2, 1940, in Arad, Gutman, and Margolit, *Documents on the Holocaust*, 220–21.

13. On the Warsaw Blue Police, see Jan Grabowski and Dariusz Libionka, "Reports on the Jews Apprehended in Warsaw during May–July 1943 Submitted by the 'Praga' District of the Polish Police," *Holocaust Studies and Materials*, no. 4 (2017): 487–518. On Polish Kriminalpolizei (Criminal Police) in Warsaw, see Jan Grabowski, "Hunting Down Emanuel Ringelblum: The Participation of the Polish Kriminalpolizei in the 'Final Solution of the Jewish Question,'" *Holocaust Studies and Materials*, no. 4 (2017): 9–41; Dariusz Libionka, "Zapisy dotyczące Żydów w warszawskich kronikach policyjnych z lat 1942–1944," *Zagłada Żydów: Studia i Materiały*, no. 10 (2014): 558–91.

14. Aleksander Reszczyński (1892–1943)—prewar commandant of the Polish State Police in Vilna, L'viv, Cracow, and Poznań. On June 26, 1941, after the arrest of Marian Kozielewski, he was appointed commandant of the Blue Police in Warsaw. He was assassinated by Gwardia Ludowa, an armed communist underground

organization created by the Polish Workers' Party. Franciszek Przymusiński (1889–1945)—officer of the Polish State Police. From 1932 to 1939, commandant of the state police in Rypin. From June 1940, deputy commandant of the Blue Police in Warsaw. After Reszczyński's assassination in March 1943, commandant of the Blue Police in Warsaw. In January 1945, deported to the Soviet Union, where he died. Marek Getter, Franciszek Przymusiński, Internetowy Polski Słownik Biograficzny, http://ipsb.nina.gov.pl/index.php/a/franciszek—august—przymusinski. See AIPN, MBP 2355, Komenda Policji Polskiej m.st. Warszawy, Skład osobowy Korpusu Oficerskiego.

15. Archiwum Akt Nowych (AAN), 203/III/123, Relacja z odprawy u komendanta m. Warszawy, 4.

16. APW, PRŻ, RG 21, "40 Weekly Report of the Chairman of the Jewish Council for the Period from January 17 to January 23, 1941." The Nazi-introduced term "Aryan" denoting non-Jewish was commonly used in the ghetto and appeared in ghetto diaries and documents. It will therefore also be used in this book.

17. JHIA, ARG I 646 (I/502), T. Witelson, study on the [Jewish] Order Service in the Warsaw Ghetto, 19. Printed in *Archiwum Ringelbluma: Konspiracyjne Archiwum Getta Warszawy*, vol. 34, *Getto warszawskie, cz. II*, ed. T. Epsztein (Warsaw: Żydowski Instytut Historyczny, 2016), 583–626.

18. Stanisław Adler, *In the Warsaw Ghetto 1940–1943: An Account of a Witness; The Memoirs of Stanisław Adler*, trans. Sara Philip (Jerusalem: Yad Vashem, 1982), 134.

19. The Ordnungsdienst in Cracow was set up in July 1940 at the same time as the Judenrat, even though the ghetto was closed in March 1941. Alicja Jarkowska-Natkaniec, "Jüdischer Ordnungsdienst in Occupied Cracow during the Years 1940–1945," *Scripta Judaica Cracoviensia* 11 (2013): 147–60.

20. See Dieter Pohl, *Nationalsozialistische Judenverfolgung in Ostgalizien: 1941–1944; Organisation und Durchführung eines staatlichen Massenverbrechens* (Munich: Oldenbourg, 1997), 165.

21. "Półrocze Służby Porządkowej w Warszawie," [Half a year of the Order Service in Warsaw]), *Gazeta Żydowska*, May 13, 1941.

22. Adam Czerniaków, *Adama Czerniakowa dziennik getta warszawskiego 6 IX 1939–23 VII 1942*, ed. M. Fuks (Warsaw: Wydawnictwo Naukowe PWN, 1983), entry from October 13, 1940, 158.

23. There is no further information regarding T. Witelson. There are three men with this surname in the Jewish Order Service name register: Samuel (no. 162), Abraham (no. 896), and Gecel (no. 908). Leopold Kupczykier (1891–1943)—factory owner, social activist, and member of the Warsaw Jewish Council, where he was the head of the Welfare Department and of the Judenrat Department of the Jewish Order Service. He was murdered at the Majdanek concentration camp in November 1943. JHIA, ARG I 646 (I/502), Witelson, study on the [Jewish] Order Service, 3. According to Wittelson this meeting was to take place on October 9. There is no confirmation of this information in Czerniaków's diary.

24. Edward Kobryner (1880–1943)—prewar judge of the Commercial Court; in the ghetto, member of the Warsaw Jewish Council, director of the Bank of the Jewish District. Murdered in the first days of the Warsaw Ghetto Uprising.

25. See "Utworzenie referatu prasowego w Kom. Gł. P.P." [Setting up of the press department in the headquarters of the state police], *Na Posterunku*, no. 15 (1929), May 14, 1929.

26. AAN, Komenda Główna Policji Państwowej, RG 81. Wykaz oficerów PP Komendy Głównej i będących na etacie Komendy Głównej PP. See also Robert Litwiński, *Policja Państwowa w województwie lubelskim w latach 1919–1939* (Lublin: Wydawnictwo UMCS, 2001), 314. It is not known when Szeryński changed his name and religion. In the Polish State Police documentation preserved in the AAN, he appears only under the name "Szeryński." Leszek Smolak, who wrote about police publications in the interwar period, points out an article published in the December 8, 1919, issue of *Gazeta Policyjna Państwowa* authored by a Szenkman, whom Smolak identifies as Szeryński. Leszek Smolak, *Prasa Policji Państwowej 1918–1939* (Warsaw: Vipart, 2003), 57, 87n12.

27. JHIA, 302/129 ([Stanisław Gombiński?], memoir), 44.

28. On that, see Ziemowit Bernard Kayzer, "Kadry urzędów Bezpieczeństwa Publicznego i ich rozmieszczenie w autonomicznym województwie śląskim w latach 1922–1939," *Zeszyty Naukowe WSOWL* 3, no. 161 (2011): 277–78, and Janusz Mikitin and Grzegorz Grześkowiak, *Policja Województwa Śląskiego 1922–1939* (Piekary Śląskie: ZP Grupa, 2008).

29. Józef Szeryński, "Granatowe mundury na polu chwały" [Navy-blue uniforms in the field of glory], *Polska Zbrojna*, no. 77-a (March 19, 1929): 19–28. See, among others, Józef Szeryński, "Co dają nam nowe przepisy dyscyplinarne?" [What do we gain from new disciplinary regulations?], *Przegląd Policyjny*, no. 2 (1939): 91–99, and H. Walczak, A. Barta, J. Płotnicki, A. Robaczewski, and J. Szeryński, and Z. Krzyżanowski, eds., *Obowiązujące Rozkazy i Okólniki Komendanta głównego Policji Państwowej w układzie rzeczowym* (Warsaw: n.p., 1927). Józef Szeryński, "Jeszcze o prze-mytnikach" [More on the smugglers], *Na Posterunku*, October 23, 1938.

30. Józef Szeryński, "Jak Cię widzą—tak Cię piszą" [How they see you], *Na Posterunku*, July 21, 1935; Józef Szeryński, "Uprzejmość nacodzień" [Everyday politeness], *Na Posterunku*, May 12, 1935.

31. *Dobry Wieczór Warszawa*, no. 260 (November 10, 1930).

32. J. S., "W mieście stu minaretów (korespondencja własna 'Polski Zbrojnej')" [In the city of a hundred minarets (Correspondence of "Polska Zbrojna")], *Polska Zbrojna*, September 10, 1930.

33. Gombiński, *Wspomnienia policjanta,* 220–22. Leon Berenson (1882–1941)—well-known prewar attorney, member of the City Council of Warsaw, and a counselor of the Polish embassy in the United States. He gained fame defending political prisoners in 1905–8. Berenson died in the ghetto of natural causes in April 1941. Survivng fragments of Berenson's wartime diary were published in M. Czajka and T. Epsztein, eds., "Nieznany dziennik z getta warszawskiego," *Kwartalnik Historii Żydów*, no. 1 (2013): 32–67. On Stanisław Gombiński, see M. Janczewska, "Wstęp," in Gombiński, *Wspomnienia policjanta.*

34. Adler, *In the Warsaw Ghetto*, 23. Berenson repeatedly mentions his health in his diary. See Czajka and Epsztein, "Nieznany dziennik z getta warszawskiego."

35. Maksymilian Schönbach (1876–1942)—lawyer, social activist, and head of the secretariat of the Directorate of the Jewish Order Service. Died of natural causes in February 1942.

36. "Zmiany personalne kierownictwa Służby Porządkowej w Warszawie" [Changes in the leadership of the Order Service in Warsaw], *Gazeta Żydowska*, December 17, 1940.

37. Ewa Koźmińska-Frejlak, "Świadectwo milczenia: Rozmowa z Jerzym Lewińskim, byłym funkcjonariuszem Służby Porządkowej getta warszawskiego," *Zagłada Żydów: Studia i Materiały* (2006), 258.

38. Gombiński, *Wspomnienia policjanta*, 156.

39. For example, the commandant and a number of high-ranking officers in the Jewish Order Service in the Częstochowa Ghetto served before the war in the Polish State Police. See Isaiah Trunk, *Judenrat: The Jewish Councils in Eastern Europe under Nazi Occupation* (New York: Macmillan, 1972), 486.

40. Marian Kozielewski (1897–1964)—from 1934 until 1939, commandant of the state police in Warsaw. From 1939, commandant of the Blue Police in Warsaw. From 1940, involved in the Polish Underground. In May 1940, arrested and deported to Auschwitz. He was freed in May 1941 and became involved in the Polish Underground state. Committed suicide in Washington, DC, in 1964. Bolesław Buyko (1899–1947)—lawyer; in 1930s, deputy superintendent of the state police in Warsaw. During the war, deputy superintendent of the Blue Police there.

41. AAN, AK, 203/III/124, 113.

42. Litwiński, *Policja Państwowa*, 75.

43. Gombiński, *Wspomnienia policjanta*, 156.

44. JHIA, ARG I 646 (I/502), Witelson, study on the [Jewish] Order Service, 3.

45. Czerniaków, *Adama Czerniakowa dziennik*, October 27, 1940, 160.

46. Gombiński, *Wspomnienia policjanta*, 160.

47. Adler, *In the Warsaw Ghetto*, 103. Bernard Zundelewicz (1886–1943)—before the war, president of the Small Traders Society, lawyer. In the ghetto, member of the Jewish Council. From December 1940, he headed the Jewish Order Service Department of the Jewish Council.

48. YVA, O.3/2996 (Marceli Reich, testimony).

49. Adler, *In the Warsaw Ghetto*, 108.

50. Czerniaków, *Adama Czerniakowa dziennik*, April 25, 1940, 107; also June 5, 1940, 119.

51. Marian Händel (1905–83)—originating from L'viv, before the war he worked in trade and in cinemas. After the war, he lived in Venezuela.

52. Gombiński, *Wspomnienia policjanta*, 160.

53. Waldemar Schön (1904–69)—from January 1940, head of the Ressettlement Division of the Warsaw District (Umsiedlung). In May 1941, replaced in the authority over the Warsaw Ghetto by Heinz Auerswald.

54. Marcin Urynowicz, *Adam Czerniaków, 1880–1940: życie i działalność* (Warsaw, IPN: 2008), 273; Czerniaków, *Adama Czerniakowa dziennik*, May 31, 1940, 118.

55. Adler writes that due to Szeryński's negative attitude, it was in fact Schönbach who acted as his deputy. Adler, *In the Warsaw Ghetto*, 63.

56. JHIA, ARG I 646 (I/502), Witelson, study on the [Jewish] Order Service, 9.

57. On the Czapliński brothers, see JHIA, ARG I 646 (I/502), Witelson, study on the [Jewish] Order Service, 31–32. See also *Nasz Przegląd Ilustrowany: Dodatek specjalny do "Naszego Przeglądu,"* March 26, 1939, photograph on p. 8.

58. JHIA, ARG I 435 (I/100), Z. Millet, memories of working in the [Jewish] Order Service, 1, trans. in *The Ringelblum Archive: Underground Archive of the Warsaw Ghetto*, vol. 1: *Warsaw Ghetto: Everyday Life*, ed. K. Person (Warsaw: ŻIH, 2017), 590.

59. Adler, *In the Warsaw Ghetto*, 9.

60. See APW, Starostwo Miejskie w Warszawie (SW), RG 17, "Report on the Organization of the Jewish Order Service by the Jewish Council in Warsaw together with the Organizational Rules of the Service," 14–18. In comparison, candidates for the Blue Police were required to have no criminal record, Polish nationality, be twenty to thirty years of age, have four years of secondary school education, and to be, with their wives, of Aryan background. See Adam Hempel, *Pogrobowcy klęski: rzecz o policji "granatowej" w Generalnym Gubernatorstwie 1939–1945* (Warsaw: PWN, 1990), 94.

61. "Utworzenie Służby Porządkowej przy Gminie Żydowskiej w Warszawie" [Setting up of the Order Service by the Judenrat in Warsaw], *Gazeta Żydowska*, November 8, 1940. According to Stanisław Gombiński, applications were no longer accepted already a day after *Gazeta Żydowska* published information about the intake. Gombiński, *Wspomnienia policjanta*, 154. In his 1940 notes regarding the Jewish Order Service, Hersz Wasser writes that seven thousand applications were filed. There is no other confirmation of this number. JHIA, ARG I 52 (I/1088), Hersz Wasser, notes.

62. APW, PRŻ, RG 6, "Report on the Activities of the Jewish Council in Warsaw from October 7 to December 31, 1940."

63. Gombiński, *Wspomnienia policjanta*, 165.

64. Imion, "Panie Władzo . . ." (Reportaż z życia Żydowskiej Służby Porządkowej w Warszawie.)" ["Mr. Constable . . ." (Feature on the life of the Jewish Order Service in Warsaw)], *Gazeta Żydowska*, December 10, 1940.

65. APW, PRŻ, RG 16, "29, 30 i 31 Weekly Report of the Chairman of the Jewish Council for the Period from November 1 to November 21, 1940"; APW, SW, RG 17, "Report on the Organization of the Jewish Order Service by the Jewish Council in Warsaw together with the Organizational Rules of the Service"; "Szkolenie żydowskiej służby porządkowej" [Training of the Jewish Order Service], *Gazeta Żydowska*, November 8, 1940.

66. Adler, *In the Warsaw Ghetto*, 13.

67. "Z Żydowskiej Służby Porządkowej w Warszawie" [From the Jewish Order Service in Warsaw], *Gazeta Żydowska*, December 24, 1940. Yiddish-language courses for members of the Jewish Order Service were set up in January 1941. "Kursy języka żydowskiego" [Yiddish language courses], *Gazeta Żydowska*, January 31, 1941.

68. Helena Szereszewska, *Krzyż i mezuza* (Warsaw: Czytelnik, 1993), 52–53.

69. Mejer Bałaban (1877–1943)—historian of the history and culture of Polish Jews, professor at the University of Warsaw, cofounder of the Institute for Judaic Studies (Instytut Nauk Judaistycznych) in Warsaw. In the ghetto, he was the head of the Archival Department of the Jewish Council. He died in the ghetto in January 1943.

70. JHIA, Kolekcja rodziny Melchior, S/373, j. 42. Mojsze Bursztyn most likely did not join the Jewish Order Service; he worked in the Jewish Social Self-Help. JHIA, Kolekcja rodziny Melchior, S/373, j. 42.

71. JHIA, ARG I 435 (I/100), Z. Millet, memories of working in the [Jewish] Order Service, 4.

72. USC Shoah Foundation Visual History Archive, Jacob Epstein, interview 14342.

73. "Z Żydowskiej Służby Porządkowej w Warszawie" [From the Jewish Order Service in Warsaw], *Gazeta Żydowska*, December 24, 1940.

74. "Współpraca obywateli z Radą Żydowską w Warszawie" [Citizens' cooperation with the Jewish Council in Warsaw], *Gazeta Żydowska*, January 17, 1942.

75. APW, Urząd Szefa Okręgu Warszawskiego—Komisarz dla żydowskiej dzielnicy mieszkaniowej w Warszawie (KŻDM), RG 18, "Weekly Report of the Jewish Order Service in the Jewish Residential District in Warsaw, September 14–September 20, 1941"; "Reorganizacja służby zdrowia" [Reorganization of health care], *Gazeta Żydowska*, September 17, 1941.

76. According to Witelson, it was 130 people. See Witelson, study on the [Jewish] Order Service, 10.

77. Witelson, 71.

78. APW, PRŻ, "Weekly Report of the Chairman of the Jewish Council on Activities of the Jewish Council for January–June 1942."

79. YIVO, HWC, 42.2, Hersz Wasser, ekspertyza.

80. JHIA, ARG I 648 (I/181), Amas Freund, "Modern Tales by Hoffman: Stories about the Bribe Service, Otherwise Known as the [Jewish] Order Service," 4, trans. in *Ringelblum Archive*, vol. 1, 605.

81. JHIA, ARG I 646 (I/502), Witelson, study on the [Jewish] Order Service, 10.

82. JHIA, ARG I 648 (I/181), Freund, "Modern Tales by Hoffman," 4. Such certificates were not always accepted. See Czerniaków, *Adama Czerniakowa dziennik*, May 16, 1941, 181.

83. USC Shoah Foundation Visual History Archive, Richard Jacobs, interview 25500.

84. Koźmińska-Frejlak, "Świadectwo milczenia," 257. Jerzy Lewiński (1911–2006)—administrative head of the Third District. In September 1942, he transferred to the Werterfassung (institution for takeover of property left behind by deported Jews). After the war, he worked as a lawyer and sports activist.

85. JHIA, 313/35, Sąd Społeczny przy Centralnym Komitecie Żydów w Polsce, Oświadczenie Ludwiki Oliszewskiej.

86. Adler, *In the Warsaw Ghetto*, 181.

87. JHIA, 313/141 (Sąd Społeczny przy Centralnym Komitecie Żydów w Polsce, Abram Wolfowicz), protokół zeznania Zdenka Wolańskiego (Abrama Wolfowicza) z 15 marca 1948 r.

Berthold Dobrin (Drobin)—lawyer from Bydgoszcz, from November 1939 in Warsaw. In the ghetto, chairman of the Central Refugee Commission.

Abraham Gepner (1872–1943)—prewar member of the Warsaw City Council and chairman of the Union of Jewish Merchants. In the ghetto, member of the Jewish Council and head of its Supply Department. Murdered in the Warsaw Ghetto Uprising.

88. JHIA, ARG I 646 (I/502), Witelson, study on the [Jewish] Order Service, 8.

89. As Barbara Engelking and Jacek Leociak point out, this can explain lack of recruits from the working class, which was at that point the most pauperized. See Barbara Engelking and Jacek Leociak, *Warsaw Ghetto: Guide to the Perished City* (New Haven, CT: Yale University Press, 2009), 193.

90. Gabriela Zalewska, *Ludność żydowska w Warszawie w okresie międzywojennym* (Warsaw: PWN, 1996), 231.

91. Dz. U. 1938 no. 40, poz. 334, Rozporządzenie Ministra Sprawiedliwości z dnia 4 czerwca 1938 o zamknięciu list adwokatów i list aplikantów adwokackich. On limits on the numbers of Jewish attorneys, see Tomasz Kotliński, "Kwestie narodowościowe i wyznaniowe w adwokaturze polskiej dwudziestolecia międzywojennego: Wybrane

zagadnienia," in *Cuius regio, eius religio?*, ed. G. Górski, L. Ćwikła, and M. Lipska (Lublin: Wydawnictwo KUL, 2008), 335–42, and Szymon Rudnicki, "Walka o zmianę ustawy o adwokaturze w II Rzeczypospolitej," in Szymon Rudnicki, *Równi, ale niezupełnie* (Warsaw: Biblioteka Midrasza, 2008), 171–89.

92. See Janczewska, "Wstęp," in Gombiński, *Wspomnienia policjanta*, 1.

93. On the generational aspect of Third Reich administrative apparatus, see Michael Wildt, *Generation des Unbedingten: Das Führungskorps des Reichssicherheitshauptamtes* (Hamburg: Hamburger Edition, 2002).

94. Gombiński, *Wspomnienia policjanta*, 167.

95. JHIA, 313/109 (Sąd Społeczny przy Centralnym Komitecie Żydów w Polsce, Szapsel Rotholc), Oświadczenie Racheli Auerbach.

96. USC Shoah Foundation Visual History Archive, Jack Pressman, interview 12401.

97. USC Shoah Foundation Visual History Archive, Henry Nusbaum, interview 10658.

98. USC Shoah Foundation Visual History Archive, Jacob Epstein, interview 14342.

99. Icchak Cukierman, "Antek," in *Nadmiar pamięci (siedem owych lat): Wspomnienia 1939–1946*, trans. Z. Perelmuter (Warsaw: PWN, 2000), 80. According to Józef Gitler, Arie Grzybowski went through the Bergen-Belsen concentration camp and was murdered in Auschwitz-Birkenau. Józef Gitler, *Leben am seidenen Faden: Tagebuch aus dem Austauschlager Bergen-Belsen*, trans. J. Liedke, ed. K. Liedke (Göttingen: Wallstein Verlag, 2015), 33.

100. Cukierman, *Nadmiar pamięci*, 80. Most likely Ignacy Engelman (service number 306). JHIA, 221/15, Rada Żydowska w Warszawie, Wykaz imienny funkcjonariuszy Służby Porządkowej.

101. Izrael Kanał (?—1943)—beginning in 1942, a member of the Jewish Fighting Organization. He resigned from the Jewish Order Service in July 1942. In the Warsaw Ghetto Uprising, he led the fighters in the central ghetto area. Cukierman, *Nadmiar pamięci*, 147.

102. JHIA, 301/5343 (Marek Edelman, testimony). He appears on the list of Jewish Order Service members as Mieczysław Mojsiej Dąb (service number 354).

103. JHIA, 221/15, Rada Żydowska w Warszawie, Wykaz imienny funkcjonariuszy Służby Porządkowej. See also Cukierman, *Nadmiar pamięci*, 236, and the editor's note in Yitzhak Zuckerman, *A Surplus of Memory: Chronicle of the Warsaw Ghetto Uprising*, trans. and ed. B. Harshav (Berkeley: University of California Press, 1993), 205n64.

104. Koźmińska-Frejlak, "Świadectwo milczenia," 265–66.

105. JHIA, ARG I 646 (I/502), Witelson, study on the [Jewish] Order Service, 3.

106. Melania (Maria) Wassermanówna-Wisłowska (1907–75)—famous translator from German (H. Mann), French (S. de Beauvoir), English, and Russian.

107. JHIA, 302/129 ([Stanisław Gombiński?], memoir), 25.

108. According to one of the Jewish Order Service medical doctors, Ignacy Rejder, doctors were given this privilege only in 1941 to safeguard them during forced-labor camps roundups. JHIA, 313/101 (Sąd Społeczny przy Centralnym Komitecie Żydów w Polsce, Ignacy Rejder-Romejko), Protokół z dnia 9 czerwca 1949 w sprawie dr.

Ignacego Romejko. The term "civilian officers" is used by Henryk Makower (Henryk Makower, *Pamiętnik z getta warszawskiego październik 1940—styczeń 1943* (Wrocław: Ossolineum, 1987), 126).

109. Zygmunt Fajncyn (1889–1941)—dermatologist and chief physician of the Judenrat and the Jewish Order Service. Julian Lewinson (1900–43)—radiographer, medical doctor. After the Warsaw Ghetto Uprising, deported to Majdanek where he died. Włodzimierz Zadziewicz (1906–43)—laryngologist. See the testimony of his wife, Maria (JHIA, 301/2225). Henryk Makower (1904–64)—medical doctor; after the war, virologist, professor of microbiology at the Medical Academy in Wrocław. See Makower, *Pamiętnik z getta warszawskiego*, as well as a memoir by his wife, Noemi Makower, *Miłość w cieniu śmierci: Wspomnienia z getta warszawskiego* (Wrocław: Erechtejon, 1996).

110. Józef Jaszuński (1881–1943)—engineer, social activist, and educator. In the ghetto, member of the Judenrat and deputy head of the Jewish Social Self-Help. Murdered on January 18, 1943.

111. APW, KŻDM, RG 18, Heinz Auerswald, letter to Adam Czerniaków, December 11, 1941.

112. Szeryński did not leave any personal notes. His visits in KdS are described by Czerniaków, *Adama Czerniakowa dziennik*, November 21, 1941, 229.

113. On that, see Stephan Lehnstaedt, *Okkupation im Osten: Besatzeralltag in Warschau und Minsk 1939–1944* (Munich: R. Oldenbourg Verlag, 2010), 278–79.

114. See Wolfgang Curilla, *Der Judenmord in Polen und die deutsche Ordnungspolizei 1939–1945* (Paderborn: Schöningh, 2011), 533–682, and Stefan Klemp, *Vernichtung: Die deutsche Ordnungspolizei und der Judenmord im Warschauer Ghetto 1940–43* (Berlin: Prospero, 2013). None of these authors writes in detail about the relations between the German Order Police and the Jewish Order Service. On the participation of the Warsaw KdS in executions of Jews outside Warsaw, see Lehnstaedt, *Okkupation im Osten*, 40.

115. The Transferstelle was the German authority that from December 1940 controlled the exchange of goods between the ghetto and the Aryan side. On German workshops in the Warsaw Ghetto, see Helge Grabitz and Wolfgang Scheffler, *Letzte Spuren: Ghetto Warschau—SS-Arbeitslager Trawniki—Aktion Erntefest: Fotos und Dokumente über Opfer des Endlösungswahns im Spiegel der historischen Ereignisse* (Berlin: Hentrich, 1988).

116. See Czerniaków, *Adama Czerniakowa dziennik*, November 27, 1940, 168.

117. JHIA, ARG I 646 (I/502), Witelson, study on the [Jewish] Order Service, 68.

118. JHIA, ARG I 646 (I/502), Witelson, 44.

119. See nine weekly reports on the internal matters of the Warsaw Ghetto in *Ludność żydowska w Warszawie w latach 1939–1943—życie-walka-zagłada*, ed. J. Kazimierski (Warsaw: ŻIH, 2012) (CD). In English, the reports were published in "The Reports of a Jewish 'Informer' in the Warsaw Ghetto: Selected Documents," ed. Ch. Browning and Y. Gutman, *Yad Vashem Studies* 17 (1986): 247–93.

120. Adam Rutkowski, "O agenturze gestapowskiej w getcie warszawskim," *Biuletyn Żydowskiego Instytutu Historycznego*, nos. 3–4 (1956): 38–59.

121. JHIA, 302/27 (Samuel Puterman, memoir), 9. For more on that, see Ghetto Fighters House Archive (GFH), Adolf Berman Collection, 5647, "Komitet Ścisły," 8–9.

122. JHIA, ARG I 1342 (I/730), *Żagiew* [Torch], no. 5 (May 1942), 8. The spring of 1942 issues of *Żagiew* were published by a ghetto organization of assimilationists, while the 1943 issues were most likely published by Gestapo collaborators.

123. JHIA, ARG II 281 (II/155), Józef Ehrlich, letter dated May 27, 1941, to Sicherheitspolizei (Security Police).

124. JHIA, ARG II 281 (II/155), Józef Ehrlich, letter dated May 27, 1941, to Sicherheitspolizei.

125. JHIA, ARG II 281 (II/155), Józef Ehrlich, letter August 8, 1941, to Hauptzollamt West.

126. Czerniaków, *Adama Czerniakowa dziennik*, November 4, 1940, 162. On other interpretations of this event, see Czajka and Epsztein, "Nieznany dziennik z getta warszawskiego," 48.

127. Czerniaków, *Adama Czerniakowa dziennik*, May 16, 1941, 181.

128. Samuel Puterman suggested that Kohn and Heller were supported by the Gestapo but not by Auerswald. JHIA, 302/27 (S. Puterman, Pamiętnik), 56.

129. APW, Sąd Okręgowy w Warszawie 1946–1950, 654/III, no. 494, Akta w sprawie Juliana Gojchermana.

130. Czerniaków, *Adama Czerniakowa dziennik*, April 28, 1941, 174.

131. JHIA, ARG I 294 (I/359), Statute of the Office for the Prevention of Usury and Speculation.

132. Abraham Gancwajch (1904–1943?)—prewar journalist; in the ghetto, head of the Thirteen. From August 1941, on the Aryan side.

133. APW, Sąd Okręgowy w Warszawie 1946–1950, 654/III, no. 494, Akta w sprawie Juliana Gojchermana. The topic of the drinking parties was brought up numerous times during the trial of Wiera Gran. See JHIA, 313/36 (Sąd Społeczny przy Centralnym Komitecie Żydów w Polsce, Wiera Gran).

134. Wilhelm Ohlenbusch (1899–1997)—head of the propaganda department in the Warsaw District. From 1941 to 1943, head of the Main Propaganda Department in the General Government.

135. Rutkowski, "O agenturze gestapowskiej w getcie warszawskim," 44.

136. Adler, *In the Warsaw Ghetto*, 131. Stabenow left his testimony on the topic after the war. See USHMM, record group (RG) 14.101M, reel 2164, Zentrale Stelle der Landesjustizverwaltungen zur Aufklärung nationalsozialistischer Verbrechen, B 162/5898 "Leben und Tod in Ghettograd"—Aufsatz von Dr. Gerhard Stabenow, AR—Z 25/62.

137. APW, PRŻ, RG 20, "39 Weekly Report of the Chairman of the Jewish Council for the Period from January 19 to January 16, 1941."

138. APW, PRŻ, RG 21, "42, 43 i 44 Weekly Report of the Chairman of the Jewish Council for the Period from January 31 to February 20, 1941."

139. Rutkowski, "O agenturze gestapowskiej w getcie warszawskim," 47–48.

140. JHIA, 302/27 (S. Puterman, memoir), 19.

141. YIVO, HWC 32/1, Hersz Wasser, notes, January 7, 1941, 26.

142. Rutkowski, "O agenturze gestapowskiej w getcie warszawskim," 43.

143. Czerniaków, *Adama Czerniakowa dziennik*, August 5, 1941, 347.

144. Czerniaków, June 6, 1941, 190.

145. Ringelblum, *Pisma z getta*, July–August 1941, 280.

146. JHIA, ARG I 978 (I/236), Jankiel Henig, account titled "What's Going On."

147. See Czerniaków's commentary on Gancwajch's visits, *Adama Czerniakowa dziennik*, February 25, 1942, 256.

148. Abraham Lewin, *A Cup of Tears: A Diary of the Warsaw Ghetto*, ed. A. Polonsky (London: Blackwell, 1989), 160 (entry of August 18). In May, Czerniaków wrote that Gancwajch was interested in the position of the commander of the Jewish Order Service. Czerniaków, *Adama Czerniakowa dziennik*, May 18, 1942, 279.

149. "Karetki ratunkowe Żydowskiego Pogotowia Ratunkowego" [Ambulances of the Jewish Emergancy Service], *Gazeta Żydowska*, June 27, 1941.

150. According to *Gazeta Żydowska*, in July 1941, the Jewish Emergency Service had thirty thousand fee-paying members and planned on enlisting an additional twenty thousand. "50 tysięcy członków Żydowskiego Pogotowia Ratunkowego" [Fifty thousand members of the Jewish Emergency Service], *Gazeta Żydowska* July 18, 1941.

151. APW, Sąd Okręgowy w Warszawie 1946–1950, 654/III, no. 494, Akta w sprawie Juliana Gojchermana.

2. Organization and Objectives of the Service

1. Gombiński, *Wspomnienia policjanta*, 168.

2. Czerniaków, *Adama Czerniakowa dziennik*, November 12, 1940, 164.

3. See JHIA, ARG I 646 (I/502), Witelson, study on the [Jewish] Order Service in the Warsaw Ghetto, 14–16; Adler, *In the Warsaw Ghetto*, 118; APW, PRŻ, RG 20. "38. Weekly Report of the Chairman of the Jewish Council for the Period from January 3 to January 9, 1941."

4. The following have survived to this day: "Service Instructions for the [Jewish] Order Service" of May 21, 1942 (JHIA, ARG I 251); "Instruction for District Officers for the Maintaining of Order" (n.d., JHIA, ARG I 272); daily orders of Superintendent Józef Szeryński from November 1940 to January 1941 (JHIA, ARG I 252); and daily orders of the head of the Fifth District of the [Jewish] Order Service from December 1940 and January 1941 (JHIA, ARG I 253).

5. Members of the Jewish Order Service received uniforms only in the Vilna Ghetto. This took place in October 1942 before they participated in the executions of Jews in Ashmyany. See Trunk, *Judenrat*, 496.

6. "Służba porządkowa w dzielnicy żyd. w Warszawie" [Order Service in the Jewish District in Warsaw], *Gazeta Żydowska*, December 6, 1940; Gombiński, *Wspomnienia policjanta*, 182. On the uniforms in Cracow, see "Służba Porządkowa przy Gminie Żyd. w Krakowie" [Order Service at the Juderat in Cracow], *Gazeta Żydowska*, December 3, 1940.

7. APW, PRŻ, RG 20. "39. Weekly Report of the Chairman of the Jewish Council for the Period from January 10 to January 16, 1941." In the following month, twenty-five pairs of shoes were distributed to members of the Jewish Order Service by the Jewish Social Self-Help.

8. An exception was Vilna, where functionaries of the Jewish Order Service received firearms when carrying out the deportations. Trunk, *Judenrat*, 498.

9. "Z Żydowskiej Służby Porządkowej w Warszawie" [From the Jewish Order Service in Warsaw], *Gazeta Żydowska*, December 24, 1940.

10. Gombiński, *Wspomnienia policjanta*, 162. According to *Gazeta Żydowska*, the Directorate of the service was located in "a small, one-window room." "Półrocze

Służby Porządkowej w Warszawie" [Half a year of the Order Service in Warsaw], *Gazeta Żydowska* May 13, 1941.

11. "Półrocze Służby Porządkowej w Warszawie."

12. For example, in 1941, members of the service were trained in first aid by Jewish Order Service doctors. "Szkolenie funkcjonariuszy Sł. Porząd. z zakresu ratownictwa" [Emergency aid training of members of the Order Service], *Gazeta Żydowska*, May 30, 1941.

13. Based on JHIA, 302/129 ([Stanisław Gombiński?], memoir), 1–3, and Gombiński, *Wspomnienia policjanta*, 163–64.

14. "Utworzenie Referatu Obrony Przeciwlotniczej przy kierowniku Służby Porz" [Creation of the Anti-aircraft Defense Department by the Directorate of the Order Service], *Gazeta Żydowska*, May 30, 1941. On details regarding members of the Directorate, see Gombiński, *Wspomnienia policjanta*, 168–71.

15. Marta Janczewska, "Gazeta Żydowska" (1940–42), in *Studia z dziejów trójjęzycznej prasy żydowskiej na ziemiach polskich XIX—XX wieku*, ed. J. Nalewajko-Kulikov et al. (Warsaw: IH PAN, Neriton, 2012), 176.

16. "Szkolenie kierowników policyjnych" [Training of police leaders], *Gazeta Żydowska*, January 3, 1941. A slightly different division is provided by Gombiński, *Wspomnienia policjanta*, 180.

17. Józef Rode (1895–?)—before the war, served in the cavalry. In the ghetto, he was at the head of the Gmina Precinct and later the Central Lockup. See "List of Polish Legionnaires 1914–1918" of the Józef Pi łsudski Museum in Sulejówek, https://zolnierze-niepodleglosci.pl/.

18. The headquarters of the First District was at 15 Twarda Street (the first commander was Karol Peczenik (1897–?)—lawyer, attorney, after the war a judge and later an attorney in Cracow). The Second District was at 15 Chłodna Street (led by lawyer Henryk Nadel [1903–?]). The Third District was at 40 Leszno Street (led Albin Fleischman [1897–1943?]—captain in the Polish army). The Fourth District was at 4 Gęsia Street (led by Henryk Landau [1901–?]—attorney, born in Vienna). The Fifth District was at 19 Zamenhofa Street (led by Oskar Sekler). The Sixth District was at 42 Gęsia Street (led by lawyer Józef Jerzy Hertz [1900–?]). The Gmina Precinct's headquarters was in the building of the Jewish Council at 26/28 Grzybowska Street (led by Józef Rode).

19. See JHIA, ARG I 49 (II/136), Jewish Council in Warsaw, announcement dated May 7, 1941 about preparations for anti-aircraft defense.

20. According to Adler, Henryk Weisblat was later removed from the service for embezzlement. Adler, *In the Warsaw Ghetto*, 188–90.

21. "Utworzenie Referatu Obrony Przeciwlotniczej."

22. JHIA, 302/129 ([Stanisław Gombiński?], memoir), 68.

23. JHIA, ARG I 251 (I/227), "Official Instruction for the Order Service," art. 29.

24. "Ze Służby Porządkowej" [From the Order Service], *Gazeta Żydowska*, February 6, 1942.

25. JHIA, 302/129 ([Stanisław Gombiński?], memoir), 111.

26. APW, PRŻ, RG 6, "Report on the Activities of the Jewish Council in Warsaw from October 7, 1939, until December 31, 1940."

27. "Utworzenia Pogotowia Straży Pożarnej" [Creation of the Emergency Fire Service], *Gazeta Żydowska*, July 24, 1942.

28. "Decentralizacja i organizacja Służby Porządkowej w terenie" [Decentralization and organization of the Order Service in the field], *Gazeta Żydowska*, January 31, 1941.

29. JHIA, ARG I 435 (I/100), Z. Millet, memories of working in the [Jewish] Order Service, 5, trans. in *Ringelblum Archive*, vol. 1, 594.

30. JHIA, ARG I 413 (I/435), G., information collected in a conversation with an officer of the [Jewish] Order Service (May 2, 1942), 2.

31. JHIA, ARG I 252 (I/14), orders of the day of Józef Szeryński, November 1940–January 1941, order no. 42 of December 23, 1940. Printed in *Archiwum Ringelbluma: Konspiracyjne Archiwum Getta Warszawy*, vol. 12, *Rada Żydowska w Warszawie (1939–1943)*, ed. Marta Janczewska (Warsaw: Żydowski Instytut Historyczny, 2014), 245–317.

32. See JHIA, ARG I 252 (I/14), orders of the day of Józef Szeryński, November 1940–January 1941, and JHIA, ARG I 253 (I/206), Oskar Sekler, head of District V of the [Jewish] Order Service, daily orders, nos. 3 and 4 of January 12 and 14, 1941.

33. AIPN, 165/367, "Raporty dzienne KSP dla niemieckiego komisarza o planowanych czynnościach służbowych i stwierdzonych uchybieniach porządkowych w getcie."

34. APW, KŻDM, RG 18, "Weekly Report of the Jewish Order Service in the Jewish Residental District in Warsaw, June 22, 1941–July 10, 1942."

35. JHIA, ARG I 252 (I/14), orders of the day of Józef Szeryński, November 1940–January 1941, order no. 64 of January 13, 1941.

36. JHIA, ARG I 252 (I/14), orders of the day of Józef Szeryński, November 1940–January 1941, order no. 62 of January 12, 1941.

37. JHIA, ARG I 251 (I/227), official instructions for the [Jewish] Order Service, art. 22. Printed in *Archiwum Ringelbluma*, vol. 12, 228–44.

38. "Dorożki dla Żyd. Służby Porządkowej w nagłych wypadkach" [Cabs for the Jewish Order Service in urgent cases], *Gazeta Żydowska*, February 25, 1941.

39. JHIA, ARG I 251 (I/227), official instructions for the [Jewish] Order Service, art. 23.

40. JHIA, ARG I 251 (I/227), official instructions for the [Jewish] Order Service, art. 24.

41. Marek Passenstein, "Szmugiel w getcie warszawskim," *Biuletyn Żydowskiego Instytutu Historycznego*, no. 2 (1958): 47–48.

42. Bundesarchiv Berlin, ZM 886, A.3, 4. On German violence by the ghetto walls, see Jan H. Issinger, "Frankenstein w warszawskim getcie: Historia i legenda," *Zagłada Żydów: Studia i Materiały*, no. 12 (2016): 187–208.

43. JHIA, ARG I 646 (I/502), Witelson, study on the [Jewish] Order Service, 21.

44. Aharon Weiss, *Hamishtara hayehudit baGeneral-Gouvernement uvi-Shlezia Ha'ilit bitkufat ha-Shoa* (Jerusalem: Hebrew University, 1973), 71.

45. See Jan Grabowski, "Żydzi przed obliczem niemieckich i polskich sądów w Dystrykcie Warszawskim Generalnej Guberni, 1939–1942," in *Prowincja noc: Życie i zagłada Żydów w dystrykcie warszawskim 1939–1945*, ed. B. Engelking, J. Leociak, and D. Libionka, 75–119 (Warsaw: IFiS PAN, 2007).

46. APW, KŻDM, RG 18, "Weekly Reports of the Jewish Order Service in the Jewish Residential District in Warsaw."

47. One such person was Chaim Kaplan, who commented in his diary on how much he valued seeing the Aryan side again. Chaim Aron Kaplan, *Scroll of*

Agony: The Warsaw Diary of Chaim A. Kaplan, ed. A. I. Katsch (New York: Macmillan, 1965), 295–96. Jews released from prisons on the Aryan side signed a declaration that they would go straight to the ghetto and were aware of the possibility of the death penalty should they not do so. USHMM, Więzienie Karne Mokotów Zespół no. 657/0, Mikrofilm no. 18323. Oświadczenie.

48. APW, KŻDM, RG 2, weekly reports on the situation in the ghetto, March 24–May 19, 1942, 30.

49. APW, PRŻ, RG 19, "38. Weekly Report of the Chairman of the Jewish Council for the Period from January 3 to January 9, 1941."

50. "Żydowska dzielnica mieszkaniowa w Warszawie od 16.XI.1940 r. do 1.XI.1941 r." On the Criminal Department of the Jewish Order Service in L'viv, see "Wydział Kryminalny Żydowskiej Służby Porządkowej" [Criminal Department of the Jewish Order Service], *Gazeta Żydowska*, February 4, 1942.

51. "Nowe uprawnienia Służby Porządkowej" [New prerogatives of the Order Service], *Gazeta Żydowska*, June 3, 1942.

52. "Działalność mediacyjna Służby Porz." [Mediation activities of the Order Service], *Gazeta Żydowska*, May 6, 1941. According to *Gazeta Żydowska*, the Order Service dealt among other things with "conflicts between neighbors, between tenants and subtenants and marital quarrels."

53. JHIA, 302/129 ([Stanisław Gombiński?], memoir), 11.

54. JHIA, 302/129 ([Stanisław Gombiński?], memoir), 13.

55. "Obowiązki Żyd. Służby Porządkowej w Warszawie" [Duties of the Jewish Order Service in Warsaw], *Gazeta Żydowska*, January 3, 1941.

56. JHIA, ARG I 252 (I/14), orders of the day of Józef Szeryński, November 1940–January 1941, order no. 63 of January 13, 1941.

57. *Le Dernier des injustes* [The last of the unjust], documentary directed by Claude Lanzmann (2013).

58. On that, see Kazimierz Wyka, *Życie na niby* (Cracow: Universitas, 2010).

59. Janusz Korczak, "O projekcie 'dziecko i policja,'" in *Pamiętnik i inne pisma z getta*, ed. M. Ciesielska (Warsaw: WAB, 2012), 229.

60. Barbara Engelking and Jacek Leociak provide addresses of four of them: 20 Nowolipie Street, 12 Nowolipki Street, 6 Gęsia Street, and 21 Chłodna Street. *Warsaw Ghetto*, 201.

61. Szymon Kataszek (1898–1943)—pianist, composer, pioneer of jazz in Poland. He was murdered during the liquidation of the L'viv Ghetto.

62. "U nas w Rejonach . . ." [In our districts . . .], *Gazeta Żydowska*, January 21, 1942. Jerzy "Jerry" Ryba (1909–43?) was a film critic and author of film and revue songs.

3. Violence and Corruption in the Exercise of Daily Duties

1. Czerniaków, *Adama Czerniakowa dziennik*, May 19, 1940, 113.

2. Czerniaków, June 1, 1940, 118; June 8, 1940, 119.

3. Ringelblum, *Pisma z getta*, April 20–May 1, 1940, 102.

4. Ringelblum, April 20–May 1, 1940, 105.

5. Czerniaków, *Adama Czerniakowa dziennik*, June 7, 1940, 119.

6. Czerniaków, June 1940, 122.

7. JHIA, ARG I 646 (I/502), Witelson, study on the [Jewish] Order Service, 15.

8. JHIA, ARG I 251 (I/227), official instructions for the [Jewish] Order Service, art. 5.

9. In May 1941, Ringelblum described policemen wrongly claiming on the street that it was already past the curfew and taking bribes of "ten to twenty zlotys, a watch, or a ring." Ringelblum, May 11, 1941, *Pisma z getta*, 250.

10. Ringelblum, September 20–26, 1941, *Pisma z getta*, 299.

11. JHIA, ARG I 577 (I/154), Stanisław Różycki, "The Street," 4.

12. See M. Szwarcman, "Popularne słówka w dzielnicy żydowskiej: 'Szafa gra'" [Popular words in the Jewish district: "The jukebox is playing"], *Gazeta Żydowska*, May 2, 1941.

13. JHIA, ARG I 456 (I/429), Stanisław Różycki, "Street Scenes from the Ghetto," 26, trans. in *Ringelblum Archive*, vol. 1, 39.

14. JHIA, ARG I 502 (I/93), "Sanitary Operation at Krochmalna Street," 2. According to Samuel Puterman, three hundred members of the Jewish Order Service participated in this operation. JHIA, 302/27 (S. Puterman, memoir), 2.

15. Samuel Puterman (1915–55)—painter, in the ghetto a member of the Jewish Order Service. He left the ghetto during the Warsaw Ghetto Uprising. After the uprising, he was deported to Sachsenhausen. He died in France.

16. JHIA, 302/27 (S. Puterman, memoir), 3.

17. Czerniaków, *Adama Czerniakowa dziennik*, 211.

18. JHIA, ARG I 502 (I/93), "Sanitary Operation at Krochmalna Street," 3.

19. JHIA, ARG I 513 (I/203), "Lock-Down of an Apartment Block (Nalewki Street)," 3.

20. Peretz Opoczynski, "House No. 21," trans. in *Voices from the Warsaw Ghetto: Writing Our History*, ed. David G. Roskies (New Haven, CT: Yale University Press, 2019), 106.

21. "Orkiestra życia" [The orchestra of life], *Gazeta Żydowska*, November 22, 1940.

22. JHIA, 302/27 (S. Puterman, memoir), 8.

23. JHIA, ARG I 464 (I/270), Akiba Uryson, "A Doctor's Tales," 3, trans. in *Ringelblum Archive*, vol. 1, 400.

24. JHIA, ARG I 413 (I/435), information collected in a conversation with an officer of the [Jewish] Order Service, 7; trans. in *Ringelblum Archive*, vol. 1, 620.

25. JHIA, 301/4325 (Szapsel Rotholc, testimony), 2.

26. APW, KŻDM, RG 40, Unbefugtes der judischen Wohnbezirks, 7. See also Sonderdienst's reports on smuggling in APW, KŻDM, RG 45.

27. Marek (Mojżesz) Passenstein (1900–43)—lawyer and economist. In the ghetto, a member of the Jewish Order Service and collaborator of the Underground Archive of the Warsaw Ghetto. On the Aryan side, he was in hiding with Emanuel Ringelblum. USHMM, RG 15.471, personal files of Jewish students who studied at Warsaw before World War II, RP 10029/S.

28. Passenstein, "Szmugiel w getcie warszawskim," 43.

29. Passenstein, 45–46.

30. Barbara Engelking, *Szanowny panie gistapo: Donosy do władz niemieckich w Warszawie i okolicach w latach 1940–1941* (Warsaw: IFiS PAN, 2003), 41.

31. YIVO, HWC 32/1, Hersz Wasser, notes, December 14, 1940, 12.

32. Czerniaków, *Adama Czerniakowa dziennik*, October 14, 1941, 221.

33. JHIA, 302/27 (S. Puterman, memoir), 21.

34. APW, KŻDM, RG 18, "Weekly Report of the [Jewish] Order Service in the Jewish Residential District in Warsaw, June 22, 1941–July 10, 1942."

35. APW, KŻDM, RG 18, superintendent of the Jewish Order Service to the commissar of the Jewish Order Service, December 21, 1941.

36. Hempel, *Pogrobowcy klęski*, 103. In June 1942, the Warsaw SS und *Polizeiführer* (leader of the SS and police) received a denunciation that a Blue Policeman was seen letting one hundred Polish smugglers into the ghetto. The case also involved members of the Jewish Order Service. APW, KŻDM, RG 46, various, 34.

37. B. Engelking, and J. Grabowski, *Żydów łamiących prawo należy karać śmiercią! "Przestępczość" Żydów w Warszawie, 1939–1942* (Warsaw: IFIS PAN, 2010), 17.

38. JHIA, ARG I 251 (I/227), official instruction for the [Jewish] Order Service, art. 39.

39. APW, PRŻ, RG 21, "42, 43 and 44. Weekly Report of the Chairman of the Jewish Council for the Period from January 31 to February 20, 1941."

40. See "Broszura o zadaniach Służby Porzą" [Pamphlet on the duties of the Order Service], *Gazeta Żydowska*, July 7, 1942.

41. Józef Prussak, "Lecture on the Duties and Behaviour of a Member of the [Jewish] Order Service," in Alina Podolska, *Służba Porządkowa w getcie warszawskim w latach 1940–1943* (Warsaw: "Pro Futuro," 1996), 138.

42. "Służba porządkowa—służbą społeczno-obywatelską" [Order Service as a social-civic service], *Gazeta Żydowska*, April 11, 1941.

43. "Służba porządkowa."

44. JHIA, ARG I 251 (I/227), official instruction for the [Jewish] Order Service, art. 9.

45. JHIA, ARG I 252 (I/14), orders of the day of Józef Szeryński, November 1940–January 1941, order no. 63 of January 13, 1941.

46. Ringelblum, *Pisma z getta*, February 27–28, 1941, 212.

47. "Szulchan Aruch," *Der Oyfbroyz* [The upheaval], June 22, 1942. On that, see also AAN, 202/II/28, 50. The policeman who beat up Zusman is identified in this document as Wolf (Władysław) Can. Wolf Can appears on the list of Jewish Order Service members with service number 24.

48. See Nota., "Publiczność na ulicy" [Public on the street], *Gazeta Żydowska*, October 17, 1941.

49. JHIA, ARG I 656 (I/67), minutes of meetings of the apartment house committee at [Nalewki] in Warsaw (July 1939–April 1942) and urgent meeting of the house committee on February 23, 1942. Printed in *Archiwum Ringelbluma: Konspiracyjne Archiwum Getta Warszawy*, vol. 34, *Getto warszawskie, cz. II*, ed. Tadeusz Epsztein (Warsaw: Żydowski Instytut Historyczny, 2016), 304–498.

50. Adler, *In the Warsaw Ghetto*, 248.

51. JHIA, ARG I 588 (I/143), "Quarantine at Leszno Street," transl. *Ringelblum Archive*, vol. 1, 160.

52. JHIA, ARG I 513 (I/203), "Lock-Down of an Apartment Block (Nalewki Street)," 6, trans. in *Ringelblum Archive*, vol. 1, 397.

53. JHIA, ARG I 513 (I/203), "Lock-Down of an Apartment Block (Nalewki Street)," 9.

54. Ludwik Landau, *Kronika lat wojny i okupacji*, vol. 1, ed. Z. Landau and J. Tomaszewski (Warsaw: PWN, 1962), 694. On the transports to camps in the autumn of 1940, see Czerniaków, *Adama Czerniakowa dziennik*, October 3–19, 1940, 147–52.

55. On that, see Marta Janczewska, "Obozy pracy przymusowej dla Żydów na terenie dystryktu warszawskiego," in *Prowincja noc: Życie i zagłada Żydów w dystrykcie warszawskim 1939–1945*, ed. B. Engelking, J. Leociak, and D. Libionka (Warsaw: IFIS PAN, 2007), 272.

56. Tatiana Berenstein, "Żydzi warszawscy w hitlerowskich obozach pracy przymusowej," *Biuletyn Żydowskiego Instytutu Historycznego*, no. 3 (1967): 61.

57. Janczewska, "Obozy pracy przymusowej dla Żydów na terenie dystryktu warszawskiego," 281.

58. YIVO, HWC 31/4, "Day and Night in the Collegium," April 1941, 1.

59. YIVO, HWC 53/3, "Wilga—Kasyno," December 1941.

60. YIVO, HWC 31/4, "Day and Night in the Collegium," April 1941, 2.

61. YIVO, HWC 31/4, "Day and Night in the Collegium," April 1941, 7.

62. Ringelblum, *Pisma z getta*, April 26, 1941, 246.

63. JHIA, ARG I 1134 (I/6), "Winter Camps," 17; Janczewska, *Obozy pracy przymusowej dla Żydów na terenie dystryktu warszawskiego*, 286–99. According to this document, the number of guards proved to be too many for the needs of the camp, so only sixteen guards remained there. Seven guards were moved to the camp in Milejów; the remaining returned to Warsaw.

64. Janczewska, *Obozy pracy przymusowej dla Żydów na terenie dystryktu warszawskiego*, 291.

65. "Poszukiwani robotnicy" [Laborers sought], *Gazeta Żydowska*, June 10, 1941.

66. Gombiński, *Wspomnienia policjanta*, 195–96.

67. Janczewska, *Obozy pracy przymusowej dla Żydów na terenie dystryktu warszawskiego*, 288.

68. Landau, *Kronika lat wojny i okupacji*, vol. 1, 677–78.

69. Makower, *Pamiętnik z getta warszawskiego*, 58.

70. JHIA, ARG I 646 (I/502), Witelson, study on the [Jewish] Order Service, 25. Passensztajn to Czerniaków. See also YIVO, HWC 53/3, "Wilga—Kasyno, December 1941."

71. Czerniaków, *Adama Czerniakowa dziennik*, April 29, 1941, 174.

72. YIVO, HWC 53/6, "Pustków," January 1942.

73. YIVO, HWC 53/6, "Pustków," January 1942.

74. JHIA, ARG I 1125 (I/228), questioning of Zygmunt Dajtelbaum on May 20, 1941, regarding his experiences in the labor camp in Drewnica, quoted in Janczewska, *Obozy pracy przymusowej dla Żydów na terenie dystryktu warszawskiego*, 312.

75. Janczewska, *Obozy pracy przymusowej dla Żydów na terenie dystryktu warszawskiego*, 313.

76. For instance, Adam Czerniaków describes laborers as "delighted with the change" (*Adama Czerniakowa dziennik*, May 8, 1941, 177).

77. JHIA, ARG I 1134 (I/6), "Winter Camps," 17, printed in *Archiwum Ringelbluma: Konspiracyjne Archiwum Getta Warszawy*, vol. 24, *Obozy pracy przymusowej*, ed. M. Janczewska (Warsaw: Żydowski Instytut Historyczny, 2015).

78. YIVO, HWC 53/3, "Wilga—Kasyno," December 1941, printed in *Archiwum Ringelbluma: Konspiracyjne Archiwum Getta*, vol. 14. *Kolekcja Hersza Wassera*, 318–21,

ed. K. Person (Warsaw: Żydowski Instytut Historyczny, 2014). On a member of the Jewish Order Service, Szymon Goldman, aiding forced laborers in Pustków, see JHIA, ARG I 646 (I/502), Witelson, study on the [Jewish] Order Service, 39.

79. Member of the Jewish Order Service Szmul Śliwka reported in September 1941 that policemen from the Warsaw Ghetto were forced to bury laborers murdered in a mass execution in Osowa Camp. See APW, KŻDM, 482/108, 38, printed in *Die Verfolgung und Ermordung der europäischen Juden durch das nationalsozialistische Deutschland: 1933–1945*, vol. 9: *Polen: Generalgouvernement August 1941–1945*, ed. K.-P. Friedrich (Munich: Oldenbourg Verlag, 2014), 74–75.

80. Olga Litvak, *Conscription and the Search for Modern Russian Jewry* (Bloomington: Indiana University Press, 2006), 3.

81. YIVO, HWC 32/8, Eliasz Gutkowski, "Diary from the Warsaw Ghetto," 46, printed in *Archiwum Ringelbluma: Konspiracyjne Archiwum Getta*, vol. 23, *Dzienniki z getta warszawskiego*, ed. K. Person, M. Trębacz, and Z. Trębacz (Warsaw: Żydowski Instytut Historyczny, 2015), 364–76.

82. YIVO, HWC 31/4, "Day and Night in the Collegium," April 1941, 1.

83. In the Cracow Ghetto, a jail of the Jewish Order Service was set up in March 1941 at 37 Józefińska Street. Those imprisoned there were usually sentenced for minor offenses or remaining on the Aryan side.

84. Czerniaków, *Adama Czerniakowa dziennik*, June 6, 1941, 190.

85. JHIA, 302/129 ([Stanisław Gombiński?], memoir), 68.

86. "Wkrótce uruchomienie więzienia dzielnicy żydowskiej" [Prison in the Jewish district soon to be opened], *Gazeta Żydowska*, July 9, 1941.

87. JHIA, ARG I 687 (I/436), "Hundred and Ten," 1, printed in *Archiwum Ringelbluma*: vol. 33, 385–90.

88. Czerniaków, *Adama Czerniakowa dziennik*, July 3, 1941, 197.

89. As late as May 29, 1942, the German Court sentenced Eta Gulbas to fifty days in the Daniłowiczowska Street prison because she did not pay a 250 zloty fine for failing to wear an armband. See JHIA, ARG I 188 (I/273), "The German Court in Warsaw, Letters of 15.09.1941 and 29.05.1942 to Eta Gulbas."

90. Czerniaków, *Adama Czerniakowa dziennik*, July 3, 1941, 197, 204.

91. APW, KŻDM, RG 13, "61. Report of the Chairman of Jewish Council in Warsaw for January 1942."

92. The Ringelblum Archive contains a petition to the administration of the Central Lockup for permission to hold a literary/artistic event on the evening of December 24, 1941. The event was to include "song, dance, verse, and humor" (JHIA, ARG II 61 [II/148]).

93. YIVO, HWC 43.1, on the Jewish prison at Gęsia, 1, printed in *Archiwum Ringelbluma*, vol. 14. 63–65.

94. Czerniaków, *Adama Czerniakowa dziennik*, June 13, 1942, 289.

95. JHIA, 302/129 ([Stanisław Gombiński?], memoir), 69.

96. K. Dunin-Wąsowicz, ed., *Raporty Ludwiga Fischera gubernatora dystryktu warszawskiego, 1939–1944* (Warsaw: Książka i Wiedza, 1987), 521 (report from April 1942).

97. JHIA, 302/129 ([Stanisław Gombiński?], memoir), 75. On Roma in the Warsaw Ghetto, see Karolina Wróbel, "Romowie za murami getta warszawskiego," *Czas Kultury*, no. 4 (2016): 52–57.

98. Czerniaków, *Adama Czerniakowa dziennik*, April 22, 1942, 268.

99. Czerniaków, June 16, 1942, 290; JHIA, 302/27 (S. Puterman, memoir), 51.

100. Czerniaków, *Adama Czerniakowa dziennik*, April 25, 1942, 269.

101. "W kilku wierszach" [In a few lines], *Gazeta Żydowska*, July 11, 1941.

102. ARG II 45 (II/138), Jewish Council in Warsaw, letter dated October 20, 1941, to Transferstelle (concerns issue of a pass to Leopold Lindenfeld).

103. Izaak Rudniański, first deputy head of the First District, then deputy head of the Central Lockup, shot in July 1942.

104. Fryderyk Rose (1894–?), see *Rocznik Oficerski Rezerw* (Warsaw: Ministerstwo Spraw Wojskowych, 1934), 10.

105. "Strażniczki aresztu dzielnicy żydowskiej" [Female guards in the Jewish district detention center], *Gazeta Żydowska*, August 6, 1941.

106. JHIA, 302/27 (S. Puterman, memoir), 1.

107. JHIA, 302/215 (Chana Gorodecka, memoir), 36.

108. JHIA, 313/110 (Sąd Społeczny przy Centralnym Komitecie Żydów w Polsce, Józef Rubinrodt-Marczak); Marian Pieńkowski, "Oświadczenie." Guards from the Jewish Order Service were arrested after two prisoners escaped from Czyste Hospital. JHIA, ARG I 587 (I/292), "Note Regarding an Escape of Two Prisoners from Czyste Hospital at Stawki Street."

109. Ringelblum, *Pisma z getta*, August 1941, 288. On Blaupapier's past and his conflict with Marceli Czapliński, see JHIA, ARG I 646 (I/502), Witelson, study on the [Jewish] Order Service, 34–35.

110. JHIA, 302/129 ([Stanisław Gombiński?], memoir), 70.

111. YIVO, HWC 43.1, "On the Jewish Prison at Gęsia," 2. See also the dramatic description in Ludwik Hirszfeld's memoir, where he speaks of "air so thick, that after a few minutes I have to leave, I feel like fainting." Ludwik Hirszfeld, *Historia jednego życia* (Warsaw: Wydawnictwo Literackie, 2011), 348–49.

112. JHIA, ARG I 427 (I/95), Menachem Mendel Kon, "My Visit in the Ghetto Prison," printed in *Archiwum Ringelbluma*, vol. 34, 379–83.

113. JHIA, ARG I 427 (I/95), Kon, 2.

114. JHIA, ARG I 427 (I/95), Kon, 7.

115. JHIA, ARG I 427 (I/95), Kon, 9–10.

116. *Żagiew*, May 1942. Most likely Aron Rozin (service number 1010), Gustaw Ber (service number 175), and Natan Sznajder (service number 73).

117. JHIA, ARG I 555 (I/130), "Prison at Gęsia (Theses)." See also JHIA, ARG I 646 (I/502), Witelson, study on the [Jewish] Order Service, 21.

118. See APW, KŻDM, RG 47, orders for arrests of Jews in the arrest at Gęsia.

119. JHIA, ARG I 184 (I/781/3), "Der Kommissar für den jüdischen Wohnbezirk in Warschau, Heinz Auerswald," announcement about the shooting of eight Jews on November 17, 1941, for illegal departure from the ghetto, on the basis of the verdict of the Special Court of November 12, 1941.

120. See JHIA, ARG I 239 (I/224), "personal details of the deceased" (cards) of fifteen Jews shot on December 15, 1941, in the prison at Gęsia.

121. JHIA, ARG I 514 (I/470), account about the fate of Bajla (Bella) Keselberg [Kaselberg] vel Kociołek based on her own memories, 16, trans. in *Ringelblum Archive*, vol. 1, 614.

122. JHIA, ARG I 550 (Ring. I/586/3), letter (author and addressees unknown), after December 15, 1941, from Warsaw Ghetto jail at Gęsia Street 24, printed in *Archiwum Ringelbluma*, vol. 1, 608.

123. Ringelblum, *Pisma z getta*, November 22, 1941, 312.

124. "Poprzez mury getta" [Through the walls of the ghetto], *Za Naszą i Waszą Wolność*, December 1941; "Pogarda mordercom—cześć zamordowanym," [Disdain to murderers—glory to the murdered], *Yugnt Shtime* [Voice of the youth], November 1941.

125. "Koszmar" [Nightmare], *El-Al*, November 1941.

126. Engelking and Leociak, *Warsaw Ghetto*, 203.

4. Police in the Eyes of the Ghetto Population

1. Gombiński, *Wspomnienia policjanta*, 184.

2. The organization of the service and its daily functioning can be followed in the daily notes of the chairman of the Warsaw Judenrat, Adam Czerniaków, in Czerniaków, *Adama Czerniakowa dziennik getta warszawskiego*. An important source for the early stage of the formation of the service is the diary of one of its founders, Leon Berenson. See Czajka and Epsztein, *Nieznany dziennik z getta warszawskiego*.

3. "Męczennicy z Pomiechówka idą" [Martyrs of Pomiechówek are coming], *Yugnt Shtime*, November 1941.

4. Ringelblum, *Kronika getta warszawskiego*, ed. Artur Eisenbach, trans. Adam Rutkowski (Warsaw: Czytelnik, 1983), 479.

5. In the current literature, the term "collaboration" in reference to the actions of the Jewish Order Service is used almost exclusively in the meaning of "forced collaboration"—that is, at a risk to one's life. See Jacek Andrzej Młynarczyk, "Pomiędzy współpracą a zdradą: Problem kolaboracji w Generalnym Gubernatorstwie—próba syntezy," *Pamięć i Sprawiedliwość*, no. 14 (2009): 120.

6. JHIA, ARG I 656 (I/67), minutes of meetings of the apartment house committee at [Nalewki] Street in Warsaw (July 1939–April 1942), 371–72.

7. Hersh Wasser named among the Underground Archive collaborators policemen Witelson and Millet. YIVO, HWC 42.2, Wasser, ekspertyza (expert statement), 18.

8. JHIA, 302/129 (N.N. [Stanisław Gombiński?], memoir), 162.

9. On that, see Kamil Kijek, "Was It Possible to Avoid "Hebrew Assimilation"? Hebraism, Polonization, and Tarbut Schools in the Last Decade of Interwar Poland," *Jewish Social Studies* 21, no. 2 (2016), 105–41.

10. "Objawy degeneracji" [Signs of degeneration], *Neged Hazerem*, nos. 7–8 (September/October 1941): 1. Vikund Quisling nominally headed the government of Norway during the occupation by Nazi Germany.

11. Chaim Storch, "Obowiązek służbowy (na tle "Dziesięciorga przykazań")" [Service duty (in light of the ten commandments)], *Gazeta Żydowska*, April 1, 1942.

12. On the reaction of Orthodox Holocaust diarists to assimilation, see among others Alexandra Garbarini, *Numbered Days: Diaries and the Holocaust* (New Haven, CT: Yale University Press, 2006), 45–46.

13. On that, see Sander L. Gilman, *Jewish Self-Hatred: Anti-Semitism and the Hidden Language of the Jews* (Baltimore: Johns Hopkins University Press, 1986).

14. Michael Mazor, *The Vanished City: Everyday Life in the Warsaw Ghetto*, trans. D. Jacobson (New York: Marsillio, 1993), 78.

15. "Z życia getta warszawskiego" [On life in the Warsaw Ghetto], *Awangarda Młodzieży: Pismo Żydowskiej Młodzieży Marksistowskiej*, December 1, 1941, 10.

16. JHIA, ARG I 646 (I/502), Witelson, study on the [Jewish] Order Service, 7.

17. Ringelblum, *Pisma z getta*, March 18, 1941, 223. A more likely explanation can be found in the reports of an anonymous informer from the Warsaw Ghetto: "On the Christian holidays the lively attendance at the church in Gerichtsstrasse was, as always, a spectacle for the Jewish population, who came to gaze at the Jewish Christians entering the church. The Jewish police had mobilized special troops to maintain order in front of the church." "The Reports of a Jewish Informer in the Warsaw Ghetto: Selected Documents," *Yad Vashem Studies* 17 (1986): 263; from a weekly report dated April 7, 1942.

18. YVA, O.3/2996 (Marceli Reich), 12–13.

19. JHIA, 301/2274 (Róża Dobrecka, testimony), 7.

20. Ezra Mendelsohn, *On Modern Jewish Politics* (Oxford: Oxford University Press, 1993), 65.

21. Calel Perechodnik, *Am I a Murderer? Testament of a Jewish Ghetto Policeman*, trans. and ed. Frank Fox (Boulder, CO: Westview, 1996), xxii. Adam Mickiewicz (1798–1855)—poet, dramatist, publicist, a key figure of Polish Romanticism. Regarded as the national poet of Poland.

22. Kijek, "Was It Possible to Avoid 'Hebrew Assimilation?,'" 108.

23. On that, see Justyna Majewska, "'Czym wytłumaczy Pan . . .?': Inteligencja żydowska o polonizacji i asymilacji w getcie warszawskim," *Zagłada Żydów: Studia i Materiały*, no. 11 (2015): 325–46.

24. JHIA, ARG I 661a (I/50), Stanisław Różycki, "Theater in the Ghetto," 13, trans. in *Ringelblum Archive*, vol. 1, 67.

25. JHIA, ARG I 494 (I/1010), diary, May 1, 1941, 3, printed in *Archiwum Ringelbluma*, vol. 23, 263–68.

26. Adler, *In the Warsaw Ghetto*, 48.

27. *Iton ha—Tnua*, December 1940 / January 1941, 98.

28. Stefan Ernest, *O wojnie wielkich Niemiec z Żydami Warszawy*, ed. M. Młodkowska (Warsaw: Czytelnik, 2003), 73.

29. JHIA, ARG I 455 (I/428), Stanisław Różycki, "This Is Ghetto!," 4.

30. The ritual of entry is often discussed in the studies of concentration camps. See, for example, Primo Levi, "The Grey Zone," in *The Holocaust: Origins, Implementation, Aftermath*, ed. Omer Bartov (London: Routledge, 2002), 254.

31. Alexandra Garbarini, Alexandra, *Numbered Days: Diaries and the Holocaust* (New Haven, CT: Yale University Press, 2006), 162.

32. JHIA, ARG I 456 (I/429), Stanisław Różycki, "Street Scenes from the Ghetto," 31, trans. in *Ringelblum Archive*, vol. 1, 45.

33. Seweryn Stendt, "Mój syn został porządkowym" [My son became a constable], *Gazeta Żydowska*, April 1, 1942. The same is described by Ringelblum, who wrote that policemen wore high boots to gain recognition. Ringelblum, *Pisma z getta*, winter 1942, 424.

34. "Ogłoszenia warszawskie" [Warsaw ads], *Gazeta Żydowska*, March 29, 1941.

35. "Nasza Policja" [Our police], *Za Naszą i Waszą Wolność*, January/February 1942, 12.

36. Adler, *In the Warsaw Ghetto*, 205.

37. Czerniaków, *Adama Czerniakowa dziennik*, November 15, 1941, 228.

38. JHIA, ARG I 659 (I/92), Stanisław Różycki, "Polish-Jewish Relations," 10, trans. in *Ringelblum Archive*, vol. 1, 528. "Half-Poles" were Polish citizens of German ancestry who registered in the Deutsche Volksliste (German People's List). Called *Volksdeutsche*, they were often regarded by other Poles as traitors.

39. Ringelblum, *Pisma z getta*, May 12, 1942, 345.

40. According to an anonymous informer from the Warsaw Ghetto: "People are generally disturbed by the activities of Polish policemen in the ghetto. It is said that many of them seek a source of income in the ghetto at any price. Common articles are confiscated. People walking in the streets are arrested and released only after having paid a ransom, often a very small amount—two zlotys." "The Reports of a Jewish Informer in the Warsaw Ghetto: Selected Documents," 265.

41. USHMM, Więzienie Karne Mokotów, Zespół no. 657/0, microfilm no. 18323. Szyja Urlik, suspected of theft, was arrested after attempting to bribe a policeman with fifty zlotys.

42. See AAN, 203/III/123, Protokoły odprawy u Komendanta Policji Polskiej m. Warszawy; AIPN, MBP 2355, Komenda Policji Polskiej m.st. Warszawy, Skład osobowy Korpusu Oficerskiego na dz. 10 XII [19]41, 32 (Bernard Brzozowski).

43. Hempel, *Pogrobowcy klęski*, 172–73; Marek Getter, "Policja granatowa w Warszawie," in *Warszawa lat wojny i okupacji 1939–1944*, vol. 2, ed. K. Dunin-Wąsowicz, J. Kaźmierska and H. Winnicka (Warsaw: PWN, 1972), 220–21.

44. AAN, 203/III/123, 6.

45. AAN, 203/III/123, 3. Protokół no. 5 odprawy tygodniowej u Komendanta P.P. m. Warszawy w dniu 20 stycznia 1942. Sylwia Szymańska-Smolkin, in her article on the Blue Police, mentions policeman Mikołaj Klimenko, who was moved to serve outside the ghetto as a punishment for tolerating smuggling. APW, Komenda Policji Polskiej w Warszawie, 12, 422, quoted in Sylwia Szymańska-Smolkin, "Rola policji granatowej jako pośrednika w utrzymywaniu łączności między gettem a stroną aryjską," in *Narody i polityka: Studia ofiarowane profesorowi Jerzemu Tomaszewskiemu*, ed. A. Grabski and A. Markowski (Warsaw: ŻIH, 2010), 222.

46. "Nasza Policja" [Our police]. On that, see also APW, Komenda Policji Polskiej Miasta Warszawy, RG 17, Akta śledztwa VII.S.108/41, a case against Blue Policeman S. Krzemiński, accused in December 1941 of taking bribes from Jews and caught on the Aryan side.

47. One contributor to the Underground Archive of the Warsaw Ghetto describes a policeman who warned him of an impending forced confiscation of furs. ARG I/484 (I/430), Natan Koniński, "Hand Over Your Furs," 2.

48. For more on that, see Szymańska-Smolkin, "Rola policji granatowej," 215–26.

49. "Kary za stawianie oporu funkcjonariuszom Służby Porządkowej" [Punishment for resisting members of the Order Service], *Gazeta Żydowska*, March 4, 1941.

50. "Wypadki dnia w Warszawie" [Daily accidents in Warsaw], *Gazeta Żydowska*, March 14, 1941.

51. "Z warszawskiego getta" [From the Warsaw Ghetto], *Biuletyn*, May 1941.

52. "Żydowska policja" [Jewish police], *Dos Fraye Vort* [Free word], May 23, 1942.

53. "Życie w żydowskiej dzielnicy mieszkaniowej" [Life in the Jewish Residential District], *Nowy Kurier Warszawski*, January 10, 1941.

54. "Sześćdziesięciu bohaterów" [Sixty heroes], *Nowy Kurier Warszawski*, August 12, 1941.

55. "Za murami getta" [Behind the walls of the ghetto], *Wiadomości Polskie*, August 13, 1942, quoted in Dariusz Libionka, "ZWZ—AK i Delegatura rządu RP wobec eksterminacji Żydów polskich," in *Polacy i Żydzi pod okupacją niemiecką 1939–1945: Studia i materiały*, ed. A. Żbikowski (Warsaw: IPN, 2006), 41.

56. *Wielka Polska*, quoted in PawełSzapiro, ed. *Wojna żydowsko-niemiecka: Polska prasa konspiracyjna 1943–1944 o powstaniu w getcie Warszawy* (London: Aneks, 1992), 115.

5. Policemen's Voices

1. JHIA, 302/ 129 ([Stanisław Gombiński?], memoir), 33.
2. JHIA, 302/ 129, 33.
3. JHIA, 302/ 129, 32.
4. JHIA, 302/ 129, 34.
5. Rumors about the preferential treatment of Jewish Order Service officers appeared, for example, after the decree on the confiscation of furs belonging to Jews. See JHIA, ARG I 484 (I/430), Natan Koniński, "Hand over the Furs," 2.
6. Zygmunt Millet describes how he was able to get a pass in the summer of 1941, for a large fee and with great effort, allowing him to visit a family living in Tarnów and Dębica. JHIA, ARG I 721 (I/610), Zygmunt Millet, account "On Vacation from the Ghetto" (February 1942).
7. See also Boruch Jakubowicz's benefit application to the chairman of the Jewish Council, Adam Czerniaków, where he writes, "I live with my wife, child, and mother-in-law in very difficult material conditions. Our house was burned down, and we were displaced from Żyrardów in a cruel manner. We are without clothing and footwear. . . . We eat only bread, received for vouchers. . . . I sold everything that would . . . represent any value for a trader." The same applies to the application to the SEPOR by the orderly Jaskółka, who wrote, "I have a polite and urgent request for [SEPOR] to lend me a sum of 94.50 zlotys for weekly repayments of ten zlotys each. This amount is indispensable to me to pay for 150 coal briquettes I am entitled to from 'SEPOR.' Since I do not have that sum in full, and 'SEPOR' refused to accept the payment in installments, I am forced to ask for a loan, otherwise I will lose . . . fuel . . . for the coming winter." Despite the subsequent pleas by the commander of the platoon where Jaskółka served and by the commander of the First Precinct, in which he served, testifying to the difficult material conditions that the man endured, no aid was granted. Czapliński, as Witelson wrote, justified the refusal to grant aid by the lack of specific data confirming Jaskółka's material situation. JHIA, ARG I 646 (I/502), Witelson, study on the [Jewish] Order Service, 56.
8. JHIA, ARG I 413 (I/435), G., account titled "Information Collected in Conversations with a Jewish Order Service Officer" (February 5, 1942), 15.
9. Adler, *In the Warsaw Ghetto*, 145.
10. USC Shoah Foundation Visual History Archive, Adela Roser, interview 9132. See also Kristine Turek, interview 13721, and Halina Mitchley, interview 40467.
11. YVA, O.33/1158 (Roma Elster), 7.
12. Koźmińska-Frejlak, *Świadectwo milczenia*, 257.
13. See JHIA, 313/110 (Józef Reinhordt-Marczak).
14. Adler, *In the Warsaw Ghetto*, 75.

15. Adler, 249.

16. JHIA, ARG I 527 (I/268), account of a member of a sanitary brigade, 19, trans. in *Ringelblum Archive*, vol. 1, 373.

17. JHIA, ARG I 527 (I/268), account of a member of a sanitary brigade, 19, 373.

18. JHIA, ARG I 646 (I/502), Witelson, study on the [Jewish] Order Service, 10.

19. Adler, *In the Warsaw Ghetto*, 52–53.

20. YVA microfilm JM/1112, letter of November 24, 1941, from Heinz Auerswald to Juliusz von Medeazza, Hans Frank plenipotentiary in Berlin. Cited in Trunk, *Judenrat*, 261

21. JHIA, 302/129 ([Stanisław Gombiński?], memoir), 56.

22. JHIA, 301/2225 (Maria Zadziewicz).

23. JHIA, 302/129, 39.

24. "Publiczność na ulicy" [Public on the street], *Gazeta Żydowska*, October 17, 1941.

25. "Porządkowi biją (zagadnienie nie tylko warszawskie)" [Members of the service are beating (not only a Warsaw case)], *Gazeta Żydowska*, June 21, 1942 2.

26. See Wolfgang Curilla, *Der Judenmord in Polen und die deutsche Ordnungspolizei 1939–1945* (Paderborn: Ferdinand Schöningh, 2011), 533–682, and Stefan Klemp, *Vernichtung: Die deutsche Ordnungspolizei und der Judenmord im Warschauer Ghetto 1940–43* (Berlin: Prospero, 2013). Neither of these authors, however, thoroughly describes the contacts between German Order Police and the Jewish Order Service officers. See also the trial of Ludwig Hahn, former commandant of Sipo and the SD in Warsaw, Staatsarchiv der Hansestadt Hamburg, Aus den Ermittlungen der Staatsanwaltschaft Hamburg gegen den ehemaligen Chef der Warschauer SIPO, Ludwig Hahn, 213–12–70, no. 8, 3868. Instructions on serving at the ghetto gates can be found in APW, KŻDM, syg. 131, "Kurze Instruktion für die Posten der Gettowachen in Warschau."

27. Ringelblum, *Pisma z getta*, November 19–20, 169.

28. JHIA, ARG I 462/6 (I/1040), Mordechaj Szwarcbard, "Aktualności," 7. The Michał Konarski Craft School was located at 72 Leszno Street.

29. YIVO, HWC 32/1, Wasser, notes, February 5, 1941, 40.

30. Adler, *In the Warsaw Ghetto*, 212.

31. Ringelblum, *Pisma z getta*, April 26, 1941, 245.

32. JHIA, ARG I 588 (I/143), Salomea Ostrowska, report "Quarantine at Leszno 109/III," 77.

33. James Waller, *Becoming Evil: How Ordinary People Commit Genocide and Mass Killing* (Oxford: Oxford University Press 2002), 310.

34. Sofsky, *Order of Terror*, 195.

35. Adler, *In the Warsaw Ghetto*, 143.

36. Mina Tomkiewicz, *Of Bombs and Mice: A Novel of War-Time Warsaw* (London: George Allen & Unwin, 1970), 137. The topic of alcohol comes up in policemen's memories very often. However, it is not limited to the Warsaw Ghetto, as Tadeusz Pankiewicz wrote about the Jewish Order Service in Cracow: "Mostly pure ethyl alcohol was consumed, but getting actually drunk was rare. People who did not know the taste of alcohol at all were drinking; in vodka they sought relief and help. Many began to break down mentally. Insomnia has become a common disease." Tadeusz Pankiewicz, *Apteka w getcie krakowskim* (Cracow: Wydawnictwo Literackie, 2012), 161. For

more, see Ed Westermann, *Drunk on Genocide: Alcohol, Masculinity and the Intoxication of Mass Murder in Nazi Germany*, which is forthcoming with the Cornell University Press in association with the United States Holocaust Memorial Museum.

37. On organization and ego needs, see Waller, *Becoming Evil*, 321.

38. Barbara Engelking, *Holocaust and Memory: The Experience of the Holocaust and Its Consequences. An Investigation Based on Personal Narratives* (Leicester: Leicester University Press, 1994), 130.

39. Adler, *In the Warsaw Ghetto*, 204.

40. JHIA, 302/129 ([Stanisław Gombiński?], memoir), 88. "Dudziński" is probably Leon Dymiński, the commander of the Eighth Polish Police Precinct.

41. IPN BU MBP 2355, Polish police headquarters in Warsaw, composition of the officer corps on December 10, 1941 (Karol Moniak), 38.

6. Response to Violence

1. JHIA, ARG I 252 (I/14), orders of the day of Józef Szeryński, November 1940–January 1941.

2. Józef Prussak, "Lecture on the Duties and Behavior of a Member of the [Jewish] Order Service," in Alina Podolska, *Służba Porządkowa w getcie warszawskim* (Warsaw: Pro Futuro, 1996), 138.

3. "Selekcja żyd. Służby Porządkowej w Warszawie" [Selection in the Jewish Order Service in Warsaw], *Gazeta Żydowska*, December 27, 1940.

4. Mieczysław Goldstein (Goldsztejn)—lawyer; in the ghetto, deputy head of the Jewish Order Service administrative office and later head of the Order and Disciplinary Section. His brother, Nikodem Goldsztejn, was the head of the Jewish Order Service's human resources office. See USHMM, RG 15.471, personal files of Jewish students who studied at Warsaw University before World War II, RP 117705/S.

Henryk Nowogródzki (?–1992)—lawyer and court reporter for *Nasz Przegląd*; in the ghetto, employed in the Jewish Order Service human resources office and from September 1941 head of the Order and Disciplinary Section. After the war, he worked as an attorney.

5. JHIA, ARG I 251 (I/227), official instruction for the Order Service, art. 11.

6. See APW, KŻDM, sygn. 18, "Weekly Report of the Jewish Order Service in the Jewish Residential District in Warsaw, June 22, 1941– July 10, 1942."

7. Engelking and Grabowski, *Żydów łamiących prawo należy karać śmiercią!*, 32–33.

8. Ringelblum, *Pisma z getta*, April 26, 1942, 246.

9. Rachela Auerbach, "Dziennik," in *Pisma z getta warszawskiego*, ed. and trans. K. Szymaniak (Warsaw: Żydowski Instytut Historyczny, 2016), 166.

10. JHIA, ARG I 646 (I/502), Witelson, study on the [Jewish] Order Service, 11–12.

11. JHIA 302/129 ([Stanisław Gombiński?], memoir), 25.

12. JHIA, ARG I 645 (I/233), memorandum of the reform of the [Jewish] Order Service in the Warsaw Ghetto. According to Zygmunt Millet, the opposition group consisted of, among others, Mieczysław Goldsztejn, Józef Herc and Henryk Nowogródzki. The memorandum was handed over to Czerniaków by Berenson. JHIA, ARG I 435 (I/100), Z. Millet, memories of working in the [Jewish] Order

Service, 10–11. On other memorandums, see JHIA, ARG I 647 (I/115), fragment of a study on the [Jewish] Order Service in the Warsaw Ghetto, 2.

13. JHIA, ARG I 435 (I/100), Z. Millet, memories of working in the [Jewish] Order Service, 1, trans. in *Ringelblum Archive*, vol. 1, 600.

14. JHIA, ARG I 435 (I/100), 11.

15. JHIA, 302/129 ([Stanisław Gombiński?], memoir), 85–86.

16. Czerniaków, *Adama Czerniakowa dziennik*, June 11, 1941, 289.

17. JHIA, 302/129 ([Stanisław Gombiński?], memoir), 105.

18. "Opłaty na rzecz Służby Porządkowej" [Fees for the Order Service], *Gazeta Żydowska*, April 22, 1941. The payment from individuals amounted to eighty groszys and was paid via house committees. Ghetto entrepreneurs paid from ten to one hundred zlotys a month.

19. Adler, *In the Warsaw Ghetto*, 192.

20. APW, PRŻ, sygn. 22. "41. Weekly Report of the Chairman of the Jewish Council for the period January 24 to January 30, 1941."

21. JHIA, ARG I 646 (I/502), Witelson, study on the [Jewish] Order Service, 6.

22. Adler, *In the Warsaw Ghetto*, 196.

23. "Inauguracja 'Kuchen Policyjnych' pod kierownictwem Służby Porządk." [Opening of "police kitchens" under the leadership of the Order Service], *Gazeta Żydowska*, June 20, 1941.

24. Czerniaków, *Adama Czerniakowa dziennik*, June 19, 1941, 194. According to Tadeusz Witelson, the soups were not tasty. JHIA, ARG I 646 (I/502), Witelson, study on the [Jewish] Order Service, 70.

25. Adler, *In the Warsaw Ghetto*, 147.

26. Czerniaków, *Adama Czerniakowa dziennik*, October 23, 1941, 223.

27. JHIA, ARG I 289 (I/1197), Szmul Winter, letter, "To the Chairman of the Jewish Council in Warsaw."

28. Czerniaków, *Adama Czerniakowa dziennik*, January 6, 1942, 239.

29. "Informować-Zespolić-Pomagać" [Inform-Unite-Help], *Gazeta Żydowska*, July 23, 1940.

30. "Listy, listy" [Letters, letters], *Gazeta Żydowska* April 10, 1942.

31. "Służba porządkowa—służbą społeczno-obywatelską" [Order Service as a social-civic service], *Gazeta Żydowska*, April 11, 1941.

32. Samuel Iarkai, "W sprawie służby porządkowej" [On the topic of the Order Service], *Gazeta Żydowska*, December 17, 1940.

33. On the Judenrat as a successor of the *kehilla*, see "Gminy żydowskie dawniej a obecnie" [Jewish communities then and now], *Gazeta Żydowska*, May 9, 1941. See also "Żydowska Służba Porządkowa w dalszej Warszawie" [Jewish Order Service in Warsaw of the past], *Gazeta Żydowska*, January 21, 1941.

34. Ringelblum, *Pisma z getta*, June 10, 1942, 365.

7. Spring 1942

1. Auerbach, *Pisma z getta warszawskiego*, 138.

2. YIVO, HWC 32.3, Szymon Huberband, diary, May 22, 1942, 1.

3. JHIA, 302/129 ([Stanisław Gombiński?], memoir), 74.

4. Ernest, *O wojnie wielkich Niemiec z Żydami Warszawy*, 138–39.

5. JHIA, 302/144 (Marek Stok, diary), 22–23.

6. Czerniaków, *Adama Czerniakowa dziennik*, April 18, 1942, 267.

7. Czerniaków, May 1, 1942, 271; JHIA, 302/129 ([Stanisław Gombiński?], memoir), 99.

8. JHIA, 302/188, Ber Warm, Befehlstelle (Żelazna 103), 9.

9. On the order, see JHIA, ARG I/484 (I/430), Natan Koniński, "Hand Over Your Furs," trans. in *Ringelblum Archive*, vol. 1, 566–70.

10. Czerniaków, *Adama Czerniakowa dziennik*, 272. This proves as groundless a rumor circulating in the ghetto that claimed Czerniaków did not undertake any actions to free Szeryński. JHIA, 302/129 ([Stanisław Gombiński?], memoir), 90.

11. Czerniaków, *Adama Czerniakowa dziennik*, May 11, 1942, 275.

12. JHIA, 302/129 ([Stanisław Gombiński?], memoir), 100.

13. "Reports of a Jewish 'Informer' in the Warsaw Ghetto," 272.

14. Czerniaków, *Adama Czerniakowa dziennik*, May 8, 1942, 274.

15. Czerniaków, May 13, 1942, 277.

16. Czerniaków, May 30, 1942, 284.

17. Two other candidates mentioned in testimonies were Berthold Drobin, a lawyer from Bydgoszcz and chairman of the Central Refugee Commission, and a converted prewar persecutor named Nizsenzon. See JHIA, 302/129 [Stanisław Gombiński?], memoir), 102.

18. Czerniaków, *Adama Czerniakowa dziennik*, May 4, 1942, 273.

19. Czerniaków, May 2, 1942, 271.

20. Czerniaków, May 5, 1942, 273.

21. Czerniaków, May 6, 1942, 274.

22. JHIA, 302/27 (S. Puterman, memoir), 3.

23. JHIA, ARG I 648 (I/181), Amas Freund, "Modern Tales by Hoffman: Stories about the Bribe Service, Otherwise Known as the [Jewish] Order Service," 5, trans. in *Ringelblum Archive*, vol. 1, 607.

24. Czerniaków, *Adama Czerniakowa dziennik*, May 4, 1942, 273.

25. "Z dziennika Punktu Uchodźców," *Dror*, May–June 1941.

26. APW, KŻDM, RG 18, "Weekly Reports of the Jewish Order Service in the Jewish Residential District in Warsaw, June 22, 1941–July 10, 1942."

27. Auerbach, *Dziennik z getta warszawskiego*, 140.

28. JHIA, ARG II 63 (II/150), notes concerning the transfer of sixteen prisoners to the Germans on March 25, 1942, printed in *Archiwum Ringelbluma*, vol. 12, 558–59. *Junak* was a colloquial name for members of the Building Service (Baudienst), a paramilitary organization consisting mostly of Ukrainians, Lithuanians, Latvians, and Volksdeutsche.

29. Czerniaków, *Adama Czerniakowa dziennik*, May 29, 1942, 283. See also Engelking and Grabowski, *Żydów łamiących prawo należy karać śmiercią!*, 164.

30. JHIA, 302/129 ([Stanisław Gombiński?], memoir), 83.

31. JHIA, 302/129, 84.

32. Gombiński, *Wspomnienia policjanta*, 58.

33. "Służba Porządkowa na posterunku" [Order Service on duty], *Gazeta Żydowska*, July 17, 1942.

34. Abraham Lewin noted that Jewish Order Service members participated in taking women from a building at 39 Dzielna Street. They were then filmed taking part in staged sexual encounters. Lewin, *Cup of Tears*, May 13, 1942.

35. APW, KŻDM, RG 18, "Weekly Reports of the Jewish Order Service in the Jewish Residential District in Warsaw, April 1942–July 1942."

36. JHIA, ARG I 414 (I/29), Jechiel Górny, daily notes, 33.

37. "Kronika warszawska" [Warsaw chronicle], *Yedies* [News], May 1942.

38. Ringelblum, *Pisma z getta*, June 1942, 377. On attempts to limit smuggling, see APW, KŻDM, RG 2, "Weekly Reports on the Situation in the Ghetto," March 24, 1942, 104.

39. An anonymous ghetto inhabitant described in his diary the arrest of seven Jews who were trying to climb the ghetto wall. They were executed in the courtyard of his building in presence of a Jewish policemen. YIVO, HWC 31.14, N.R., notes from the ghetto, 5.

40. Czerniaków, *Adama Czerniakowa dziennik*, June 30, 1942, 294.

41. Janusz Szczepański, *Społeczność żydowska Mazowsza w XIX–XX wieku* (Pułtusk: Wyższa Szkoła Humanistyczna im. Aleksandra Gieysztora, 2005), 430–31.

42. JHIA, 302/27 (S. Puterman, memoir), 24; JHIA, 302/129 (memoir), 109.

43. JHIA, ARG I 687 (I/436), account titled "Hundred-and-Ten," 6. An unknown ghetto inhabitant wrote that among those taken was a policeman leading his captured colleagues.

44. Czerniaków, *Adama Czerniakowa dziennik*, July 1 1942, 294.

45. See Landesarchiv Nordrhein—Westfalen, Abteilung Westfalen, Aus den Ermittlungen der Staatsanwaltschaft Dortmund gegen ehemalige Angehörige des Reserve-Polizeibataillons 61, LAV, NRW, W, Q 223, no. 1486, 118 (Rückseite).

46. On the execution, see Klemp, *Vernichtung*, 115–16.

47. Czerniaków, *Adama Czerniakowa dziennik*, July 8, 1942, 297.

48. JHIA, ARG I 414 (I/29), Jechiel Górny, daily notes, 8.

49. Czerniaków, *Adama Czerniakowa dziennik*, July 20, 1942, 302.

8. Umschlagplatz

1. Hermann Julius Höfle (1911–62)—Austrian-born prewar auto mechanic. From 1942, he was in charge of the organization of Operation Reinhard (Leiter der Hauptabteilung Aktion Reinhard) and personally oversaw the deportations from the Warsaw Ghetto. In November, he played a key role in Operation Erntefest—the mass murder of the surviving Jews in the Lublin District. He was arrested in 1961 in Vienna and committed suicide before the trial started.

2. On Lejkin's presence at that point, see Marcin Urynowicz, *Adam Czerniaków, 1880–1940: Życie i działalność* (Warsaw, IPN: 2008), 323; Koźmińska-Frejlak, *Świadectwo milczenia*, 265.

3. JHIA, 302/129 ([Stanisław Gombiński?], memoir), 118.

4. Koźmińska-Frejlak, *Świadectwo milczenia*, 265. Lewiński described that information as uncertain. Ber Warm claimed that this was on Brandt's initiative. JHIA, 302/188, Ber Warm, *Befehlstelle* (command post) (Żelazna 103), 9.

5. Czerniaków, *Adama Czerniakowa dziennik*, July 22, 1942, 306.

6. Makower cites in his memoir the information he heard, which well reflects the change in the balance of power in the police: "When, after a few days, Colonel Szeryński was brought from Pawiak . . . and in the evening he had a meal after the prison board and after a day's work, Stach Czapliński raised the goblet with vodka and made a toast not for Szeryński's health, but for the health of Lejkin." Makower, *Pamiętnik z getta warszawskiego*, 63.

7. JHIA, ARG II 301 (II/196), study on the first liquidation action in the Warsaw Ghetto (07–09.1942 r.), 30. printed in *Archiwum Ringelbluma*, vol. 33, 423–42.

8. JHIA, ARG II 58 (II/191), Jewish Council in Warsaw, report for the period July 22–September 30, 1942, 2.

9. Seweryn Spotkowski—attorney; from June 1942, head of the Gmina Precinct.

10. JHIA, ARG II 301 (II/196), study on the first liquidation action in the Warsaw Ghetto (07–09.1942 r.), 2.

11. According to the postwar testimony of Jerzy Lewiński, prisoners went to Umschlagplatz willingly, expecting to be sent to labor camps, where the living conditions would presumably be better than in the prison. Koźmińska-Frejlak, *Świadectwo milczenia*, 265.

12. Leon Najberg, *Ostatni powstańcy getta* (Warsaw: Żydowski Instytut Historyczny, 1993), 13. According to postwar testimonies, some of the prisoners managed to escape from the transport. JHIA 313/110 (Józef Rubinrodt-Marczak), Protokół przesłuchania świadka Rafała Pragi.

13. According to Jerzy Lewiński, the blockade at Muranowska was carried out on July 23 only by Germans, as the Jewish policemen were not effective. This could be confirmed by a note from that day by Adam Czerniaków, who wrote down that by 4:00 p.m., the Jewish Order Service brought to the Umschlagplatz only four thousand people out of the required nine thousand. This is, however, not confirmed elsewhere. See Koźmińska-Frejlak, *Świadectwo milczenia*, 268, and Czerniaków, *Adama Czerniakowa dziennik*, July 23, 1942, 306.

14. Gombiński, *Wspomnienia policjanta*, 78.

15. According to the notice that appeared on the walls of the ghetto buildings around midday of July 22, 1942, exempted from deportation were "a) everyone employed by the authorities or in German enterprises who can present appropriate evidence of this; b) all Jews who are members or employees of the Judenrat at the date of the publication of this order; c) all Jews employed in firms belonging to the German Reich who can present appropriate evidence of this; d) all Jews who are fit for work, who to date have not been included in the employment process; these should be put in barracks in the Jewish District; e) all Jews who are members of the Jewish Order Service; f) all Jews who are part of the personnel of Jewish hospitals and who are in the Jewish disinfection columns; g) all Jews who are close family members of the persons named in a to f. Only wives and children are counted as family members; h) all Jews, who on the first day of the deportations are in one of the Jewish hospitals and are not fit to be discharged. Unfitness for discharge must be certified by a doctor appointed by the Judenrat." JHIA, ARG II 52 (II/186), quoted in Engelking and Leociak, *Warsaw Ghetto*, 705.

16. JHIA, 302/129 ([Stanisław Gombiński?], memoir), 157.

17. Lewin, *Cup of Tears*, 137.

18. Ringelblum, *Pisma z getta*, autumn/winter 1942, 414. The Jewish Emergency Service de facto merged at that point with the Jewish Order Service—its members received help from SEPOR and the same food rations as members of the Jewish Order Service. "Dwa lata pracy Żyd. Pogotowia Ratunkowego" [Two years of the Jewish Emergency Service], *Gazeta Żydowska*, August 14, 1942. According to Mina Tomkiewicz, members of the Emergency Service were meant to be placed in a block next to the police block and deported in September 1942. Tomkiewicz, *Of Bombs and Mice*, 233.

19. Makower, *Pamiętnik z getta warszawskiego*, 63.

20. According to one testimony, Szmerling was for a short time replaced on the Umschlagplatz by Marian Händel's adjutant, Jerzy Furstenberg. JHIA, 313/141 (Abram Wolfowicz), Oświadczenie Majera Rubinsztajna.

21. Adler, *In the Warsaw Ghetto*, 75. See also a satirical take on Szmerling's brutality in the Jewish Order Service revue: JHIA, ARG I 1349 (I/35), profiles of famous figures of the [Jewish] Order Service.

22. JHIA, 302/129 ([Stanisław Gombiński?], memoir), 153; JHIA, 302/27 (S. Puterman, memoir), 181–83.

23. JHIA, 302/27 (S. Puterman, memoir), 179. According to Puterman, twelve members of the service were employed as the loaders.

24. JHIA, ARG II 301 (II/196), study on the first liquidation action in the Warsaw Ghetto (07–09.1942 r.), 12. According to this testimony, Germans assisted members of the Jewish Order Service during the blockades of buildings at Lubeckiego and Gliniana Streets on July 24.

25. JHIA, ARG II 68 (II/188), announcement of July 29, 1942. On July 1, 1942, this order was prolonged by three days.

26. JHIA, ARG II 300 (II/192), report titled "Liquidation of Jewish Warsaw," 15.

27. JHIA, ARG II 301 (II/196), study on the first liquidation action in the Warsaw Ghetto (07–09.1942 r.), 14.

28. Lewin, *Cup of Tears*, 142.

29. Ringelblum wrote that "90 percent of those uncovering the hideouts are Jewish policemen. They first found the hideouts themselves and then pointed them out to the Ukrainians and Germans." Ringelblum, *Pisma z getta*, December 24, 1942, 428.

30. Korczak, "O projekcie 'dziecko i policja,'" 274.

31. Halina Birenbaum, *Hope Is the Last to Die: A Personal Documentation of Nazi Terror* (Oświęcim: Publishing House of the State Museum in Oświęcim, 1994), 52.

32. JHIA, 302/49 (Henryk Rudnicki, "History of the Martyrology and Ending of the Warsaw Ghetto, 1942," unpublished memoir), 31.

33. Lewin, *Cup of Tears*, August 20, 1942, 161.

34. Natalia Aleksiun, "Intimate Violence: Jewish Testimonies on Victims and Perpetrators in Eastern Galicia," *Holocaust Studies* 23, nos. 1–2 (2017): 17–33.

35. Kaplan, *Scroll of Agony*, 325.

36. Kaplan, 327.

37. Kaplan, 329.

38. Ringelblum, *Pisma z getta*, December 5, 1942, 416.

39. Lewin, *Cup of Tears*, July 25, 1942, 137. On deportation as a punishment for looting, see JHIA, 302/129 ([Stanisław Gombiński?], memoir), 153.

40. JHIA, 302/49 (Rudnicki, "History of "Martyrology," 23.

41. Stefan Chaskielewicz, "Rozmowa z panem J.B.D.," in *Ukrywałem się w Warszawie: Styczeń 1943–1945* (Cracow: Znak, 1988), 120.

42. Ringelblum, *Pisma z getta*, October 15, 1942, 393.

43. Ringelblum, December 24, 1942, 428.

44. Lewin, *Cup of Tears*, July 29, 1942, 141.

45. Gombiński, *Wspomnienia policjanta*, 109; JHIA, 301/4511 (Estera Rozin, testimony). According to a report of the ghetto underground, Kapłański was to save seventy people from the Umschlagplatz. See JHIA, ARG II 300 (II/192), report titled "Liquidation of Jewish Warsaw," 20. Among those mentioned are the head of the Central Lockup, Ludwik Lindenfeld, and his deputy, Izaak Rudniański. An anonymous member of the Jewish Order Service (perhaps Stanisław Gombiński) estimated that twenty to thirty policemen were shot on the Umschlagplatz. JHIA, 302/129 ([Stanisław Gombiński?], memoir), 159.

46. Władysław Szlengel, "Pożegnanie z czapką" [Farewell to the cap], JHIA, utwory literackie [literary works], 226, j. 270. Transl. Krzysztof Heymer. Władysław Szlengel (1914–43)—poet, very popular songwriter; perished during the Warsaw Ghetto Uprising.

47. Some of them managed to find refuge in the Central Lockup. See YVA, O.33/129.

48. JHIA, 301/3334 (Maria Kasmanowa, testimony).

49. Tomkiewicz, *Of Bombs and Mice*, 218–19.

50. JHIA, 302/27 (S. Puterman, memoir).

51. Any member of the Jewish Order Service who allowed anyone other than his wife and children to live in his apartment was to be executed. See Makower, *Pamiętnik z getta warszawskiego*, 73.

52. Janina Bauman, *Winter in the Morning: A Young Girl's Life in the Warsaw Ghetto and Beyond, 1939–1945* (London: Virago, 1986), 73.

53. Janina David, *A Square of Sky, a Touch of Earth: A Wartime Childhood in Poland* (Harmondsworth, UK: Penguin, 1981), 164.

54. USC Shoah Foundation Visual History Archive, Stefania Staszewska, interview 4286.

55. Perechodnik, *Am I a Murderer?*, 17.

56. JHIA, 301/688 (Aron Czechowicz, testimony); Kaplan, *Scroll of Agony*, 325.

57. JHIA, 302/49 (Rudnicki, "History of Martyrology"), 23.

58. JHIA, memoir, quoted in Engelking and Leociak, *Warsaw Ghetto*, 714.

59. JHIA, ARG II 303 (II/199), Yehoshua Perle, "Destruction of Warsaw," 28.

60. Cywia Lubetkin, *Zagłada i powstanie*, trans. in M. Krych (Warsaw: Książka i Wiedza, 1999), 71.

61. Lubetkin, *Zagłada i powstanie*, 72.

62. According to JHIA, ARG II 301 (II/196), study on the first liquidation action in the Warsaw Ghetto (07–09.1942 r.), 15, such blockades involved only a few members of the Jewish Order Service.

63. Gombiński, *Wspomnienia policjanta*, 114.

64. Makower, *Pamiętnik z getta warszawskiego*, 118.

65. Bauman, *Winter in the Morning*, 75.

66. JHIA, ARG II 303 (II/199), Y. Perle, "Destruction of Warsaw," 111.

67. Bauman, *Winter in the Morning,* 75–76.

68. JHIA, 302/129 ([Stanisław Gombiński?], memoir), 168. Makower writes that almost none of the "civil functionaries" (among them doctors and office employees) received life numbers. Makower, *Pamiętnik z getta warszawskiego,* 126.

69. JHIA, 302/188 (B. Warm, Befehlstelle [Żelazna 103]), 7. Makower writes that the Directorate of the Jewish Order Service brought their families to the Directorate offices on Ogrodowa Street. Makower, *Pamiętnik z getta warszawskiego,* 119.

70. JHIA, 302/27 (S. Puterman, memoir), 239–40. Also, Mina Tomkiewicz confirms that the numbers were distributed by Lejkin. Tomkiewicz, *Of Bombs and Mice* 240.

71. I base this description mainly on JHIA, 302/129 ([Stanisław Gombiński?], memoir), 169, which contains the most detailed information about the September selection.

72. Some write that the policemen's wives and children were deported while the policemen were called to a participate in a pretend blockade on Szczę śliwa Street. Ringelblum, *Pisma z getta,* September 24, 1942, 426.

73. Lewin, *Cup of Tears,* September 23, 1942, 184.

74. Makower, *Pamiętnik z getta warszawskiego,* p.

75. Makower, 127.

76. They were, for example, to calm others by showing them fabricated letters supposedly sent by previous deportees JHIA, ARG II 303 (II/199), Y. Perle, "Destruction of Warsaw," 36.

77. Ernest, *O wojnie wielkich Niemiec z Żydami Warszawy,* 177. Such letters were also shown around by other policemen. See Eugenia Szajn-Lewin, *W getcie warszawskim: lipiec 1942—kwiecień 1943* (Poznań: A5, 1989), 34. According to Ringelblum, (*Pisma z getta,* October 15, 1942, 400), false positive news about letters from "the East" was spread in the ghetto by Gestapo collaborators.

78. JHIA, 302/167 (Stefania Szochur [Staszewska], memoir), 29.

79. JHIA, ARG II 300 (II/192), report titled "Liquidation of Jewish Warsaw," 13. Tadeusz Epsztein and Aleksandra Bańkowska, who prepared the Polish-language edition of this document, noted that its final version was much less openly negative regarding the behavior of the Jewish Order Service than the first one. See *Archiwum Ringelbluma: Konspiracyjne Archiwum Getta Warszawy,* vol. 11, *Ludzie i prace "Oneg Szabat,"* ed. Aleksandra Bańkowska and Tadeusz Epsztein (Warsaw: Żydowski Instytut Historyczny, 2013), lxiv.

9. After Resettlement

1. Perechodnik, *Am I a Murderer?,* 77.

2. JHIA, ARG II 58 (II/191, II/189), Jewish Council in Warsaw, report for the period July 22–September 30, 1942, 9.

3. JHIA, ARG II 56 (II/262), Jewish Council in Warsaw, announcement on Week of Cleanliness, January 3–9, 1943, 1.

4. Stanisław Holckener's recollections of imprisonment at Żelazna can be found in the Ghetto Fighters House Archives. In them, he thanks Czapliński, who by not

informing the Gestapo about his attempted bribery of Blue Policemen saved him from immediate execution. GFH, Adolf Berman Collection, 6086 (Stanisław Holckener), 10–11.

5. JHIA, 302/188 (B. Warm, Befehlstelle [Żelazna 103]), 18.

6. JHIA, ARG II 423 (II/338/1), *Wiadomości. ARG* [News. ARG], December 22, 1942, no. 3, 30.

7. GFH, Adolf Berman Collection, 5967, Emanuel Ringelblum's notes on a publication called *Na oczach świata* [In front of the eyes of the world] by Maria Kann.

8. JHIA, 302/49 (Rudnicki, "History of Martyrology"), 51.

9. JHIA, ARG II 426 (II/333), "Announcement," printed in *Archiwum Ringelbluma,* vol. 34, 560–61.

10. David Engel, "Why Punish Collaborators?," in *Jewish Honor Courts: Revenge, Retribution, and Reconciliation in Europe and Israel after the Holocaust,* ed. Laura Jockusch and Gabriel N. Finder (Detroit: Wayne State University Press, 2015), 35.

11. JHIA, ARG I 414 (I/29), Jechiel Górny, daily notes, November 5, 1942, 2.

12. Lubetkin, *Zagłada i powstanie,* 80; Cukierman, *Nadmiar pamięci,* 232. For details on Brzeziński's death see JHIA, 301/1308 (Ryszard Mitelberg, testimony).

13. Ringelblum, *Kronika,* 497.

14. Author's conversation with Kalman Teigman, a survivor of Treblinka death camp, Tel Aviv, January 2012.

15. Władysław Szlengel, "Zahlen bitte," JHIA, Utwory literackie, 226, j. 270, transl. Krzysztof Heymer.

16. JHIA, 302/49 (Rudnicki, "History of Martyrology"), 51. Jakub Lejkin's grave can be still found at the Jewish Cemetery in Warsaw.

17. Ringelblum, *Pisma z getta,* December 5, 1942, 415.

18. Leon Najberg, *Ostatni Powstańcy Getta* (Warsaw: Żydowski Instytut Historyczny, 1993), 34.

19. JHIA, ARG II 423 (II/338/1), *Wiadomości* [News], December 22, 1942, no. 3, printed in *Archiwum Ringelbluma: Konspiracyjne Archiwum Getta Warszawy,* vol. 11, *Ludzie i prace Oneg Szabat,* ed. A. Bańkowska, T. Epsztein (Warsaw: Żydowski Instytut Historyczny, 2013), 258–98.

20. David, *Square of Sky,* 248.

21. On the January uprising, see Cukierman, *Nadmiar pamięci,* 191–249.

22. Makower, *Pamiętnik z getta warszawskiego,* 150. Alina Brewda (1905–88) was an obstetrician. She worked as a doctor in the ghetto and later at Majdanek and Auschwitz-Birkenau.

23. Gombiński, *Wspomnienia policjanta,* 144.

24. Cukierman, 210. Information about this institution appears in the memoirs of Maria Lewi-Kurowska, who described it in mid-1943 (after the Warsaw Ghetto Uprising): "A typical camp, fenced with barbed wire. At the entrance and around, armed German guards. . . . I could only stand across, on the other side of the road and watch helplessly. . . . [Prisoners] found the right moment and threw a stone wrapped in a note in my direction, in which they wrote that the workplace was changed, that they go out less frequently, and that one day they will work along the tracks along the East Railway Station." Maria Lewi-Kurowska, *Pamięć pozostanie* (Warsaw: Wydawnictwo Myśl, 1993), 96.

25. APW, KŻDM, RG 13, "Report of the Chairman of the Jewish Council for the Month of January 1943."

26. Makower, *Pamiętnik z getta warszawskiego*, 203.

27. APW, KŻDM, RG 14, "Report of the Chairman of the Jewish Council for the Month of February 1943."

28. Szapiro, *Wojna żydowsko-niemiecka*, 22–23.

29. JHIA, 302/129 ([Stanisław Gombiński?], memoir), 212. Ber Warm writes in his memoir that members of the Jewish Order Service were alongside the Germans shot at by the Jewish insurgents. JHIA, 302/188 (B. Warm, "Niska i Prosta czyli ostatnie dni legalnego żywota Żydów w Warszawie"), 6.

30. JHIA, 302/188 (B. Warm, "Niska i Prosta czyli ostatnie dni legalnego żywota Żydów w Warszawie"), 20–21. According to Warm, the Jewish Order Service also performed auxiliary duties on the Umschlagplatz at that point.

31. Marian Berland, *Dni długie jak wieki* (Warsaw: Niezależna Oficyna Wydawnicza, 1992), 102–3.

32. According to Polish Radio in London, this took place on April 30. Komunikat z 6 maja 1943, quoted in Szapiro, *Wojna żydowsko-niemiecka*, 123. Ber Warm (JHIA, 302/188, B. Warm, "Niska i Prosta czyli ostatnie dni legalnego żywota Żydów w Warszawie," 39) writes that it took place in the night of April 28–29. An anonymous description of these events can be found in the files of Henryk Nowogrodzki's postwar trial. Its author, who dated this event April 29 or 30, writes, "After bringing all Jewish policemen to the Judenrat on Gęsia Street and holding them a dozen or so days— the exact date I do not remember, I remember Thursday or Friday after a meal at 1700—they brought under the escort of Germans to 37 Pawiak and 39 Dzielna Streets over 150 to 200 Jewish policemen, and there were officers, acquaintances of mine. They were ordered to strip naked and were all shot by the SS at Pawiak." JHIA, 313/89 (Sąd Społeczny przy Centralnym Komitecie Żydów w Polsce, Henryk Nowogródzki), anonymous letter to the Social Court.

33. Ringelblum, *Pisma z getta*, December 24, 1942, 426.

34. JHIA, ARG I 414 (I/29), Jechiel Górny, daily notes, November 5, 1942, 6.

10. The Courts

1. Quoted in Gabriel N. Finder, "Proces Szepsla Rotholca a polityka kary w następstwie Zagłady" *Zagłada Żydów: Studia i Materiały*, no. 2 (2006): 225.

2. I did not come across any trials of members of the Jewish Order Service held in Polish state courts. Investigation materials can be found in, among other places, IPN GK, 453/1004 (akta sprawy Szapsla Rotholca); and IPN BU, 0423/3315 (sprawa operacyjna dot. Zygmunta Klumel-Kluczyka).

3. JHIA, 313/1 (Sąd Społeczny przy Centralnym Komitecie Żydów w Polsce, Aleksander Eintracht), verdict.

4. Finder, "Proces Szepsla Rotholca," 221–41.

5. JHIA, 313/109 (Szapsel Rotholc), uzasadnienie wyroku w sprawie Szepsla Rotholca z dnia 29.11.1946.

6. JHIA, 313/92 (Sąd Społeczny przy Centralnym Komitecie Żydów w Polsce, Karol Peczenik), Protokół przesłuchania Karola Peczenika.

7. JHIA, 313/35 (Sąd Społeczny przy Centralnym Komitecie Żydów w Polsce, Stanisław Gombiński), Wyjaśnienie Stanisława Gombińskiego.

8. YIVO, HWC 42.2, Hersz Wasser, ekspertyza.

9. Raul Hilberg, "The Nature of the Process," in *Survivors, Victims, and Perpetrators: Essays on the Nazi Holocaust*, ed. Joel E. Dimsdale (Washington, DC: Hemisphere Publishing, 1980), 5–54.

10. Ringelblum, *Pisma z getta*, December 5, 1942, 415.

11. JHIA, 313/65 (Sąd Społeczny przy Centralnym Komitecie Żydów w Polsce, Jerzy Lewiński), Oświadczenie Rozali Landsberg-Englowej.

12. Gombiński, *Wspomnienia policjanta*, 127.

13. Marian Händel emigrated after the war to Venezuela, and Abram Wolfowicz emigrated to Australia. They both changed their last names.

14. JHIA, 302/129 ([Stanisław Gombiński?], memoir); JHIA, 302/27 (Stanisław Puterman, memoir).

15. JHIA, 301/4325 (Szapsel Rotholc, testimony). On Rotholc, see Finder, *Proces Szepsla Rotholca*, 221–41.

16. Adler's diary was published in English thirty-six years after his death. It was published in the original Polish only in 2018.

17. GFH, Adolfa Berman Collection, 6040, Józef Fels, "Wspomnienia. . . ."

18. Jacek Leociak, *Text in the Face of Destruction: Accounts from the Warsaw Ghetto Reconsidered* (Warsaw: Żydowski Instytut Historyczny, 2004), 127.

19. On writing as therapy in Perechodnik's case, see Garbarini, *Numbered Days*, 142–43.

20. See Henryk Nowogródzki, *Ze wspomnień warszawskiego adwokata* (Warsaw: Wydawnictwo Prawnicze, 1986).

21. Christopher R. Browning, *Remembering Survival: Inside a Nazi Slave-Labor Camp* (New York: W. W. Norton, 2010), 9.

22. JHIA, 303/I 12, "Protokół posiedzenia Prezydium z dnia 8 X 1946." On that, see also Andrzej Żbikowski, *Sąd Społeczny przy CKŻP. Wojenne rozliczenia społeczności żydowskiej w Polsce* (Warsaw: Żydowski Instytut Historyczny, 2015).

23. Browning, *Remembering Survival*, 10.

24. On the trials in Israel of prisoner functionaries, see Rivka Brot, *Be'eyzor haafor: Hakapo hayehudi kemishpat* (Tel Aviv: Open University Publishing House, 2019).

25. Raul Hilberg, *The Politics of Memory: The Journey of a Holocaust Historian* (Chicago: Ivan R. Dee, 1996), 69.

26. Noe Grüss, *Rok pracy Centralnej Żydowskiej Komisji Historycznej* (Łódź: CKŻP, 1946), 10.

27. On the early research on the ghetto as a "Jewish space," see Tim Cole, "Ghettoization," in *The Historiography of the Holocaust*, ed. D. Stone (London: Palgrave, 2004), 67–77. On the historiography of collaboration and forced cooperation during the Holocaust, see Laura Jockusch and Gabriel Finder, "Introduction," in Jockusch and Finder, *Jewish Honor Courts*, 1–28, and Dan Michman, "Kontroversen über die Judenräte in der jüdischen Welt: Das Ineinandergreifen von öffentlichem Gedächtnis und Geschichtsschreibung 1945–2005," in *Judenrat von Białystok: Dokumente aus dem Archiv des białystoker Ghettos 1941–1943*, ed. F. Anders, K. Stoll, and K. Wilke (Paderborn: Schöningh, 2010), 311–17.

28. Hannah Arendt, *Eichmann in Jerusalem: A Report on the Banality of Evil* (New York: Viking, 1963); Raul Hilberg, *The Destruction of the European Jews* (Chicago: Quadrangle, 1961). See also Philip Friedman's 1957 lecture "Preliminary and Methodological Aspects of Research on the Judenrat," in *Roads to Extinction: Essays on the Holocaust* (New York: Jewish Publication Society, 1980), 539–53.

29. Trunk, *Judenrat*, 499. See also Aharon Weiss, "The Relations between the Judenrat and the Jewish Police," in *Patterns of Jewish Leadership in Nazi Europe, 1933–1945: Proceedings of the Third Yad Vashem International Historical Conference, Jerusalem, April 4–7, 1977* (Jerusalem: Yad Vashem, 1979), 201–18.

30. The first academic work on the Jewish Order Service was Aldona Podolska's *Służba Porządkowa w getcie warszawskim*. See also Engelking and Leociak, *Warsaw Ghetto*, 190–218.

31. Documents from the underground archive of the Kovno police were published in *The Clandestine History of the Kovno Jewish Ghetto Police*, ed. Samuel Schalkowsky (Bloomington: Indiana University Press in association with the United States Holocaust Memorial Museum, 2014). See also Dov Levin, "How the Jewish Police in the Kovno Ghetto Saw Itself," *Yad Vashem Studies* no. 29 (2001): 183–241, and Dalia Ofer, "Swearing-in Ceremony: The Police in the Kovno Ghetto, November 1, 1942," *Partial Answers: Journal of Literature and the History of Ideas*, no. 2 (2009): 229–41.

32. See, among others, Ryszard Gontarz, "Samotni wśród współbraci" [Lonely among their brothers], *Kurier Polski*, March 29, 1968; Adam W. Wysocki, "W obronie pamięci bohaterów getta" [In defense of the memory of ghetto heroes], *Kurier Polski*, April 13–15, 1968; and B. C., "Fałsz i oszczerstwo" [Falsification and slander], *Żołnierz Wolności*, April 4, 1968.

33. Sławomir Buryła, *Opisać Zagładę: Holocaust w twórczości Henryka Grynberga* (Toruń: Wydawnictwo UMK, 2014), 43.

Conclusion

1. JHIA, ARG I 414 (I/29), Jechiel Górny, daily notes, November 5, 1942, 4.

2. On that, see Primo Levi, "The Grey Zone," in *The Holocaust: Origins, Implementation, Aftermath*, ed. Omer Bartov (London: Routledge, 2002), 251–72.

3. Levi, "Grey Zone," 257.

4. Browning, *Remembering Survival*, 297–98.

5. Hilberg, *Politics of Memory*, 193.

BIBLIOGRAPHY

Archival Collections

Archiwum Akt Nowych, Warsaw
Archiwum Instytutu Pamięci Narodowej, Warsaw
Archiwum Państwowe w Warszawie, Warsaw
Jewish Historical Institute Archive, Warsaw
Ghetto Fighters House Archive, Lohamei Hagetaot, Israel
Landesarchiv Nordrhein–Westfalen, Abteilung Westfalen, Münster
Muzeum Historii Żydów Polskich Archive, Warsaw
Staatsarchiv der Hansestadt Hamburg, Hamburg
United States Holocaust Memorial Museum Archive, Washington, DC
USC Shoah Foundation Visual History Archive, Los Angeles
Yad Vashem Archive, Jerusalem
YIVO Archive, New York

Newspapers and Periodicals

Biuletyn (Warsaw Ghetto)
Dos Fraye Vort (Warsaw Ghetto)
Dror (Warsaw Ghetto)
El-Al (Warsaw Ghetto)
Gazeta Policyjna Państwowa (Warsaw)
Gazeta Żydowska (Warsaw Ghetto)
Kurier Polski (Warsaw)
Na Posterunku (Warsaw)
Nasz Przegląd (Warsaw)
Nasz Przegląd Ilustrowany: Dodatek specjalny do "Naszego Przeglądu" (Warsaw)
Nowy Kurier Warszawski (Warsaw)
Wiadomości ARG (Warsaw Ghetto)
Nowy Kurier Warszawski (Warsaw)
Der Oyfbroyz (Warsaw Ghetto)
Polska Zbrojna (Warsaw)
Przegląd Policyjny (Warsaw)
Wiadomości Polskie (London)
Żagiew (Warsaw Ghetto)
Yedies (Warsaw Ghetto)
Yugnt Shtime (Warsaw Ghetto)

Za Naszą i Waszą Wolność (Warsaw Ghetto)
Żołnierz Wolności (Warsaw)

Published Primary Sources

Adler, Stanisław. *In the Warsaw Ghetto 1940–1943: An Account of a Witness; The Memoirs of Stanisław Adler.* Translated by Sara Philip. Jerusalem: Yad Vashem, 1982.

Archiwum Ringelbluma: Konspiracyjne Archiwum Getta Warszawy. Vol. 2, *Dzieci—tajne nauczanie w getcie warszawskim.* Edited by Ruta Sakowska and Felix Tych. Warsaw: Żydowski Instytut Historyczny, 2000.

Archiwum Ringelbluma: Konspiracyjne Archiwum Getta Warszawy. Vol. 6, *Generalne Gubernatorstwo: Relacje i dokumenty.* Edited by Aleksandra Bańkowska. Warsaw: Żydowski Instytut Historyczny, 2012.

Archiwum Ringelbluma: Konspiracyjne Archiwum Getta Warszawy. Vol. 11, *Ludzie i prace "Oneg Szabat."* Edited by Aleksandra Bańkowska and Tadeusz Epsztein. Warsaw: Żydowski Instytut Historyczny, 2013.

Archiwum Ringelbluma: Konspiracyjne Archiwum Getta Warszawy. Vol. 12, *Rada Żydowska w Warszawie (1939–1943).* Edited by Marta Janczewska. Warsaw: Żydowski Instytut Historyczny, 2014.

Archiwum Ringelbluma: Konspiracyjne Archiwum Getta Warszawy. Vol. 14, *Kolekcja Hersza Wassera.* Edited by Katarzyna Person. Warsaw: Żydowski Instytut Historyczny, 2014.

Archiwum Ringelbluma: Konspiracyjne Archiwum Getta Warszawy. Vol. 16, *Prasa getta warszawskiego: Bund i Cukunft.* Edited by Martyna Rusiniak-Karwat and Alicja Jarkowska-Natkaniec. Warsaw: Żydowski Instytut Historyczny, 2016.

Archiwum Ringelbluma: Konspiracyjne Archiwum Getta Warszawy. Vol. 17, *Prasa getta warszawskiego: Poalej Syjon Lewica i Poalej Syjon Prawica.* Edited by Eleonora Bergman, Tadeusz Epsztein, and Maciej Wójcicki. Warsaw: Żydowski Instytut Historyczny, 2016.

Archiwum Ringelbluma: Konspiracyjne Archiwum Getta Warszawy. Vol. 19, *Prasa getta warszawskiego: Hechaluc-Dror i Gordonia.* Edited by Piotr Laskowski and Sebastian Matuszewski. Warsaw: Żydowski Instytut Historyczny, 2015.

Archiwum Ringelbluma: Konspiracyjne Archiwum Getta Warszawy. Vol. 20, *Prasa getta warszawskiego: Ugrupowania prawicowe.* Edited by Marcin Urynowicz. Warsaw: Żydowski Instytut Historyczny, 2015.

Archiwum Ringelbluma: Konspiracyjne Archiwum Getta Warszawy. Vol. 23, *Dzienniki z getta warszawskiego.* Edited by Katarzyna Person, Zofia Trębacz, and Michał Trębacz. Warsaw: Żydowski Instytut Historyczny, 2015.

Archiwum Ringelbluma: Konspiracyjne Archiwum Getta Warszawy. Vol. 24, *Obozy pracy przymusowej.* Edited by Marta Janczewska. Warsaw: Żydowski Instytut Historyczny, 2015.

Archiwum Ringelbluma: Konspiracyjne Archiwum Getta Warszawy. Vol. 26, *Utwory literackie z getta warszawskiego.* Edited by Agnieszka Żółkiewska and Marek Tuszewicki. Warsaw: Żydowski Instytut Historyczny, 2017.

Archiwum Ringelbluma: Konspiracyjne Archiwum Getta Warszawy. Vol. 31, *Pisma Pereca Opoczyńskiego.* Edited by Monika Polit. Warsaw: Żydowski Instytut Historyczny, 2017.

Archiwum Ringelbluma: Konspiracyjne Archiwum Getta Warszawy. Vol. 32, *Pisma rabina Szymona Huberbanda*. Edited by Anna Ciałowicz. Warsaw: Żydowski Instytut Historyczny, 2017.

Archiwum Ringelbluma: Konspiracyjne Archiwum Getta Warszawy. Vol. 33, *Getto warszawskie, cz. I*. Edited by Tadeusz Epsztein and Katarzyna Person. Warsaw: Żydowski Instytut Historyczny, 2016.

Archiwum Ringelbluma: Konspiracyjne Archiwum Getta Warszawy. Vol. 34, *Getto warszawskie, cz. II*. Edited by Tadeusz Epsztein. Warsaw: Żydowski Instytut Historyczny, 2016.

Auerbach, Rachela. "Dziennik." In *Pisma z getta warszawskiego*, edited and translated by K. Szymaniak, 79–206. Warsaw: Żydowski Instytut Historyczny, 2016.

Bauman, Janina. *Winter in the Morning: A Young Girl's Life in the Warsaw Ghetto and Beyond, 1939–1945*. London: Virago, 1986.

Berenstein, Tatiana, Artur Eisenbach, Adam Rutkowski, eds. *Eksterminacja Żydów na ziemiach polskich w okresie okupacji hitlerowskiej: Zbiór dokumentów*. Warsaw: Żydowski Instytut Historyczny, 1957.

Berland, Marian. *Dni długie jak wieki*. Warsaw: Niezależna Oficyna Wydawnicza, 1992.

Birenbaum, Halina. *Hope Is the Last to Die: A Personal Documentation of Nazi Terror*. Oświęcim: Publishing House of the State Museum in Oświęcim, 1994.

Browning, C., and Y. Gutman, eds. "The Reports of a Jewish 'Informer' in the Warsaw Ghetto: Selected Documents." *Yad Vashem Studies* 17 (1986): 247–93.

Chaskielewicz, Stefan. "Rozmowa z panem J.B.D." In *Ukrywałem się w Warszawie: Styczeń 1943–1945*. Cracow: Znak, 1988.

Cukierman, Icchak. *Nadmiar pamięci (siedem owych lat): Wspomnienia 1939–1946*. Translated by Zoja Perelmuter. Warsaw: PWN, 2000.

Czajka, Michał, and Tadeusz Epsztein, eds. "Nieznany dziennik z getta warszawskiego." *Kwartalnik Historii Żydów*, no. 1 (2013): 32–67.

Czerniaków, Adam. *Adama Czerniakowa dziennik getta warszawskiego 6 IX 1939–23 VII 1942*. Edited by M. Fuks. Warsaw: Wydawnictwo Naukowe PWN, 1983.

Datner, Helena, and Olga Pieńkowska, eds. *70 lat historii ŻIH w dokumentach źródłowych*. Warsaw: Żydowski Instytut Historyczny, 2017.

David, Janina. *A Square of Sky, a Touch of Earth: A Wartime Childhood in Poland*. (Harmondsworth, UK: Penguin, 1981.

Dunin-Wąsowicz, K., ed. *Raporty Ludwiga Fischera gubernatora dystryktu warszawskiego, 1939–1944*. Warsaw: Książka i Wiedza, 1987.

Ernest, Stefan. *O wojnie wielkich Niemiec z Żydami Warszawy*. Edited by Marta Młodkowska. Warsaw: Czytelnik, 2003.

Friedrich, K.-P., ed. *Die Verfolgung und Ermordung der europäischen Juden durch das nationalsozialistische Deutschland: 1933–1945*. Vol. 9: *Polen: Generalgouvernement August 1941–1945*. Munich: Oldenbourg Verlag, 2014.

Gitler, Józef. *Leben am seidenen Faden: Tagebuch aus dem Austauschlager Bergen-Belsen*. Translated by J. Liedke. Edited by K. Liedke. Göttingen: Wallstein Verlag, 2015.

Gombiński, Stanisław. *Wspomnienia policjanta z warszawskiego getta*. Edited by Marta Janczewska. Warsaw: Centrum Badań nad Zagładą Żydów, 2010.

Grabitz, Helge, and Wolfgang Scheffler. *Letzte Spuren: Ghetto Warschau–SS-Arbeitslager Trawniki–Aktion Erntefest; Fotos und Dokumente über Opfer des Endlösungswahns im Spiegel der historischen Ereignisse*. Berlin: Hentrich, 1988.

Hirszfeld, Ludwik. *Historia jednego życia*. Warsaw: Wydawnictwo Literackie, 2011.

Kaplan, Chaim Aron. *Scroll of Agony: The Warsaw Diary of Chaim A. Kaplan*. Edited by A. I. Katsch. New York: Macmillan, 1965.

Kazimierski, Józef, ed. *Ludność żydowska w Warszawie w latach 1939–1943: Życie—walka—zagłada*. Warsaw: DiG, 2012.

Koźmińska-Frejlak, Ewa. "Świadectwo milczenia: Rozmowa z Jerzym Lewińskim, byłym funkcjonariuszem Służby Porządkowej getta warszawskiego." *Zagłada Żydów: Studia i Materiały* 2 (2006): 245–79.

Korczak, Janusz. *Pamiętnik i inne pisma z getta*, edited by Maria Ciesielska. Warsaw: WAB, 2012.

Landau, Ludwik. *Kronika lat wojny i okupacji*. Vol. 1. Edited by Z. Landau and J. Tomaszewski. Warsaw: PWN, 1962.

Lewi-Kurowska, Maria. *Pamięć pozostanie*. Warsaw: Wydawnictwo Myśl, 1993.

Lewin, Abraham. *A Cup of Tears: A Diary of the Warsaw Ghetto*. Edited by Antony Polonsky. Translated by Christopher Hutton. London: Blackwell, 1989.

Lubetkin, Cywia. *Zagłada i powstanie*. Translated by Maria Krych. Warsaw: Książka i Wiedza, 1999.

Makower, Henryk. *Pamiętnik z getta warszawskiego październik 1940—styczeń 1943*. Wrocław: Ossolineum, 1987.

Makower, Noemi. *Miłość w cieniu śmierci: Wspomnienia z getta warszawskiego*. Wrocław: Erechtejon, 1996.

Mazor, Michael. *The Vanished City: Everyday Life in the Warsaw Ghetto*. Translated by D. Jacobson. New York: Marsillio, 1993.

Najberg, Leon. *Ostatni powstańcy getta*. Warsaw: Żydowski Instytut Historyczny, 1993.

Pankiewicz, Tadeusz. *Apteka w getcie krakowskim*. Cracow: Wydawnictwo Literackie, 2012.

Passenstein, Marek. "Szmugiel w getcie warszawskim." *Biuletyn Żydowskiego Instytutu Historycznego*, no. 2 (1958): 42–72.

Perechodnik, Calel. *Am I a Murderer? Testament of a Jewish Ghetto Policeman*. Translated by and edited by Frank Fox. Boulder, CO: Westview, 1996.

Ringelblum, Emanuel. *Kronika getta warszawskiego*. Edited by Artur Eisenbach. Translated by Adam Rutkowski. Warsaw: Czytelnik, 1983.

——. *Pisma z getta warszawskiego*. Edited by Joanna Nalewajko-Kulkov. Translated by Agata Kondrat. Warsaw: Żydowski Instytut Historyczny, 2018.

Ringelblum Archive: Underground Archive of the Warsaw Ghetto. Vol. 1, *Warsaw Ghetto: Everyday Life*. Edited by Katarzyna Person (Warsaw: Żydowski Instytut Historyczny, 2017).

Rocznik oficerski 1928. Warsaw: Ministerstwo Spraw Wojskowych, 1928.

Roskies, David G., ed. *Voices from the Warsaw Ghetto: Writing Our History*. New Haven, CT: Yale University Press, 2019.

Schalkowsky, Samuel, ed. *The Clandestine History of the Kovno Jewish Ghetto Police*. Bloomington: Indiana University Press in association with the United States Holocaust Memorial Museum, 2014.

Szapiro, Paweł, ed. *Wojna żydowsko-niemiecka: Polska prasa konspiracyjna 1943–1944 o powstaniu w getcie Warszawy*. London: Aneks, 1992.

Szajn-Lewin, Eugenia. *W getcie warszawskim, lipiec 1942—kwiecień 1943*. Poznań: A5, 1989.

Szereszewska, Helena. *Krzyż i mezuza*. Warsaw: Czytelnik, 1993.
Tomkiewicz, Mina. *Of Bombs and Mice: A Novel of War-Time Warsaw*. London: George Allen & Unwin, 1970.
Walczak, H., A. Barta, J. Płotnicki, A. Robaczewski, J. Szeryński, and Z. Krzyżanowski, eds. *Obowiązujące Rozkazy i Okólniki Komendanta głównego Policji Państwowej w układzie rzeczowym*. Warsaw: n.p., 1927.

Secondary Sources

Arendt, Hannah. *Eichmann in Jerusalem: A Report on the Banality of Evil*. New York: Viking, 1963.
Berenstein, Tatiana. "Żydzi warszawscy w hitlerowskich obozach pracy przymusowej," *Biuletyn Żydowskiego Instytutu Historycznego*, no. 3 (1967): 39–65.
Brot, Rivka. *Be'eyzor haafor: Hakapo hayehudi kemishpat*. Tel Aviv: Open University Publishing House, 2019.
Browning, Christopher R. *Remembering Survival: Inside a Nazi Slave-Labor Camp*. New York: W. W. Norton, 2010.
Buryła, Sławomir. *Opisać Zagładę: Holocaust w twórczości Henryka Grynberga*. Toruń: Wydawnictwo UMK, 2014.
Cole, Tim. "Ghettoization." In *The Historiography of the Holocaust*, edited by D. Stone, 67–77. London: Palgrave, 2004.
Curilla, Wolfgang. *Der Judenmord in Polen und die deutsche Ordnungspolizei 1939–1945*. Paderborn: Ferdinard Schoningh, 2011.
Engelking, Barbara. *Holocaust and Memory: The Experience of the Holocaust and Its Consequences; An Investigation Based on Personal Narratives*. Leicester, UK: Leicester University Press, 2002.
——. *Szanowny panie gistapo: Donosy do władz niemieckich w Warszawie i okolicach w latach 1940–1941*. Warsaw: IFiS PAN, 2003.
Engelking, Barbara, and Jan Grabowski. *Żydów łamiących prawo należy karać śmiercią! "Przestępczość" Żydów w Warszawie, 1939–1942*. Warsaw: IFIS PAN, 2010.
Engelking, Barbara, and Jacek Leociak, *Warsaw Ghetto: Guide to the Perished City*. New Haven, CT: Yale University Press, 2009.
Finder, Gabriel N. "Proces Szepsla Rotholca a polityka kary w następstwie Zagłady." *Zagłada Żydów: Studia i Materiały*, no. 2 (2006): 221–41.
Friedman, Philip. "Preliminary and Methodological Aspects of Research on the Judenrat." In *Roads to Extinction: Essays on the Holocaust*, 539–53. New York: Jewish Publication Society, 1980.
Garbarini, Alexandra. *Numbered Days: Diaries and the Holocaust*. New Haven, CT: Yale University Press, 2006.
Getter, Marek. "Policja granatowa w Warszawie." In *Warszawa lat wojny i okupacji 1939–1944*, z. II, edited by K. Dunin-Wąsowicz, J. Kaźmierska, and H. Winnicka, 213–37. Warsaw: PWN, 1972.
Gilman, Sander L. *Jewish Self-Hatred: Anti-Semitism and the Hidden Language of the Jews*. Baltimore: John Hopkins University Press, 1986.
Grabowski, Jan. "Hunting down Emanuel Ringelblum: The Participation of the Polish Kriminalpolizei in the 'Final Solution of the Jewish Question.'" *Holocaust Studies and Materials*, no. 4 (2017): 28–56.

———. "Żydzi przed obliczem niemieckich i polskich sądów w Dystrykcie Warszaw-skim Generalnej Guberni, 1939–1942." In *Prowincja noc: Życie i zagłada Żydów w dystrykcie warszawskim 1939–1945*, edited by B. Engelking, J. Leociak, and D. Libionka, 75–119. Warsaw: IFiS PAN, 2007.

Grabowski, Jan, and Dariusz Libionka, "Reports on the Jews Apprehended in War-saw during May–July 1943 Submitted by the 'Praga' District of the Polish Police." *Holocaust Studies and Materials*, no. 4 (2017): 487–518.

Grüss, Noe. *Rok pracy Centralnej Żydowskiej Komisji Historycznej*. Łódź: CKŻP, 1946.

Hempel, Adam. *Pogrobowcy klęski: rzecz o policji "granatowej" w Generalnym Guberna-torstwie 1939–1945*. Warsaw: PWN, 1990.

Hilberg, Raul. *The Destruction of the European Jews*. Chicago: Quadrangle, 1961.

———. "The Nature of the Process." In *Survivors, Victims, and Perpetrators: Essays on the Nazi Holocaust*, edited by Joel E. Dimsdale, 5–54. Washington, DC: Hemi-sphere Publishing, 1980.

———. *The Politics of Memory: The Journey of a Holocaust Historian*. Chicago: Ivan R. Dee, 1996.

Issinger, Jan H. "Frankenstein w warszawskim getcie: Historia i legenda." *Zagłada Żydów: Studia i Materiały*, no. 12 (2016): 187–208.

Janczewska, Marta. "Gazeta Żydowska (1940–1942)." In *Studia z dziejów trójjęzycznej prasy żydowskiej na ziemiach polskich XIX–XX wieku*, edited by J. Nalewajko-Kulikov, 167–81. Warsaw: IH PAN, Neriton, 2012.

———. "Obozy pracy przymusowej dla Żydów na terenie dystryktu warszawskiego." In *Prowincja noc: Życie i zagłada Żydów w dystrykcie warszawskim 1939–1945*, edited by B. Engelking, J. Leociak, and D. Libionka, 271–320. Warsaw: IFIS PAN, 2007.

Jarkowska-Natkaniec, Alicja. "Jüdischer Ordnungsdienst in Occupied Cracow during the Years 1940–1945." *Scripta Judaica Cracoviensia* 11 (2013): 147–60.

Jockusch, Laura, and Gabriel Finder, eds. *Jewish Honor Courts: Revenge, Retribution, and Reconciliation in Europe and Israel after the Holocaust*. Detroit: Wayne State University Press, 2015.

Kassow, Samuel D. *Who Will Write Our History? Emanuel Ringelblum, the Warsaw Ghetto, and the Oyneg Shabes Archive*. Bloomington: Indiana University Press, 2007.

Kayzer, Ziemowit Bernard. "Kadry urzędów Bezpieczeństwa Publicznego i ich roz-mieszczenie w autonomicznym województwie śląskim w latach 1922–1939." *Zeszyty Naukowe WSOWL* 3, no. 161 (2011): 277–78.

Kijek, Kamil. "Was It Possible to Avoid 'Hebrew Assimilation'? Hebraism, Poloniza-tion, and Tarbut Schools in the Last Decade of Interwar Poland." *Jewish Social Studies* 21, no. 2 (2016): 105–41.

Klemp, Stefan. *Vernichtung: Die deutsche Ordnungspolizei und der Judenmord im Warschauer Ghetto 1940–43*. Berlin: Prospero, 2013.

Kotliński, Tomasz. "Kwestie narodowościowe i wyznaniowe w adwokaturze polskiej dwudziestolecia międzywojennego: Wybrane zagadnienia." In *Cuius regio, eius religio?*, edited by G. Górski, L. Ćwikła, and M. Lipska, 335–42. Lublin: Wydawnictwo KUL, 2008.

Lehnstaedt, Stephan. *Okkupation im Osten: Besatzeralltag in Warschau und Minsk 1939–1944*. Munich: R. Oldenbourg Verlag, 2010.

Leociak, Jacek. *Text in the Face of Destruction: Accounts from the Warsaw Ghetto Reconsidered*. Warsaw: Żydowski Instytut Historyczny, 2004.

Levi, Primo. "The Grey Zone." In *The Holocaust: Origins, Implementation, Aftermath*, edited by Omer Bartov, 251–72 London: Routledge, 2002.

Levin, Dov. "How the Jewish Police in the Kovno Ghetto Saw Itself." *Yad Vashem Studies*, no. 29 (2001): 183–241.

Libionka, Dariusz. "Zapisy dotyczące Żydów w warszawskich kronikach policyjnych z lat 1942–1944." *Zagłada Żydów: Studia i Materiały*, no.10 (2014): 558–91.

——. "ZWZ—AK i Delegatura rządu RP wobec eksterminacji Żydów polskich." In *Polacy i Żydzi pod okupacją niemiecką 1939–1945: Studia i materiały*, edited by Andrzej Żbikowski, 15–207. Warsaw: IPN, 2006.

Litvak, Olga. *Conscription and the Search for Modern Russian Jewry*. Bloomington: Indiana University Press, 2006.

Litwiński, Robert. *Policja Państwowa w województwie lubelskim w latach 1919–1939*. Lublin: Wydawnictwo UMCS, 2001.

Löw, Andrea. "Ordnungsdienst im Ghetto Litzmannstadt." In *Fenomen getta łódzkiego 1940–1944*, edited by P. Samuś and W. Puś, 155–67. Łódź: Wydawnictwo Uniwersytetu Łódzkiego, 2006.

Majewska, Justyna. "'Czym wytłumaczy Pan . . .?' Inteligencja żydowska o polonizacji i asymilacji w getcie warszawskim." *Zagłada Żydów: Studia i Materiały*, no. 11 (2015): 325–46.

Mendelsohn, Ezra. *On Modern Jewish Politics*. Oxford: Oxford University Press, 1993.

Michman, Dan. "Kontroversen über die Judenräte in der jüdischen Welt: Das Ineinan—dergreifen von öffentlichem Gedächtnis und Geschichtsschreibung 1945–2005." In *Judenrat von Białystok: Dokumente aus dem Archiv des białystoker Ghettos 1941–1943*, edited by F. Anders, K. Stoll, and K. Wilke, 311–17. Paderborn: Schöningh, 2010.

Mikitin, Janusz, and Grzegorz Grześkowiak. *Policja Województwa Śląskiego 1922–1939*. Piekary Śląskie: ZP Grupa, 2008.

Młynarczyk, Jacek Andrzej. "Pomiędzy współpracą a zdradą: Problem kolaboracji w Generalnym Gubernatorstwie—próba syntezy." *Pamięć i Sprawiedliwość*, no. 14 (2009): 103–32.

Ofer, Dalia. "Swearing-in Ceremony: The Police in the Kovno Ghetto, November 1, 1942." *Partial Answers: Journal of Literature and the History of Ideas*, no. 2 (2009): 229–41.

Podolska, Alina. *Służba Porządkowa w getcie warszawskim w latach 1940–1943*. Warsaw: Pro Futuro, 1996.

Pohl, Dieter. *Nationalsozialistische Judenverfolgung in Ostgalizien: 1941–1944; Organisation und Durchführung eines staatlichen Massenverbrechens*. Munich: Oldenbourg, 1997.

Rudnicki, Szymon. "Walka o zmianę ustawy o adwokaturze w II Rzeczypospolitej." In Szymon Rudnicki, *Równi, ale niezupełnie*. Warsaw: Biblioteka Midrasza, 2008).

Rutkowski, Adam. "O agenturze gestapowskiej w getcie warszawskim." *Biuletyn Żydowskiego Instytutu Historycznego*, nos. 3–4 (1956): 38–59.

Smolak, Leszek. *Prasa Policji Państwowej 1918–1939*. Warsaw: Vipart, 2003.

Sofsky, Wolfgang. *The Order of Terror: The Concentration Camp.* Princeton, NJ: Princeton University Press, 2013.

Szczepański, Janusz. *Społeczność żydowska Mazowsza w XIX–XX wieku.* Pułtusk: Wyższa Szkoła Humanistyczna im. Aleksandra Gieysztora, 2005.

Szymańska-Smolkin, Sylwia. "Rola policji granatowej jako pośrednika w utrzymywaniu łączności między gettem a stroną aryjską." In *Narody i polityka: Studia ofiarowane profesorowi Jerzemu Tomaszewskiemu,* edited by August Grabski and Artur Markowski, 97–115 Warsaw: ŻIH, 2010.

Trunk, Isaiah. *Judenrat: The Jewish Councils in Eastern Europe under Nazi Occupation.* New York: Macmillan, 1972.

Urynowicz, Marcin. *Adam Czerniaków, 1880–1940: Życie i działalność.* Warsaw, IPN: 2008.

Weiss, Aharon. *Hamishtara hayehudit baGeneral-Gouvernement uvi-Shlezia Ha'ilit bitkufat ha-Shoa.* Jerusalem: Hebrew University, 1973.

——. "The Relations between the Judenrat and the Jewish Police." In *Patterns of Jewish Leadership in Nazi Europe, 1933–1945: Proceedings of the Third Yad Vashem International Historical Conference, Jerusalem, April 4–7, 1977,* 201–18. Jerusalem: Yad Vashem, 1979.

Wildt, Michael. *Generation des Unbedingten: Das Führungskorps des Reichssicherheitshauptamtes.* Hamburg: Hamburger Edition, 2002.

Wróbel, Karolina. "Romowie za murami getta warszawskiego." *Czas Kultury,* no. 4 (2016): 52–57.

Wyka, Kazimierz. *Życie na niby.* Cracow: Universitas, 2010.

Zalewska, Gabriela. *Ludność żydowska w Warszawie w okresie międzywojennym.* Warsaw: PWN, 1996.

NAME INDEX

Page numbers followed by letter *f* refer to figures.

Adler, Stanisław: on bonding of Jewish Order Service members, 98; on corruption of Jewish Order Service, 60, 82, 85, 92; on formation of Jewish Order Service, 7, 16, 18; on Gancwajch, 30; memoirs of, 152, 213n16; in postwar era, 152; on roundups, Jewish policemen's participation in, 97; on Sienna Street, 94; and Statute of Jewish Order Service, 33; survival of, 146; on Szeryński, 100; work for Jewish Order Service, 16, 21, 33; on Zundelewicz, 12

Ajzenberg, J., 16

Aleksiun, Natalia, 128

Alter, M., 19

Arendt, Hannah, 154

Auerbach, Rachela, 23, 78, 105, 111, 116

Auerswald, Heinz, 14, 26, 57, 95, 183n53; and executions of policemen, 120; roundups ordered by, 116, 117; Szeryński's arrest and, 113

Bałaban, Mejer, 19, 184n69

Bańkowska, Aleksandra, 210n79

Bauman, Janina, 131, 134–35

Ber, Gustaw, 197n116

Berenson, Leon, 10, 11, 16, 23, 113, 182n33, 198n2

Berenstein, Tatiana, 62

Berensztajn, Srul, 23

Berland, Marian, 145

Biebów, Hans, 151

Birenbaum, Halina, 127

Blaupapier, Ignacy, 70, 71, 72

Blumstein, Moszek, 57

Brandt, Karl, 26, 27; and deportation operations, 121, 140; deputy of, 26, 49; and Lejkin, 114, 121; and Szeryński, 112, 122

Brendel, Jakub, 37–38

Brewda, Alina, 143, 211n22

Browning, Christopher, 152, 153, 156

Brzeziński, Mieczysław, 125, 134, 141

Bursztyn, Mojsze, 19, 184n70

Buyko, Bolesław, 12, 183n40

Can, Wolf, 194n47

Czapliński, Marceli, 16, 122, 135, 140

Czapliński, Stanisław, 11f, 16; attack on, 140; during deportations, 122, 135; leadership change and, 121, 207n6

Czerniaków, Adam, 2f, 4, 7f, 179n1; on Central Lockup, 66–70; on corruption, 49; deportation plans and, 121; on executions of policemen, 119, 120; on Gestapo protégés, 28; and Händel, 14; irregularities in Jewish Order Service and, 106, 107; and Jewish Order Service, establishment of, 4, 6, 8, 9; on Labor Battalion of Jewish Council, 5; on labor camps, 195n76; on Lejkin, 113–14; at military-style ceremonies, 85f, 100; and Passenstein, 65; after pogrom of April 17, 1942, 112; on police kitchens, 108; and recruitment for Jewish Order Service, 20, 82; and responsibilities of Jewish Order Service, 46; on Roma deported to Warsaw ghetto, 69; on smuggling operations, 57; suicide of, 122, 124, 143, 151, 179n1; suspension of policemen by, 107; and Szeryński, 10, 11, 12–13, 17, 26, 109, 112–13, 205n10; on Szeryński and Blue Police, 85; on the Thirteen, 29; weekend getaway of, 14

Dąb, Mieczysław, 24, 186n102

Dajelbaum, Zygmunt, 195n74

David, Janina, 132, 143

Dobrin (Drobin), Berthold, 22, 185n87, 205n17
Dudziński, 100
Dymiński, Leon, 39, 203n40

Edelman, Marek, 186n102. *See also* Dąb, Mieczysław
Ehrlich, Józef, 19, 27–28, 122
Engel, David, 141
Engelking, Barbara, 99, 104, 185n89
Engelman, Yehuda, 24
Epsztajn, Jakub, 24
Epsztein, Tadeusz, 210n79
Ernest, Stefan, 82–83, 112

Fajcyn, Zygmunt, 25, 25f, 187n109
Finder, Gabriel, 148
First, Israel, 14, 141
Fischer, Ludwig, 6, 180n12
Fiszbaum, Motek, 73
Fleischman, Albin, 38, 190n18
Fogel, Mojżesz, 109
Frank, Hans, 5, 6, 180n9, 180n11
Furstenberg, Jerzy, 141, 208n20

Gac, Luba, 73
Gancwajch, Abraham, 30, 31, 188n132, 189n148
Garbarini, Alexandra, 83
Gepner, Abraham, 22, 185n87
Goldman, Szymon, 196n78
Goldstein (Goldsztejn), Mieczysław, 103, 203n4, 203n12
Goldsztejn, Nikodem, 203n4
Gombiński, Stanisław: on attitudes toward Jewish Order Service, 76; on Berenson, 10; on deportations, 121, 124, 149; drafts of memoir of, 152; on Händel, 14; on offices of Jewish Order Service, 35; on policemen in labor camps, 63; in postwar era, 149, 151; on recruitment for Jewish Order Service, 17, 33, 184n61; on roundups of children, 117–18; Szeryński and, 16, 144; on Umschlagplatz, 134; after Warsaw Uprising, 146; work at Jewish Order Service, 16, 21, 23
Górny, Jechiel, 119, 120, 141, 146, 155
Gorodecka, Chana, 70
Grabowski, Jan, 104
Gran, Wiera, 188n133
Grüss, Noe, 153
Grzybowski, Arie, 24, 186n99
Gulbas, Eta, 196n89

Hahn, Ludwig, 202n26
Halber, Maurycy, 49
Händel, Marian, 14, 15f, 183n51; adjutant of, 141, 208n20; in postwar era, 213n13; and recruitment for Jewish Order Service, 19, 22; role in Jewish Order Service, 35, 36, 113; rumors about, 27
Heller, Zelig, 28, 188n128
Herc (Hertz), Józef Jerzy, 190n18, 203n12
Heydrich, Reinhard, 5–6, 180n10
Hilberg, Raul, 150, 153, 154, 157
Hirszfeld, Ludwik, 197n111
Höfle, Hermann, 121, 206n1
Hofman (SS Hauptsturmführer), 121
Holckener, Stanisław, 210n4
Huberband, Shimon, 111
Hurwicz, Izaak, 70
Hurwicz, Sylwia, 70

Jakubowicz, Boruch, 201n7
Janczewska, Marta, 36
Jaszuński, Józef, 26, 187n110
Jof, Alfred, 59

Kac, Herman, 144
Kacenelson, Icchak, 138
Kanał, Israel, 24, 133, 186n101
Kapłan, Chaim, 128, 191n47
Kapłański (member of HeHalutz), 129, 209n45
Kaselberg, Bajla (Bella), 197n121
Kasman, Salomon, 130
Kataszek, Szymon, 48, 192n61
Katz, Jakub, 57
Keselberg, Bajla (Bella), 197n121
Kijek, Kamil, 81
Kleczkowski, Wacław, 39, 100
Kligerman, Rywka, 73
Klimenko, Mikołaj, 200n45
Kobryner, Edward, 9, 26, 181n24
Kohn, Moryc, 28, 188n128
Kon, Menachem Mendel, 72–73
Korczak, Janusz, 47, 127
Kosman, Salomon, 125
Kozielewski, Marian, 12, 180n14, 183n40
Krüger, Friedrich-Wilhelm, 6
Krzemiński, S., 200n46
Kubliński, Edmund, 97
Kupczykier, Leopold, 9, 12, 35, 181n23
Kwiek, Janusz, 69

Landau, Eliezer, 58–59
Landau, Henryk, 190n18

Landau, Ludwik, 61, 64
Lederman, Rafał, 38, 100
Leist, Ludwig, 4, 14, 179n1
Lejkin, Jakub: as acting commander
    of Jewish Order Service, 113–14,
    121; assassination of, 140; in chain
    of command, 100, 140, 207n6; and
    deportation operations, 120, 121, 122,
    124; efficiency in carrying out roundups,
    114; grave of, 211n16; life numbers
    distributed by, 135, 210n70; reputation for
    violence, 101
Leociak, Jacek, 152, 185n89
Levi, Primo, 156
Lewi-Kurowska, Maria, 211n24
Lewin, Abraham, 78; on brutality of Jewish
    policemen, 125, 127, 128, 206n34; on
    policemen committing suicide, 129; on
    policemen taken to Umschlagplatz,
    135
Lewin, Mendel, 57
Lewiński, Jerzy, 21, 92, 149, 150–51, 185n84;
    postwar testimony of, 207n11, 207n13
Lewinson, Julian, 26, 187n109
Lewkowicz (Lindenfeld's deputy), 70
Libionka, Dariusz, 88
Lichtenbaum, Mieczysław, 122
Lindenfeld, Leopold, 70, 94, 209n45
Litvak, Olga, 66
Lubliner, Stefan, 11
Luksenberg, Abram, 24

Makower, Henryk, 26, 187n109; on
    deportations, 125, 134, 136; after
    deportations, 144; on labor camps, 64;
    on leadership change, 207n6; on life
    numbers, distribution of, 210n68; on
    Szeryński's suicide, 143
Margules, Fajga, 73
Mende, Gerhard, 26, 49, 140
Mendelsohn, Ezra, 80
Michelson, Mr., 61
Mickiewicz, Adam, 81, 199n21
Millet, Zygmunt, 16, 19, 106, 198n7, 201n6,
    203n12
Moniak, Karol, 100
Murmelstein, Benjamin, 46

Nadel, Henryk, 190n18
Najberg, Leon, 123
Nowogródzki, Henryk, 103, 203n4, 203n12;
    postwar trial of, 149, 212n32
Nusbaum, Szaja, 24

Ohlenbusch, Wilhelm, 30, 188n134
Opoczynski, Peretz, 53
Ostrowska, Salomea, 60, 97

Pajkus, Josek, 73
Pankiewicz, Tadeusz, 202n36
Passenstein, Marek, 56, 64, 65, 193n27
Pasztejn, Sala, 73
Peczenik, Karol, 149, 190n18
Pelzhausen, Walter, 152
Perechodnik, Calel, 80–81, 132, 139, 152,
    213n19
Perle, Yehoshua, 133, 134, 137, 138
Piżyc, Leon, 91, 144, 145
Podolska, Aldona, 214n30
Prussak, Józef, 58, 102
Przymusiński, Franciszek, 6, 85–86,
    181n14
Puterman, Irena, 146
Puterman, Samuel, 52, 131, 135, 145–46,
    152, 193n15

Reich-Ranicki, Marcel, 80
Rejder, Ignacy, 26, 186n108
Reszczyński, Aleksander, 6, 12, 100,
    180n14
Ringelblum, Emanuel, 5, 23, 157, 179n5;
    on attacks on policemen, 142; on Blue
    Police, 86; on brutality of Jewish Order
    Service, 59, 125, 128, 137, 138; on closing
    of Warsaw Ghetto, 5; on corruption of
    Jewish Order Service, 31, 49, 71, 193n9;
    during deportations, 129; on disciplining
    of policemen, 105; on executions at
    Central Lockup, 74; on executions of
    policemen, 145; on exploitation of Jewish
    masses, 110; on Jewish Underground
    after deportations, 140; on Oneg Shabbat,
    77; and Passenstein, 64, 193n27; on
    policemen's claims of innocence, 150;
    on roundups, Jewish Order Service's
    participation in, 97, 208n29; sources of
    information for, 78
Rode, Józef, 36, 190n17, 190n18
Rodkiewicz, Władysław, 39, 100
Rose, Fryderyk, 70, 197n104
Rotholc, Szapsel, 56, 148, 149, 151, 152
Różański, Eliasz, 140
Rozenberg, Dwojra, 73
Rozensztat (lawyer), 16
Rozin, Aron, 197n116
Różycki, Stanisław, 50–51, 83
Rudniański, Izaak, 70, 197n103, 209n45

Rudnicki, Henryk, 128, 132, 140
Rutkowski, Adam, 27
Ryba, Jerzy "Jerry," 48, 192n62

Schön, Waldemar, 14, 26, 183n53
Schönbach, Maksymilian, 10–11, 23, 34f,
    113, 182n35
Sekler, Oskar, 190n18
Śliwka, Szmul, 196n79
Sofsky, Wolfgang, 98
Solnik, Abram, 92
Spotkowski, Seweryn, 123, 207n9
Stabenow, Gerhard, 30
Syrkisowa, Dacha, 59
Szejnberg, Jerzy, 57
Szeryński, Józef, 9–10; alienation from
    Jewish community, 14; and appointments
    to Jewish Order Service, 14–16, 17; arrest
    of, 112–13; attempted assassination of,
    133, 140; and Blue Police, 84–85; during
    the Cauldron, 135; closest associates of,
    14–16, 70; as convert to Christianity,
    12, 24, 76, 79, 80; and Czerniaków,
    10, 11, 12–13, 17, 26, 109, 112–13,
    205n10; after deportations, 140; during
    deportations, 122, 125, 126; disciplinary
    problems addressed by, 102, 103, 110;
    executions at Central Lockup and, 74;
    and German authorities, 26, 27; as head
    of Jewish Order Service, 11, 11f, 14, 25;
    at headquarters of Jewish Order Service,
    35; at military-style ceremonies, 100;
    in Pawiak Prison, 113; Qualification
    Commission and, 107; on responsibilities
    of Jewish Order Service, 40, 41; return
    to Jewish Order Service, 122, 207n6; roll
    calls organized by, 39; selection as head of
    Jewish Order Service, 9, 10, 11–12; suicide
    of, 143–44; weekly reports of, 44; wife of,
    80, 112, 143, 144; and Zundelewicz, 13–14
Szlengel, Władysław, 129–30, 142, 209n46

Szmerling, Mieczysław, 43, 126f; and
    deportation operations, 122, 125, 128,
    134; predisposition to violence, 101, 125,
    156
Sznajder, Natan, 197n116

Talmus, Manfred, 43
Tarwid, Mieczysław, 6, 100
Teigman, Kalman, 211n14
Teszner, Fryderyk, 16
Tomkiewicz, Mina, 131, 202n36, 208n18,
    210n70
Trunk, Isaiah, 154

Urlik, Szyja, 200n41
Urynowicz, Marcin, 14

Waller, James, 97
Warm, Ber, 140, 145, 146, 212n29, 212n30,
    212n32
Wasser, Hersz, 20, 149; on recruitment
    for Jewish Order Service, 184n61; on
    the Thirteen, 30, 32; on Underground
    Archive collaborators, 198n7
Wasserman, Melania, 25, 186n106
Weisblat, Henryk, 37, 190n20
Weiss, Aharon, 44
Winter, Szmuel, 109
Witelson, T. (Tadeusz?), 9, 22, 91, 93,
    181n23, 198n7, 201n7, 204n24
Wolfowicz, Abram, 21–22, 149, 213n13
Worthoff, Hermann, 122

Zadziewicz, Maria, 95
Zadziewicz, Włodzimierz, 26, 187n109
Zajdenwach, Chana, 73
Załek, Wiktor, 75
Zalewska, Gabriela, 22
Zundelewicz, Bernard, 12–14, 13f, 16,
    183n47
Zusman, Dr., 59, 194n47

SUBJECT INDEX

Page numbers followed by letter *f* refer to figures.

alcohol consumption, Jewish Order Service and, 82, 85, 98, 99, 132, 142, 202n36

Anti-aircraft Defense Department, Jewish Order Service, 35, 36–37, 38*f*

Anti-epidemic Company, Jewish Order Service, 20, 43, 51*f*, 126*f*

antisemitism: in interwar Poland, impact on Jewish intelligentsia, 22, 23, 80; in postwar Poland, and perceptions of Jewish Order Service, 147, 154

assimilation, Jewish Order Service as symbol of, 11, 76, 78–81

Auschwitz extermination camp, 12, 183n40, 186n99, 211n22

Austria, Jewish displaced persons (DP) camps in, 149

Bełżec (Belzec) death camp, 111

Blue Police (Polish Blue Police), 5; activities in Warsaw Ghetto, 44, 52; and Central Lockup, 68, 70; corruption of, 21, 44, 85–87; and disinfection operations, 52, 53; and Jewish Order Service, 6–7, 11–12, 21, 27, 29, 36, 39, 44, 84–87, 88; Jewish Order Service compared to, 4; looting by, 128, 145; official instructions of, 33; Orpo and, 6, 27; and smuggling operations, 57, 85–86

Central Lockup (Gęsia prison), Warsaw Ghetto, *xiii*, 44, 66–70, 67*f*; children in, 68, 69*f*, 72–73; deportations of prisoners from, 123; dissolution of, 144; executions at, 73–75, 97; female guards in, 70, 71*f*; head of, 94; Jewish Order Service members in, 120; labor-camp roundups at, 116; women in, 70, 72, 73, 74

Chełmno (Kulmhof) death camp, 111

children, in Warsaw Ghetto: abandoned and orphaned, 47, 123, 127; beggars, roundups of, 117–18, 123–24; deportations of, 123–24, 127, 132–33, 135, 137, 138; imprisoned in Central Lockup, 68, 69*f*, 72–73; smugglers, 60, 72

Chłodna Street, Warsaw Ghetto, *xiii*; deportations from, 124; high-ranking officers living on, 94; Jewish Order Service precinct at, 190n18; sentry post at, 64

Ciepła Street, Warsaw Ghetto, *xiii*; disinfection of apartment buildings on, 52

class struggle, Jewish Order Service presented as part of, 154

corruption: of Blue Police, 21, 44, 85–87; of Jewish Order Service, 50–57, 61, 63, 66, 71, 81, 82–83, 90, 91, 92–93, 98, 105, 107–8, 128–29, 155; of Labor Battalion, 49

Cracow Ghetto: alcohol consumption in, 202n36; Gestapo informers in, 27; Jewish Order Service jail in, 196n83; Ordnungsdienst in, 181n19; postwar trials of policemen from, 148

death penalty: for former Thirteen leaders, 31; for Jews found outside Warsaw Ghetto, 87, 192n47; for smuggling, 57, 119

deportations, from Warsaw Ghetto: "the Cauldron" during, 133–35; exemptions from, 207n15; first (Operation Reinhard), 101, 121–38, 141, 143; of Jewish Order Service members/families, 135, 145; resistance to, 132–33; role of Jewish Order Service during, 121–38, 141, 143, 144, 148, 149, 155, 156; second ("January action"), 143–44

Dobry Wieczór (newspaper), 10
Drewnica, labor camp in, 65, 195n74
Dzielna Street, Warsaw Ghetto, *xiii*;
    deportations from, 206n34; execution of
    Jewish policemen at, 212n32; police
    block at, 131
Dzika Street, Warsaw Ghetto, *xiii*;
    deportations from, 123, 124, 137

Elektoralna Street, Warsaw Ghetto, *xiii*;
    high-ranking officers living on, 94

Galicia District, expulsion of Jews from,
    111
Garwolin, 64
Gazeta Żydowska (newspaper): on Central
    Lockup, 67, 70; crime section of, 88; on
    insignia of power, 84; justifications for
    policemen's behavior in, 50, 59, 95–96; on
    labor camps, 61, 63; on police kitchens,
    108; as propaganda tool, 8, 30, 35–36, 109;
    on resistance, 87; on role of Jewish Order
    Service, 37, 38, 45, 53, 58, 79, 118; on
    staffing of Jewish Order Service, 11, 17,
    18, 20, 103
German authorities: and Jewish Order
    Service, 6, 26–28, 47, 52, 81, 94–95, 96,
    110, 153; and Judenrat (Jewish Council),
    46, 153. *See also* Gestapo; Orpo
Germany, Jewish displaced persons (DP)
    camps in, 149
Gęsia Street, Warsaw Ghetto, *xiii*;
    deportations from, 123, 124; headquarters
    of Jewish Order Service at, 140; Jewish
    Order Service precinct at, 190n18. *See also*
    Central Lockup
Gestapo: and Jewish Order Service, 27, 81,
    145–46; and Operation Reinhard, 112,
    122; and the Thirteen, 30, 31
Gestapo informers: in Jewish Order Service,
    27–28, 31, 32, 60, 122, 144–45; in Warsaw
    Ghetto, 8, 14, 27–28
Ghetto Fighters House Archives, 152,
    210n4
Gmina (Judenrat) company, 36, 92, 94,
    123, 144, 176; functionaries of, 37*f*;
    headquarters of, 190n18
Grzybowska Street, Warsaw Ghetto, *xiii*;
    gate on corner with Żelazna Street, 2*f*;
    Gmina Precinct's headquarters at, 190n18;
    Judenrat building at, 35, 85*f*, 100
Grzybowski Square, Warsaw Ghetto: gate
    at, 157*f*; high-ranking officers living on, 94

HeHalutz (Zionist organization), 129
Honor Court of the Central Committee of
    Jews in Poland, 147–48, 153

Israel, trials of policemen and prisoner-
    functionaries in, 153
Italy, Jewish displaced persons (DP) camps
    in, 149

Jewish Cemetery gate, Warsaw Ghetto,
    55*f*
Jewish Council, Warsaw. *See* Judenrat
Jewish Emergency Service, 31–32, 32*f*,
    189n150, 208n18
Jewish Fighting Organization, resistance by,
    133, 140–41
Jewish Military Union, 141
Jewish Order Service, Warsaw: alienation
    from community, 81–83, 87, 132,
    136–37, 157; Anti-aircraft Defense
    Department of, 35, 36–37, 38*f*; Anti-
    epidemic Company of, 20, 43, 51*f*, 126*f*;
    antisemitism in postwar Poland and
    perceptions of, 147, 154; apartment block
    of, during deportations, 131–32, 134;
    attempts to improve, 102–9; auxiliary
    activities of, 7, 47–48, 112, 143, 145;
    Blue Police and, 6–7, 11–12, 21, 27, 29,
    36, 39, 44, 84–87, 88; bonding factors
    for, 98–100; and Central Lockup, 68,
    70, 74–75, 97; compared to Blue Police,
    4; compared to German soldiers,
    1; corruption of, 50–57, 61, 63, 66,
    71, 81, 82–83, 90, 91, 92–93, 98, 105,
    107–8, 128–29, 155; defiance of orders
    by, 97, 129–30; during deportations,
    121–38, 141, 143, 144, 148, 149, 155,
    156; after deportations, 139–40, 144;
    deportations of members/families of,
    135, 145; disciplinary problems in, 102–3;
    disinfection operations by, 51–54, 61,
    89; doctors in, 25–26, 25*f*, 131, 187n109;
    drinking culture in, 82, 85, 98, 99, 132,
    142, 202n36; earliest research on, 153–54;
    elite vs. rank-and-file members of, 90–91,
    93–94; equipment of members, 34–35,
    84; fire brigade of, 37–38; gates guarded
    by, 42, 54–55, 55*f*, 96, 119; German
    authorities and, 6, 26–28, 47, 52, 81, 94–95,
    96, 110, 153; Gestapo collaborators in,
    27–28, 31, 32, 60, 122, 144–45; Gmina
    (Judenrat) company of, 34–36, 37*f*, 64,
    144; hatred of, 89–90, 95, 98, 120, 136–37,

143, 146; headquarters of, 35, 140;
Hospital Sentinel Unit of, 37; instructions
for, 33–34, 57–58, 159–77; internal
structure of, 34–36; Jewish population's
views on, 76–83, 98, 120; Judenrat and, 7,
8, 12–14, 17, 19, 23, 26, 36, 46, 84, 108–9;
labor-camp roundups by, 61–63, 66, 97,
115, 116–17; lawyers in, 14, 16, 22–23;
Lejkin as acting commander of, 113–14;
limited power of, 8, 100; looting by,
52, 128–29, 137; messengers in, 19, 21;
military-style ceremonies of, 41, 99–100;
as model for other security formations,
8; moral collapse of, 74–75, 77, 78, 82–83,
97–98, 100, 106; motivation for joining,
19, 20, 21, 90, 156–58; "no assignment"
policemen in, 21–22; officers of, selection
of, 14–16; Order and Disciplinary
Section of, 103–5, 104f; origins of, 4–7;
pauperization of members, 91–92; Polish
language used by, 18; portrayal outside
of ghetto, 88; postwar trials of members
of, 90, 147–52, 157; presented as part
of class struggle, 154; privileges for,
108, 143; propaganda tool of, 8, 35–36,
109; Qualification Commission of, 31,
107; rationalization of activities of,
89–90, 150–51, 155; records of wartime
experiences of members of, 145, 152–53;
recruitment of members, 1, 14–24, 81;
resistance against, 115–16, 132–33,
140–43, 144; salaries for members of,
91, 106, 107; sanitary platoons in, 43;
sanitation instructions for, 159–60;
SEPOR, 35, 107–8, 108f, 201n7, 208n18;
smuggling operations and, 24, 42–43,
55–57, 76, 82, 91, 92, 98, 105–6, 108;
supporting staff of, 24–25; as symbol of
assimilation, 11, 76, 78–81; Szeryński
as head of, 9, 10, 11–12, 14, 25; tasks of,
1, 29, 30, 39–48, 112, 114–15; Thirteen
members incorporated into, 20, 31;
training of recruits, 38–39; underground
Jewish press on, 83–84, 87–88; as victims,
57, 96, 118–20, 143, 145; violence of,
57–61, 66, 73, 83, 90, 95–96, 98, 99,
101, 137–38, 155; work as factory
guards, 143, 144; work in labor camps,
63–65
Jewish underground: on Jewish policemen's
role in deportations, 137; resistance by,
133, 140–43, 144. See also underground
Jewish press

Judenrat (Jewish Council), Warsaw:
chairman of, 4; deportations and, 133;
Disciplinary Section of, 103, 104; German
authorities' demands on, 46, 153;
Gestapo protégés in, 28; ghetto residents'
dislike of, 109; and Jewish Order Service,
7, 8, 12–14, 17, 19, 23, 26, 36, 46, 84,
108–9; Labor Battalion of, 4–5, 14, 46,
49, 63

Karmelicka Street, Warsaw Ghetto:
management of apartment houses on, 29;
police block at, 131
Kielce pogrom, 152
Końskowola, labor camp in, 63, 65
Kovno (Kaunas) Ghetto, Jewish police in,
214n31; studies of, 154, 214n31
Krochmalna Street, Warsaw Ghetto, xiii;
Blue Police administration at, 39; corner
with Walicόw Street, 40f; Directorate of
Jewish Order Service at, 35; disinfection
operation at, 52, 114
Krosno, Pustków labor camp near,
65
Kulmhof (Chełmno) death camp, 111

Labor Battalion, of Warsaw Judenrat, 4–5,
46; corruption in, 49; Gestapo informers
in, 14; transfer of members to Jewish
Order Service, 14, 63, 102
labor camps: doctors in, 64; *Gazeta
Żydowska* reports on, 61, 63; membership
in Jewish Order Service to avoid, 19, 20,
21; resistance to roundups for, 115–16;
roundups for, 61–63, 66, 97, 115, 116–17;
Warsaw Ghetto policemen in, 63–65,
144
Leszno Street, Warsaw Ghetto, xiii;
bathhouse at, 52; children held at, 117;
deportations from, 124; deportees at, 60;
Jewish Order Service precinct at, 190n18;
Konarski school at, 96; meat factory at,
22; prison at, 62; quarantine facility at, 97,
124; the Thirteen at, 8, 29
Łόdź (Litzmannstadt), Jewish Order Service
recruits from, 1, 26, 30
Łόdź Ghetto, 180n7; administrator of,
postwar trial of, 151; expulsion of Jews
from, 111; Gestapo informers in, 27;
Jewish Council in, 39; Jewish criminal
police in, 45
Łowicz: refugees from, 60; Roma arrested
in, 69

Lubeckiego Street, Warsaw Ghetto: Blue
Police precinct at, 39; deportations from,
135, 208n24
Lublin: expulsion of Jews from, 111;
Szeryński in, 9, 12, 16
L'viv Ghetto, 192n61

Majdanek death camp: deportations to, 135,
181n23; doctors at, 187n109, 211n22
Miła Street, Warsaw Ghetto, xiii;
deportations from, 124
Mława Ghetto, Jewish policemen hung in,
119
Muranowska Street, Warsaw Ghetto,
deportations from, 124, 207n13
Mylna Street, Warsaw Ghetto, deportations
from, 127

Nalewki Street, Warsaw Ghetto, xiii;
detention center for children at, 68; gate
at, 145; payment demanded from house
committee at, 59
Neged Hazarem (newspaper), 78
Niska Street, Warsaw Ghetto, xiii; Blue
Police precinct at, 39
Nowolipie Street, Warsaw Ghetto, xiii;
execution of Jewish policeman near, 119;
management of apartment houses on,
29
Nowolipki Street, Warsaw Ghetto, xiii;
attacks on former policemen on, 141;
Blue Police precinct at, 39; grocery store
at, 22; police block at, 131, 133, 136
Nowy Kurier Warszawski (newspaper),
88
Nowy Zjazd Street, Warsaw Ghetto,
deportations from, 127
Nuremberg trials, 153

Ogrodowa Street, Warsaw Ghetto, xiii;
deportations from, 125; Directorate of
Jewish Order Service at, 35, 121, 149,
156, 210n69; during "the Cauldron,"
135
Oneg Shabbat, 77, 140, 143
Operation Reinhard, 121–38; "the
Cauldron" in, 133–35; preparations for,
112–20; resistance to, 132–33
Oranienburg, deportations to, 146
Orla Street, Warsaw Ghetto, xiii; corpses
left at, 112; management of apartment
houses on, 29
orphanages, deportations from, 123, 127

Orpo (German Order Police): and Blue
Police, 6, 27; and disinfection operations,
52; gates guarded by, 42; and Jewish
Order Service, 6, 26–27, 47, 52, 96
Osowa Camp, mass execution in, 196n79
Ostrowska Street, Warsaw Ghetto,
deportations from, 135
Otwock, as weekend getaway, 14
Otwock Ghetto, 8; confessions of Jewish
policeman from, 80, 132, 139, 152
Ożarów, transit camp in, 146

Pawiak Prison, Warsaw, 68; Central Lockup
compared to, 68; execution of Jewish
policemen in, 96, 212n32; Szeryński in,
113
Polish Blue Police. See Blue Police
Polish language: rising popularity among
Jews, 81; used by Jewish Order Service,
18
Polish State Police, 6
Polish Underground: on abuses committed
by Jewish Order Service, 86, 88;
cooperation with, in Jewish policemen's
testimonies, 151; on executions in
Warsaw Ghetto, 144–45
Ponary, massacre of Vilnius Jews in, 111
Praga neighborhood, Warsaw: Jewish
policemen working in, 135, 144; labor
camp in, 144, 211n24
Prosta Street, Warsaw Ghetto, xiii;
Directorate of Jewish Order Service at,
35
Pruszków, transit camp in, 146
Pustków labor camp, Jewish policemen in,
65

Radogoszcz Prison, trial of commander of,
152
Radom Ghetto, Gestapo informers in, 27,
31
reconstruction, postwar, survivors of Jewish
Order Service during, 147–52
refugee shelters, in Warsaw Ghetto, 45,
60; deportations from, 123, 124, 137;
labor-camp roundups in, 62, 115; police
activities in, 114–15
resistance: to deportations, 132–33; after
deportations, 140–43, 144; to labor-camp
roundups, 115–16
Ringelblum Archive. See Underground
Archive of the Warsaw Ghetto
Roma, in Warsaw Ghetto, 69–70

Russia, tsarist, Jews as forced conscripts in, 66

Rynkowa Street, Warsaw Ghetto, disinfection of apartment buildings on, 52

Sachsenhausen death camp, 146, 193n15

Sandomierz, Jewish policemen in, 141

SEPOR (Section of Material Assistance for Order Service Functionaries), 35, 107–8, 108f; application to, 201n7; and Jewish Emergency Service, 208n18

Sienna Street, Warsaw Ghetto, xiii; high-ranking officers living on, 94; incorporation into ghetto, 27

Silesia, 9

Śliska Street, Warsaw Ghetto, xiii; Blue Police precinct at, 39; deportations from, 127

smuggling: Blue Police and, 57, 85–86; children and, 60, 72; death penalty for, 57, 119; detention for, 72, 73; intensified fight against, prior to deportations, 119; Jewish Order Service and, 24, 42–43, 55–57, 76, 82, 91, 92, 98, 105–6, 108; the Thirteen and, 29

Sobibór, reports from, 117

Spokojna Street, Warsaw Ghetto, xiii; bathhouse at, 52

Szucha Avenue, Warsaw: Gestapo headquarters at, 30, 121; Gestapo lockup at, 112

the Thirteen, 8, 28–32; liquidation of, 20, 31

Treblinka extermination camp: construction of, 3, 128; deportations of Jews to, 3, 122, 135, 139, 141; policeman families sent to, 135, 139; survivor of, 211n14

Twarda Street, Warsaw Ghetto, xiii; clinic at, 25; deportations from, 127; Jewish Order Service precinct at, 190n18; synagogue at, 38

typhus epidemic, 43, 118; and deaths among policemen, 100, 118; disinfection operations to combat, 51–54, 91

Umschlagplatz, Warsaw Ghetto, xiii, 3; during deportations, 122, 123, 124, 127–28, 134, 135; Jewish Order Service at, 125, 145, 156, 212n30; rescues from, 129, 130, 132

Underground Archive of the Warsaw Ghetto (Ringelblum Archive), 41, 77; on

Blue Police, 86; on Central Lockup, 72; founder of, 5; on Jewish policemen in labor camps, 65; on labor-camp roundups, 116–17; on Lejkin, 114; on Operation Reinhard, 122, 126; photos from, 2f, 3

underground Jewish press: on Blue Police, 87; on Gestapo informers, 27–28; on Jewish Order Service, 59, 73, 76, 78, 83–84, 87–88

Vilna Ghetto, Jewish Order Service in, 189n5, 189n8

Walicόw Street, Warsaw Ghetto, xiii; Blue Police precinct at, 39; corner with Krochmalna Street, 40f

Wałowa Street, Warsaw Ghetto, shelter at, 70

Warsaw: Jewish Order Service recruits from, 1; Jews hiding in, 145–46; Ziemiańska café in, 10. See also Warsaw Ghetto; specific locations

Warsaw Ghetto, xiii; abandoned and orphaned children in, 47, 123, 127; "as if" world of, 46; bars, cafés, and theaters in, 81, 99; Blue Police in, 39, 44; Central Lockup (Gęsia prison) in, xiii, 44, 66–70, 67f, 69f, 71f; deportation operations in (first, Operation Reinhard), 101, 121–38, 141, 143; deportation operations in (second, "January action"), 143–44; detention center for children in, 68, 69f; disease outbreaks in, 43, 118; disinfection operations in, 51–54, 61, 89, 91; first impressions of, 83; gates to, 2f, 42, 54, 55f, 157f; German soldiers stationed in, 26; Gestapo informers in, 8, 14, 27–28, 60; Jewish cemetery in, xiii, 5; pogrom of April 17, 1942, in, 112; police block in, 131–32, 134; preparations for Operation Reinhard in, 112–20; propaganda film about, 118; refugees and deportees in, 60, 114–15, 123; residual, after deportations, 139–40; Roma in, 69–70; roundups for labor camps in, 49, 61–63, 66, 97, 115, 116–17; roundups of child beggars in, 117–18, 123–24; sanitary conditions in, 43; sealing of, 5, 14, 39, 42; smuggling in, 55–57. See also Central Lockup; Jewish Order Service; Judenrat; specific streets

Warsaw Ghetto Uprising (1943), 145, 181n24, 185n87, 186n101, 209n46

Warsaw Uprising (1944), 145–46

Wielka Polska (newspaper), 88
Wilga, labor camp in, 64
Wolność Street, Warsaw Ghetto, *xiii*;
    deportations from, 127
Wołyńska Street, Warsaw Ghetto, *xiii*;
    collection point during deportations,
    134–35, 136
women: during deportations, 132, 135,
    138; as guards in Central Lockup, 70, 71*f*;
    imprisoned in Central Lockup, 70, 72, 73,
    74; in Jewish Order Service, 144; during
    labor-camp roundups, 116; sexual abuse
    by police, 128, 206n34

Yad Vashem Archives, 152

Zamenhofa Street, Warsaw Ghetto:
    deportations from, 124; Directorate of
    Jewish Order Service at, 144; Jewish
    Order Service precinct at, 190n18; police
    block at, 140
Zamość, expulsion of Jews from, 111
Żelazna Street, Warsaw Ghetto, *xiii*; Blue
    Police command at, 39; gate on corner with
    Grzybowska Street, 2*f*; sentry post at corner
    with Chłodna Street, 64; SS Management
    Board (Befehlstelle) at, 122, 140

www.ingramcontent.com/pod-product-compliance
Ingram Content Group UK Ltd.
Pitfield, Milton Keynes, MK11 3LW, UK
UKHW040201260425
457897UK00011B/96/J